D0509564

QUICKSTART
to the Books of the Bible

Greg Brothers

Pacific Press® Publishing Association
Nampa, Idaho
Oshawa, Ontario, Canada
www.PacificPress.com

Edited by B. Russell Holt
Designed by Michelle C. Petz
Cover illustration by Susan Blubaugh, © 2001 Stock illustration Source

Copyright 2002 by
Pacific Press® Publishing Association
Printed in United States of America
All Rights Reserved

Additional copies of this book may be purchased at
http://www.adventistbookcenter.com

ISBN: 0-8163-1924-3

02 03 04 05 06 • 5 4 3 2 1

Dedication

For my parents.

Proverbs 22:6

Acknowledgments

This book began as a series of articles for *Signs of the Times*® magazine. It was my associate editor, David Jarnes, who encouraged me to write these as a regular series of columns. It was my secretary, Helen Stiles, who kept saying, "This would make a really great book." And it was my successor, Marvin Moore, who continued to run these columns and let me finish out my series on all sixty-six books of the Bible. All of these people deserve my thanks.

Over the years, I have been blessed by a number of excellent teachers who taught me to love the Bible. Many of them will probably recognize many of the ideas (and even some of the words!) in this book; a few may be appalled at my grievous mistakes and errors. To the first group, I can say only, "Thank you." The second, I can only encourage to try to do a better job with the next generation of students than they did with me.

My editors at Pacific Press have borne with courage and good humor my consistent failure to meet any deadline they set. Whatever they get paid to deal with people like me, it's not enough.

Finally, there is no way I can thank my family enough for the help they've been to me. In a very real sense, it is their book as much as my own.

May God be glorified through my work.

November 2001

Contents

Introduction

Absolutely, Positively Everything You Need to Know in Order to Read the Bible

OK, so just exactly what *do* you need to know in order to read the Bible?

The answer, of course, is nothing.

Really.

As much as it pains me to admit it, you don't need this book in order to read and enjoy the Bible, any more than you need a travel agent to have a good vacation. In both cases, all you really need to do is pick a likely-looking spot and go for it. With a little luck, a sense of humor, and several gallons of Pepto-Bismol™, you should do just fine.

Then again, if you ever had one of those vacations where you *needed* that Pepto-Bismol™ . . . well, then you know the difference that a little preparation can make. Not too much preparation, of course; there's nothing worse than traveling with one of those travel-nazis who plan *everything* in advance. ("Enough of the Grand Canyon, already—we're five minutes behind schedule!") But still, it's nice to talk things over with someone who's already been there—somebody who can tell you where he stayed, what he saw, and why you probably shouldn't drink the water.

That's the purpose of this book. It's not an elaborate, step-by-step guide to *everything* that *everyone* wants to know about the Bible; to be honest, I'm not smart enough to write a book like that. There are still large chunks of the Bible that puzzle me—and there are some that scare me silly! But over the years, I've knocked around the Bible enough to know who's who and what's what. And if I can't always tell you what a passage means, then at least I can tell you what all the arguing is about.

Keep in mind, however, that even the best travel agent can't tell you as much as you'll learn by actually making the trip. Reading this book is no substitute for reading the Bible. You need to get in there and take a look for yourself. If this book helps you to do that, then it's served its purpose. If it doesn't, then don't let that stop you.

After all, you don't *need* this book in order to read the Bible. Like any adventure, all you really need is the willingness to try.

Enjoy your trip.

How to Read This Book

My advice? Read this book as you would the Bible—just pick a spot that looks interesting, and dive in!

If you like, you can read the first two chapters straight through; after that, you're better off picking and choosing as you go.

Scattered through the text, you'll find four types of notes:

• **FastFact:** Just what it says.

• **FlashPoint:** An issue that stirs up controversy.

• **GoodWord:** A quick definition of an important word or phrase.

• **HighLight:** Where to find the most famous story or verse in a particular part of the Bible.

As you read, you'll notice that I quote the New International Version of the Bible (NIV). If you prefer another version, that's fine; I used the NIV simply because it's the most popular version out there.

One last point: If you bought this book, you're entitled to ask me one, free question. Write to me, care of the publisher, or send an email to *heybibleguy@hotmail.com.* I promise that I'll get back to you.

Chapter 1

A Quick Guide to the Bible

Think of the Bible as a city. Just like New York or Los Angeles, after all, the Bible is big. It's confusing. What's more, it's an easy place to get lost.

That's because the Bible is not just one book, anymore than a city is just one street or neighborhood. No, the Bible is like a big city with lots of neighborhoods. In fact, it's a library; it's a collection of books written by dozens of authors over hundreds of years in three different languages. And just as neighborhoods differ from each other—think of the Bronx and Wall Street, or Beverly Hills and Compton—so too, every book in the Bible has its own look and feel.

In other words, no matter what you need, you'll probably find it in the Bible. If you like poetry, for instance, try the Psalms. History? Read the books of Samuel and Kings. Need some help running a business? Study Proverbs. Want to learn more about Jesus? The Bible doesn't just have *one* biography of Him; it has four!

!GOOD! !WORD!
Bible

The word comes from the Lebanese city of *Byblos,* a seaport that became famous for making papyrus (a kind of early Egyptian paper). This made Byblos a natural place to produce books—and as a result, the Greeks and Romans came to know all books as "bibles."

Different as they are, the books of the Bible have one thing in common: they all came from a bunch of nobodies. If it weren't for the Bible, after all, you probably never would have heard of the Israelites—I mean, Tiglath-pileser* was a *lot* more important than they were, and when was the last time you ever heard of him? No, the Bible came to us from a small group of insignificant people who lived on the fringes of the world's great empires. And if you want to understand the Bible, then you need to know their story.

The Bible's history

Most of the Bible takes place in a small, rocky country on the eastern shore of the Mediterranean. Variously known as "Canaan," "Israel," or "Palestine," it's a lot like the Los Angeles metro area would be without the freeways. Same size: roughly 8,000 square miles. Same climate: hot, dry summers and cool, wet winters. Same landscape: lots of brush, dry grass, and oak trees. And pretty much the same local politics: lots of little communities that don't like each other very much. Left to itself, in other words, Canaan would have been known for its goats, grapes, and tax revolts, but not much else.

Unfortunately, Canaan was (and is) the land-bridge that connects two of the biggest hot spots in the Middle East. To the south is the Nile Valley, home of the Egyptian Empire. To the north—well, actually, it's east, but the only way you can get there without crossing the nasty desert is by circling around to the north—anyway, to the north is Mesopotamia, "the land between the rivers." Watered by the Tigris and Euphrates rivers, Mesopotamia was a broad, flat, muddy plain that gave rise to two of the nastiest empires the world has ever seen: first Assyria, and then Babylon.

When it came to Middle Eastern politics, in other words, Egypt was the anvil. Mesopotamia was the hammer. And right between them—smack-dab in the middle—was the land of Canaan.

It made for an interesting life.

---

* Just for the record, Tiglath-pileser III was the King of Assyria from 745-727 B.C. An even more famous predecessor of the same name ruled Assyria from 1114-1074 B.C.—and yes, Dave Barry would probably think that "Tiglath-pileser" is a great name for a band!

Sometime around 1200 B.C., the Egyptians started complaining about a new group in Canaan—a group known as "the Israelites." Where they came from is something that the experts love to argue about. The Israelites themselves said they were the descendants of Abraham—a wealthy nomad from Mesopotamia. Abraham's family had moved to Canaan, but drought had forced his descendants to relocate in Egypt. There they had been slaves, until their God set them free and brought them back to Canaan in "the Exodus."

FAST FACT

The Names of God

What do you call God? At first, He seemed to go by several names: *El Elyon* ("God Most High"), *El Shaddai* ("God Almighty"), *El-roi* ("the God who sees"), and *El Olam* ("the everlasting God"). In time, He came to be known as *YHWH* (Yahweh)—a name that seems to mean "I am"—and it is by this name that He is known to the present day.

1050 B.C.: God's people get a king

A common ancestor, a common history, a common God: None of these meant that the Israelites got along with each other. In truth, they were little more than a loose confederation of twelve tribes that fought each other almost as much as they did outsiders. From time to time, an *ad hoc* leader (or "judge") might unite a few tribes against some common enemy, but when the threat disappeared, so did the unity.

All this changed sometime around 1050 B.C., when a new group known as Philistines began moving inland from the coast. Faced with this threat, the Israelites united and chose Saul to lead them in battle. When he died, the Israelites split; the northern tribes backed Saul's son Ishbaal, while the southern tribe of Judah backed a disaffected general named David. When Ishbaal was killed by two of his own commanders, David took over all of Israel.

David's regime marked the high point of Israel's history. With Egypt and Assyria in the doldrums, David was free to expand the land of Israel; he also pushed back the Philistines to the coast. With the capture of Jerusalem, David found a neutral site for

FAST FACT

What do you call God's people?

Hebrews, the children of Abraham, Israelites, and Jews—God's people go by all these names, yet they don't all mean the same.

- No one knows what a "hebrew" might be—a wanderer? A descendant of Eber? All we know is that Abraham used this word to describe himself.

- God promised Abraham many heirs—heirs who are known collectively as "children of Abraham."

- But one grandchild was especially blessed: Israel, who had twelve sons.

- Then again, almost all the descendants of Israel disappeared when the Assyrians invaded their land. As a matter of fact, aside from the Levites, the only ones left were members of the tribe of Judah (or "Jews" for short).

In practical terms, what this means is that all Jews are Israelites, but not all Israelites are Jews. All Israelites are children of Abraham, but not all children of Abraham are Israelites. And all children of Abraham are Hebrews . . . but we still don't know what a Hebrew might be!

his capital—one that had not previously belonged to any of the tribes. And when God's shrine was transferred to Jerusalem, it seemed as though the twelve tribes of Israel had finally been molded into a strong and unified kingdom.

But even David couldn't end the old tribal jealousies. Revolts marred his reign as well as that of his heir; when his son Solomon died, Israel split once again along tribal lines. The northern tribes took the name of Israel; they also took most of the land, most of the people, and most of the wealth. Judah retained little more than Jerusalem and its old tribal lands. But with the House of David firmly in control, it avoided much of the palace intrigue that plagued its northern neighbor.

The empire strikes back

No sooner did Israel and Judah split up, however, than both had to face a common enemy: the newly-reborn empire of Assyria. Both Israel and Judah tried to play off Assyria against its enemies; both failed. As a result, Israel was invaded in 722 B.C. by Assyria; its capital was destroyed, its temple burnt, and its people were taken into exile where they were never seen again.

Judah managed to hold on a bit longer, mainly because it was poor and off the beaten track. But in 586 B.C., Judah was invaded by the same group that had just destroyed Assyria—the empire of Babylon. As a result, Judah suffered the same fate as its long-gone cousins to the north: Its capital was destroyed, its temple burnt, and its people taken into exile.

Where they survived.

Strange as it may seem, the "Babylonian captivity" may have been one of the best things that ever happened to Judah. Faced with the loss of their land, the Jews focused on their religion. They gathered the sacred texts of their religion into a rough-and-ready Bible of sorts. They formed small groups to discuss these texts—small groups that would later be known as "synagogues." And they developed a new type of religious leader: the scribe or rabbi—a man who knew God's laws and could teach them to others. In short, the people who *returned* to Judah after seventy years of exile were not the same as their parents and grandparents who had lived there before.

Ten Lost Tribes

No one knows what happened to the Israelites who were captured by the Assyrians. Most experts believe they were carried off to Mesopotamia, where they intermarried with the locals and gradually lost their identity as a separate people. Other theories have been suggested—they moved to America, they moved to England, or they moved to Africa—but in reality, we have no evidence for any of these views.

FlashPoint: How on earth we got the Bible

Tradition has it that Ezra the priest pulled together the documents that made up the first Bible, sometime around 450 B.C. Be that as it may, the number of books that make up today's Hebrew Bible was fixed by the Council of Jamnea, sometime around A.D. 90.

The New Testament's history is a little more involved. Faced with competing schools of thought, mainstream Christianity thought it best to include *only* those books that had been written by an apostle, i.e. one of Christ's original followers or Paul of Tarsus. Everyone agreed this included the four Gospels, the book of Acts, and the thirteen letters of Paul (arranged in order of their length).

But other books stirred controversy. Western Christians, for instance, doubted that Paul had written Hebrews; Eastern Christians disliked Revelation. Some doubted that the books of James, 2 Peter, 2 and 3 John, and Jude were important enough to be included. Others continued to agitate for books like the Shepherd of Hermas, and the Apocalypse of Ezra.

By A.D. 367, however, most of the shouting had died down, and Bishop Athanasius of Alexandria was reading from the same New Testament that most Christians do today.

This caused problems. In 539 B.C., the empire of Babylon fell to the Persians, and the Persians let the Jews go home. Fifty thousand did so . . . only to discover that Judah had been taken over by a variety of people: refugees, stragglers, converts, and people who'd been left behind when everyone else was taken to Babylon. These people thought of themselves as the true people of God—and they didn't much care for all the new-fangled changes that these refugees brought back with them from exile.

What followed next was a typical struggle over turf—a struggle that ended with the triumph of the "new Jews" from Babylon. Thanks to their leadership, both Jerusalem and the temple were rebuilt; thanks to the Persians, the next few centuries passed quite peacefully.

A.D. 70: the temple is destroyed (again)

All this changed when the Persian Empire fell to Alexander the Great in 331 B.C. Alexander had a passion for Greek culture—a passion that was shared by the generals who took over after him. For the most part, they left the Jews alone, but in 175 B.C., a new king took charge: Antiochus IV. His friends called him "Epiphanes," which means "God manifest." His enemies called him "Epimanes," which means "crazy." But to the Jews, Antiochus IV would forever be known as "the abomination that causes desolation."

Antiochus IV wanted to turn the Jews into a bunch of pork-eating, idol-worshiping, uncircumcised Greeks. He thought this would be a good way to secure the southern frontier of his kingdom against Egypt; what he got was a guerilla war. Under the leadership of the Maccabees family, the Jews rose in revolt, kicked out the Greeks, and established their own independent kingdom in 142 B.C.

It didn't last.

Palace politics led someone in the royal family to invite in the Romans; once they showed up, no one could figure out how to make them leave. The Romans got rid of the Maccabees in 63 B.C., dithered for a while, and then installed Herod the Great as their client-king. When he died in 4 B.C., the Romans split the kingdom four ways: Three parts went to Herod's sons, while Judah was ruled directly by the Roman emperor through an appointed governor. For the next seventy years, the Romans tinkered with this system—subtracting a governor *here,* adding a son of Herod *there,* moving a boundary *yonder*—all in the hope that, somehow, they could find a formula for lasting peace.

Canon

The list of books that make up the Bible.

It didn't work.

Tensions came to a climax in A.D. 66, when Greeks in the coastal city of Caesarea won a lawsuit against some Jews. The verdict led to riots. The riots led to war—a war that lasted six years, killed millions, and left both Jerusalem and the temple in ruins. A second revolt in A.D. 131 lasted four years; its failure sealed the fate of the Jews. From now on, they would live as exiles and strangers—in fact, it would be another 1,800 years before the Jews had a land of their own.

So there you have it—a brief history of a small group of insignificant people who lived in an out-of-the-way part of the world. They left us no great monuments, no awe-inspiring buildings, no graceful statues, not even so much as piece of jewelry. What they did leave us were their words—words that still speak to us today in the pages of the Bible. With that in mind, let's take a look at this Book.

What's what in the Bible

As you already know, the Bible is a collection of books written by dozens of authors in three different languages. For the sake of convenience, we've divided these books into two groups: the Hebrew Bible (known to Christians as the Old Testament), and the New Testament.

The Hebrew Bible has thirty-nine books, mostly written in . . . well, in Hebrew. (Actually, two books—Ezra and Daniel—do include sections in Aramaic, a language similar to Hebrew.) Tradition divides these books into three groups:

- *The Law: Genesis, Exodus, Leviticus, Numbers, and Deuteronomy.*

Also known as the Torah, the Pentateuch, or the Books of Moses. These five books tell us how God created a special group of people known as the Israelites; they also list the rules that God gave in order for the Israelites to *remain* a special people. (Think of this section as the *creation* of God's expectations.)

- *History: Joshua, Judges, Ruth, 1 and 2 Samuel, 1 and 2 Kings, 1 and 2 Chronicles, Ezra, Nehemiah, and Esther.*

- *Major Prophets: Isaiah, Jeremiah, Lamentations, Ezekiel, and Daniel.*

- *Minor Prophets: Hosea, Joel, Amos, Obadiah, Jonah, Micah, Nahum, Habbakuk, Zephaniah, Haggai, Zechariah, and Malachi.*

Think of the twenty-nine books in this section* as *reapplications* of God's expectations. In them, we learn how the Israelites failed to live by God's rules and what God did as a result. Some of these books are historical works. The "major prophets" and "minor prophets" are collections of essays and poetry. (And yes, the only difference between a "major prophet" and a "minor prophet" is the length of his book.)

- *Writings: Job, Psalms, Proverbs, Ecclesiastes, and Song of Solomon.*

"Writings" is a catch-all term for books that don't fit neatly into the other two sections. Some of these books are poetry, others philosophy. (I suppose you could think of this section as a series of *meditations* on God's expectations, but that might be stretching it a bit.)

---

* Hebrew Bibles count 1 and 2 Samuel, 1 and 2 Kings, and 1 and 2 Chronicles each as single books; that's why you'll often find Jewish commentaries giving different figures for the number of books in the Bible compared to the usual arrangement in most English versions.

Taken together, these thirty-nine books trace the history of God's people from the dawn of Creation down to 400 B.C. or so. If you're Jewish, that's the end of your Bible. If you're Catholic, you can read what happens next in the Apocrypha. But if you're Protestant, you're faced with a long gap before things pick up again with the New Testament.

FlashPoint: The Apocrypha

If you've read Margaret Atwood's novel, *The Poisonwood Bible,* you'll remember the part where the Protestant fundamentalist missionary is preaching from the story of Susannah and the elders.

Great scene in the novel. Unfortunately, there's no way that it could have happened.

That's because Susanah's story is in the Apocrypha—and fundamentalist Protestants (missionary or otherwise) don't include the Apocrypha in their Bible.

A little background might be helpful. The Apocrypha (meaning "hidden") includes somewhere between nine and eighteen books (or parts of books), all written in Greek between 200 B.C. and A.D. 90 or so. The Greek-speaking Jews of northern Egypt included these books in their Bible, while most Palestinian Jews (who spoke Hebrew and Aramaic) did not. In A.D. 90, Jewish leaders met at the Council of Jamnea and decided in favor of the Palestinians. That's why the Hebrew Bible does *not* include the Apocrypha.

The council didn't include Christians, however, and they continue to disagree on what should be done with these books. Most Protestants play it safe and leave the Apocrypha *out* of the Bible, while Roman Catholics and the Orthodox think it's safer to leave them *in.* Lutherans and Episcopalians, on the other hand, play it extra safe by including these books in a special "deuterocanonical" section between the Old and New Testaments; while they don't use the Apocrypha for doctrine, they do read it in church.

So what's in the Apocrypha? Catholic Bibles include the books of Tobit, Judith, the Wisdom of Solomon, Ecclesiasticus, Baruch, and 1 and 2 Maccabees, as well as additional chapters in Esther and Daniel. Orthodox Bibles include all these books, plus 1 Esdras, the Prayer of Manasseh, 3 Maccabees, and Psalm 151. (Some Orthodox Bibles also include 2 and 3 Esdras, as well as 4 Maccabees.)

Then you have the Copts of Ethiopia—twenty-five million Christians whose Bibles include such books as Jubilees, 1 Enoch, Joseph ben Gorion's history of the Jews, Sinodos, the Shepherd of Hermas, the Apostolic Constitutions, and two letters from a Roman church leader named Clement!

Why Greek?

Why was the New Testament written in Greek?

Three words: Alexander the Great.

In the fourth century B.C., Alexander conquered most of the Near and Middle East—and in the process, he made Greek the second language of anyone who even pretended to be civilized. The Romans were no exception; when they conquered the Greeks, the Romans adopted Greek culture (and the Greek language) much as people across the world today are wearing Nikes and wolfing-down Big Macs.

The New Testament has twenty-seven books, all written in Greek sometime between A.D. 50 and A.D. 90 or so. They are divided into the following groups:

• *Gospels: Matthew, Mark, Luke, and John.*

"Gospel" literally means "good news." These books tell the story of Jesus—the Jewish Carpenter who began Christianity.

• *The book of Acts.*

Written for a Roman audience, the book of Acts tells how Christianity spread from its beginnings in Palestine to the whole Roman Empire.

• *The Pauline Epistles: Romans, 1 and 2 Corinthians, Galatians, Ephesians, Philippians, Colossians, 1 and 2 Thessalonians, 1 and 2 Timothy, Titus, Hebrews, and Philemon.*

These are letters from Paul—the Jewish apostle who carried Christianity to the Roman world. Most were written to solve problems in churches that he had founded.

• *The General Epistles: James, 1 and 2 Peter, 1, 2, and 3 John, and Jude.*

Unlike Paul's letters, which were written to specific churches, these letters were meant for all Christians everywhere. They were written either by the original disciples of Jesus, or by members of His immediate family.

• *The book of Revelation.*

Revelation sums up the entire Bible and describes God's view of human history in all its terror and glory.

And with that, you know more about the Bible than you probably wanted to know. So let's take a look at what it takes to actually *read* the Bible.

Chapter 2

A Quick Guide to Reading the Bible

Some religions make it tough to read their sacred books. Good Moslems, for instance, learn how to read the Koran in Arabic—in fact, that's the *only* language in which they will read it! That's because good Moslems believe that the Koran can be properly understood *only* if it's read in Arabic.

Judaism and Christianity are different; they have *always* translated their sacred writings into everyday language. Nehemiah, for instance, describes a large, public gathering where religious leaders "read from the Book of the Law of God [in Hebrew], making it clear and giving the meaning [in the Aramaic language that everyone spoke in everyday life] so that the people could understand what was being read" (Nehemiah 8:8).

FAST FACT

The Words of Jesus

Although the New Testament is written mostly in Greek, it does contain a few fragments of Aramaic—fragments that preserve the original words of Jesus. Here they are:

"Talitha koum" (Mark 5:41)—"Little girl, I say to you, get up!"

"Ephphatha" (Mark 7:34)—"Be opened!"

"Eloi, Eloi, lama sabachthani" (Mark 15:34)—"My God, my God, why have you forsaken me?"

FAST FACT

Thee's & Thou's

Both "thee" and "thou" are nothing more than an informal way of saying "you." Once upon a time, you see, English had two ways to say "you" (just as most languages still do today). A friend would address his friend as "thou" but his boss as "you," for instance, just as a German would call one "du," but the other "sie."

The King James Version addresses God as "thou" (and not "you") because its translators wanted to stress that we may speak to Him as we would to a friend. Unfortunately, the general disappearance of "thee" and "thou" from the English language has meant that some people now use them to sound more formal and "respectful" in their prayers—something that is the exact opposite of what these words originally meant!

Likewise, Jesus probably spoke in Aramaic, but it was only a matter of decades before His words were translated into the Greek of the eastern Roman Empire. In fact, His followers did such a thorough job of spreading His sayings in Greek, that we've lost all but a few of the actual Aramaic words that Jesus spoke!

So, if you want to read the Bible, you might as well do so in a language you understand. And unless thou dost have a degree in English literature, then verily, I would bid thee get thyself something other than the King James Version of Scripture. I know, I know—it's popular. It's cheap. It's pretty accurate. And nothing else "sounds biblical." But the Bible is tough enough to read without stumbling over words like "habergeon" and "pommels."*

Fortunately, there are a lot of good translations out there. In fact, the Bible is available in roughly 2,500 of the world's 6,500 languages. And if the only language you know is English . . . well, there are at least a dozen English versions that are widely used today.

Picking a Bible

There are so many versions out there, as a matter of fact, that it can create problems. The days when everyone in church could recite the same Bible passage in unison, for example, are gone forever; try that today, and it would sound like the Tower of Babel!

---

* Just so you know, a "habergeon" is a coat of mail, and "pommels" are bowls.

Then, too, many of the books that can help you understand the Bible—dictionaries, concordances, Bible commentaries, and the like—are tied to one particular translation. I have a Hebrew dictionary, for instance, that is meant to be used with *Strong's Concordance;* unfortunately, *Strong's Concordance* can be used only with the King James Version. So, if I need to look up the meaning of a certain Hebrew word, then I'd better be using that particular version of the Bible!

So what version should you be using?

The short answer is that you should use any version that works for you. If you're comfortable with the King James Version, for instance, then stick with it. If you like the New Living Translation, then use it. There really aren't any *bad* translations out there—not the ones in common use, anyway. Buying a Bible is like buying a car: There's no *right* choice; there's only the choice that's right for you.

And to help you sort out which Bible is right for you, I've put together a list of common translations, along with my opinion of each. Keep in mind that this is not an objective evaluation; it is biased, opinionated, and subject to change without notice. Then too, I haven't included some versions (such as The Revised English Bible or The International Children's Bible), simply because I don't know much about them.

FAST FACT

How Many Bibles Are Out There?

Roughly 9 billion Bibles—either whole or in part—have been distributed since 1947. Pollsters estimate that 92 % of all American homes contain at least one Bible and that Americans spend $200 million on Bibles every year.

FAST FACT

What Bible Does Your Pastor Use?

- 34 % of all Protestant pastors surveyed prefer the New International Version.

- 24 % prefer the King James Version.

- 10 % prefer the New Revised Standard Version.

FAST FACT

Chapter and Verse

As you read the Bible, you'll notice a lot of numerals, sprinkled all throughout the text. Believe it or not, these numerals once represented the cutting edge of information technology.

Scholars had long needed a quick way to specify which part of the Bible they were arguing about. Stephen Langton, a lecturer at the University of Paris, helped meet this need in the early thirteenth century when he divided the Bible into numbered chapters.

Robert Stephanus took this one step further in the 1550s when he subdivided Langton's chapters into verses. (His son later wrote that Stephanus did this while traveling by horse from Paris to Lyons. Judging by some of the verse divisions that Stephanus made, it must have been a bumpy ride!)

Once you know what's going on, it's easy to quote "chapter and verse." If someone refers to Matthew 8:14, for instance, you know they're talking about the fourteenth *verse* in the eighth *chapter* of Matthew. The chapter itself will be marked with a large numeral "8," the verse with a small "14."

For the sake of convenience, I've lumped all translations into two groups: *Study Bibles,* and *Easy-Reading Bibles. Study Bibles* are good for church or a discussion group; *Easy-Reading Bibles* work best when you're reading the Bible on your own. If you already have a *Study* Bible, get one that's *Easy-Reading;* if you already have an *Easy-Reading* Bible, get one that's . . . well, you figure it out. (And if you don't have *any* Bible, then just flip a coin and pick one!)

With that in mind, let's take a look at what's out there:

Study Bibles

• *The King James Version (KJV).*

Also known as "The Authorized Version," this was the world's best-selling Bible, right up until 1987. Even today, it's still a strong second. And if you talk to the people who actually read their Bibles during the week (and not just in church), you'll find that they are five times more likely to use the KJV than the next most popular version. No wonder—the KJV is one of the most beautifully written books in the English language. It's still pretty accurate. And there are *scads* of reference materials out there to help you make sense of what it says. Its only major drawback, as a matter of fact, is that most people today don't understand Elizabethan English.

- *The New King James Version (NKJV).*

  Think of it as "King James *Lite*"—they've updated the language, but left most of the KJV unchanged. It's a sentimental favorite of the people who *would* read the KJV if only they could understand it. But to be honest, it's never really clicked with me.

- *The Revised Standard Version (RSV).*

  When it came out in the 1950s, the RSV stirred up lots of controversy. Some of this was due to its supposedly liberal "bias"; most of it was because the RSV was one of the first Bibles to successfully challenge the monopoly of the KJV. If you've been using the KJV, you won't find the RSV much of a switch; the language is similar, right down to using "thee's" and "thou's" in the Psalms. I like it myself, though it's rapidly being replaced by other study Bibles.

- *The New Revised Standard Version (NRSV).*

FAST FACT

Catholic Bibles

Catholic Bibles are bigger than Protestant Bibles; that's because they include extra chapters and books in the Old Testament. These chapters and books are called "the Apocrypha," and if you want a Bible that includes them, you have several choices:

- Today's English Version, The Revised Standard Version, and The New Revised Standard Version all have "Catholic" editions.

- The Jerusalem Bible is an English translation of a French translation of the Bible. Despite this, it's actually pretty good—clear, scholarly, and accurate.

- The New American Bible is a new translation that is widely admired for its accuracy. I find its language a little "earnest" at times, but that may be because I haven't used it very much.

At one time, all Catholic Bibles were based upon the Vulgate—*a* Latin translation made by Jerome between A.D. 390 and 405. Since 1943, however, Catholic scholars have been encouraged to make their translations from Greek and Hebrew manuscripts.

In 1989, the National Council of Churches finally got rid of the "thee's" and "thou's" in the RSV. They also updated the language and made it "gender inclusive"—instead of "man," for instance, God now makes "humankind" in His image. If I were a better

FAST FACT

Cheap Bibles

Bibles are expensive. Books that help you understand the Bible are even more expensive. With a little work, however, you can cut your costs dramatically.

Every thrift store I've ever been in, for instance, always has a batch of Bibles—usually the Today's English Version, but I've seen others. Likewise, second-hand bookshops are a good place to pick up commentaries and Bible dictionaries.

Need to buy Bibles in bulk? Check the Web sites of the American Bible Society and the International Bible Society—they both offer some real deals.

Finally, I've saved the best for last: Christian Book Distributors. If you know what you want (and myself, I would never buy a Bible commentary sight-unseen), they offer some incredible deals. Commentaries, for instance, go for as little as one-third the retail price at CBD. You can get a catalog by phoning 1-800-247-4784, or check the CBD site on the Web.

person, I suppose I would like this version more; as it is, I find its language too stiff and awkward.

• *The New American Standard Bible (NASB).*

The product of scholars who believe that every single word of the Bible was dictated by God, the NASB is extremely accurate—in fact, I'd say that it is excrutiatingly accurate. To be honest, I don't like the NASB—I think its language is painfully ugly—but I've learned not to say this out loud, because I've found that the people who *do* like the NASB tend to like it very, very much.

• *The New International Version (NIV).*

The NIV is the best-selling translation in the world today—not bad for a version that started out as little more than a conservative alternative to the RSV. All in all, it's a good, careful translation. Its language is smooth (though not extraordinarily beautiful). And there is a large and growing number of study helps for this version. Its only drawback is that it's written at an eighth-grade reading level; roughly a third of all adults, in other words, can read it only with difficulty.

Easy-Reading Bibles

• *New International Reader's Version (NirV).*

I'd call this version "NIV *Lite,*" except that I've already used that joke. Basically, the NirV is an *Easy-Reading* edition of the NIV. Like its ancestor, the NirV is a good, careful translation; unlike the NIV, it's written in language that a child can understand. Myself, I find it a little *too* easy to understand—the language is not "See Moses run. Run, Moses, run!" but it's close. Still, this is the Bible I'm buying for the kids in my church.

- *Contemporary English Version (CEV).*

    The CEV is a brand new translation that's accurate, gracefully written, and very easy to read. If I were you, I'd keep an eye on this one; I think it's going to be very popular in the years ahead. (And no, the American Bible Society did not pay me to write this!)

- *Today's English Version (TEV).*

    Also known as *Good News for Modern Man,* the TEV was originally meant for people who speak English as a second language. This made it extraordinarily clear and easy to read . . . and it wasn't long before it was discovered by those of us who have trouble reading English as our *first* language! Accurate, graceful, and cheap, the TEV is a sentimental favorite of mine.

- *New Living Translation (NLT).*

    Ken Taylor was a Baptist layman whose kids couldn't understand

FAST FACT

The Mother of All Translations

One of our local radio talk-show hosts likes to challenge his listeners to name "one good thing—just one good thing!—that government has ever done."

The next time he does this, I'm going to phone in and tell him, "The King James Bible."

Yes, it's true—the King James Version of Scripture was a government project. It got its start because the Church of England got tired of its people fussing about which version of the Bible they should use in church. (Sound familiar?) The common people preferred the Geneva Bible. Church leaders preferred the Bishop's Bible. So the government decided to start again from scratch—and for the next five years, fifty-four "learned men" worked at government expense to produce a new Bible.

In 1611, they unveiled the result: the King James Version of the Bible. It was beautifully written and remarkably accurate; what's more, the government required every church in England to purchase one. (And this was in the days when a Bible might cost as much as a new car does today.) As a result, the "Authorized Version" became the best-selling Bible the world has ever known.

Keep that in mind, the next time someone says, "Close enough for government work"!

FAST FACT

Marking the Bible

Some people find it helpful to make notes and mark special verses in their Bible. If you're one of those people, let me make some suggestions:

- **Don't mark the text itself.** If you do, that makes it difficult to read next time.

- **Don't use highlighters or felt-tip pens.** They "bleed" through the paper.

- **Don't get too elaborate.** The more complicated your system is, the more likely you are to forget what it means.

The best system I've found is to mark the margins with a "P" for God's promises, a "C" for God's commands, a "W" for God's warnings, and a star for any other kind of verse that I think is important.

the KJV . . . so he translated the KJV into a version they could understand. The result was The Living Bible. Critics hated it—they said it was too conservative, too Protestant, too . . . well, too *Baptist!*—but the public loved it; over the years, The Living Bible has sold something like 40 million copies.

Now a team of conservative scholars has set out to make The Living Bible a little more respectable. The result is the NLT—a version that's conservative, easy-to-read, *and* gender-inclusive. I hated The Living Bible, but I like the NLT.

- *The Message.*

The Message is *almost* more of a Bible commentary than it is a Bible. Instead of focusing on the *words* of the Bible, it takes *ideas* and rephrases them in a way that makes more sense to readers today. (Yes, all translations do this, but *The Message* does it more than most.) The result is a Bible that brings new life to old, familiar passages. If I were you, I wouldn't make this the first Bible I bought—it's a little *too* free and easy to be your only Bible—but I'd definitely make it the second.

Reading the Bible

OK, so now you have your Bible. What do you do with it?

Read it.

Just like that?

Yeah, just like that.

There's a whole industry out there, after all, that is trying to convince you the Bible is so incredibly difficult to read that you can't possibly understand it unless you buy whatever product it is that they're selling. Dictionaries. Commentaries. Study guides. Computer software. *Stuff!* And don't misunderstand me—all of it is wonderful, useful, helpful *stuff* . . .

But you don't *need* it—not to read the Bible.

No, all you *need* to do is to open the Bible and start reading. If you haven't done this before, then try reading it as you would a magazine: flip through the pages until you find something that looks interesting, and read it. If you get bored, try something else. There's no law, after all, that says you *must* read through the entire Bible in sequence, one page after the other. The Bible is a library, remember; it's a collection of books. Read it as such.

After you've done that for a while, you might try looking for specific stories. Take a look at the **FastFact** list of basic Bible stories, for instance; do you see any that you don't recognize? Read them first. Once you've done that, take a look at the chapters I've listed as a **HighLight** of each book in the Bible—and if you find one of these chapters especially interesting, then feel free to read more of that particular book.

FAST FACT

The Basic Bible

If you're not familiar with the Bible, try reading these stories first—they're fifteen of the most famous ones in all of Scripture:

- Adam and Eve's Creation and Fall (Genesis 2; 3).

- Noah and the Ark (Genesis 6–9).

- The Exodus (Exodus 3–14).

- The Ten Commandments (Exodus 20).

- The Battle of Jericho (Joshua 6).

- The Story of Gideon (Judges 6; 7).

- Samson and Delilah (Judges 13–16).

- David and Goliath (1 Samuel 17).

- David and Bathsheba (2 Samuel 11; 12).

- The Shepherd's Psalm (Psalm 23).

- The Three Hebrews in the Fiery Furnace (Daniel 3).

- Daniel in the Lions' Den (Daniel 6).

- The Birth of Jesus (Luke 2).

- The Sermon on the Mount (Matthew 5–8).

- The Death and Resurrection of Jesus (Luke 22–24).

Reading the Bible Straight Through

Sooner or later, you're going to try to read the Bible straight through—cover to cover, from Genesis to Revelation.

Fine. Go ahead. Don't let me stop you.

If you've *already* tried to do this, however, I can almost guarantee where you stopped. You made it through Genesis, right? Slogged through the last chapters in Exodus. Made it half way through Leviticus, sneaked a peak at Numbers and Deuteronomy, then gave up in despair.

How do I know this? Because I've been there and done that.

But if you want to try it again, get a copy of *The One Year Bible*—it's available in almost any translation you want. *The One Year Bible* divides the Bible into 365 daily readings; every day, you get two or three chapters of the Old Testament, a chapter or two from the New Testament, part of a Psalm, and a few verses from Proverbs. In one year's time, you've read the whole Bible . . . but you've done so in a way that makes sure you get *something* good each day.

At this point, you may be ready for something that's a little "deeper" and more systematic. If that's the case, then I'd suggest you begin with a survey of the Bible's history.

• Start with Genesis, and continue reading on through Exodus 20.

• Skip to Numbers 16, and read through to chapter 25.

• Now skip to Joshua, and read the first ten chapters.

• Pick up the story again in Judges and read all of that book, as well as the books of Samuel and Kings.

• Add the stories of Ruth, Esther, and the first six chapters of Daniel.

• Finish off with Luke and Acts.

Doing this will give you a "big picture" of the Bible—and once you have it, you're ready to start studying individual books.

Keep in mind that there has been no special trick to anything you've done so far. All that I've asked you to do is read. And the reading you've done so far has been pretty straightforward; you should have been reading the Bible the same way you'd read a newspaper or magazine. We've been trying to grasp the whole forest, remember. We've not been studying each and every tree.

By this time, however, you've probably run across a book or two that you'd like to know more about. Isaiah, perhaps. Or Mark. Maybe Paul's letter to the church in Rome. It's as though you've been dating around, but now you'd like to settle down and try a deeper relationship. So what do you do?

Myself, I'd start by reading the whole book, two or three times. As I do this, I'm watching for patterns. Let's say I'm reading through Mark, for instance, and I notice that the last five chapters—fully a third of the book—is taken up with the last week of Jesus' life.

> **!GOOD!**
> **!WORD!**
>
> **Pericope**
>
> Pronounced *puh-RIH-koh-pee,* New Testament scholars use this word to describe a single story in the Gospels, as in "Let's take a look at the *pericope* of the feeding of the five thousand." I don't expect you to use this word yourself, but at least you'll be prepared if somebody else does.

"Why does Mark spend so much time on this particular week?" I'll ask myself. "And what does that tell me about the purpose of Mark's book?"

Once I've done this, then I'll break down the book into "bite-sized pieces"—chunks of the book that I'm able to study at one setting. It may be a verse. It may be a story. It may be a whole chapter . . . but whatever it is, it's long enough to keep my interest, but short enough that I can keep the whole thing well in mind.

Let me give you an example. Suppose that I'm studying Mark's story about the time some parents brought their children to Jesus for His blessing, only to be chased off by the disciples (Mark 10:13-16). I've already read the text; what I want to do now is make it come alive.

One way to do this is by asking the "Five W's and an H" that every journalist knows:

- **Who?** In this case, Jesus and His disciples, plus some parents with small children.

- **What?** The parents wanted Jesus to bless their children; the disciples wanted them to stay away. Jesus scolded the disciples and blessed the children.

- **When?** This took place right after a very heavy discussion about divorce and remarriage.

- **Where?** The story takes place in the middle of a crowd. Apparently, there were a lot of people who wanted to be near Jesus at this time.

- **How?** Jesus rebuked the disciples—with a word? A glance? A fist upside the head?—and then reached out to take the children in His arms.

- **Why?** Jesus said that "the kingdom of heaven belongs to such as these," and that "anyone who will not receive the kingdom of God as a little child will never enter it."

Having done this, I might next add the five senses to this story:

- **What would I have tasted?** Dust.

- **What would I have smelt?** The unwashed bodies of the crowd. Sour diapers.

- **What would I have felt?** The hot sun. People crowding in against me.

- **What would I have heard?** Children crying. The angry voices of the disciples. The muttering of the crowd.

- **What would I have seen?** The impatient crowd. Anxious mothers. The blue sky overhead.

Granted, I can't do *all* of these things with *every* story—much less every book of the Bible—but I do what I can, when I can do it.

At this point I'm ready to ask what this story *meant.* Why was it included? What was the author trying to say? In the time of Jesus, for instance, children weren't all that important; is Mark trying to tell me that God puts a different value on people than society does? Check it out—what does Jesus do with some of the other outcasts that He meets? What does this tell me about Jesus?

Having done all this, I can now ask myself what this story *means* to me today. One of the easiest ways to do this is to imagine the story as a play, and then ask which character I would find it the easiest to be. In Mark's story, for instance, with whom do I identify the most? With Jesus? The disciples? The anxious mothers? So what does that tell me about the way that I treat people? Or the way that God treats me?

Another approach is to ask three questions:

- **Is there a command in this story?** Yes—be like a child!

- **Is there a warning in this story?** Yes—don't be the kind of person who keeps people away from Jesus!

- **Is there a promise in this story?** Yes—God always has time for "little people."

FAST FACT

Bible Study Guides

If you'd like some help in applying the Bible to your life (or if you've been asked to lead a group study of the Bible), there are a *lot* of good study guides out there. Take a look at the catalogs and Web sites of NavPress and InterVarsity Press—just about everything they put out in this area is excellent.

Dealing with problems

At this point, you may be ready to give up the whole idea of reading the Bible. It seems hopelessly complicated and way too "touchy-feely" for someone like you.

That's fine. You don't have to read the Bible the way I've just outlined. Read it your own way. Whatever works for you is fine.

Then again, you may want to read the Bible . . . but *nothing* seems to work for you. Whatever you do, as a matter of fact, you run into problems. Like falling asleep. Or not understanding the words. Or maybe you *do* understand the words, but you can't understand why the Bible says the kind of things that it does.

Don't worry. Reading the Bible is like riding a bicycle or eating with chopsticks; it's a learned skill—and that means you'll get better with practice. What I usually tell beginners, as a matter of fact, is to give it two weeks. If reading the Bible doesn't get easier in two weeks, then stop and try to figure out what you're doing wrong. But if you haven't given it two weeks, then you haven't been doing it long enough to find out if you're doing something right!

It may be, for instance, that you need to try a different version of the Bible. (That's why it's a good idea to make your first Bible a cheap one. Don't start by spending $75 on a leather-bound Study Bible with your name embossed in gold on the cover; if it turns out you don't like it, after all, you're stuck.)

Then too, you may find it helpful to study with a group. Most churches, high schools, and colleges have some kind of Bible study group that meets on a regular basis; ask around and find out. If you don't like meeting with strangers, try asking some of your friends. And if a group feels awkward, give it two weeks and *then* decide; you're not obligated to attend a group that makes you feel uncomfortable, of course, but you do want to give it an honest chance.

Some people are intimidated by all the strange names they find in the Bible. (Sad but true—"they set out from Bene-jaakan and camped at Hor-haggidgad" is an actual verse in Scripture.) All I can say is, "deal with it." After all, if you think that *Bible* names are hard to pronounce, then try to explain why "Arkansas" doesn't rhyme with "Kansas"!

Likewise, you may be frustrated by the sheer variety of the Bible—all those books, all those characters, all those different opinions on all those different subjects. If that's the case, then try thinking of the Bible as a party with a lot of different guests. As you're reading, you're chatting with each person in turn—and as you do so, you're learning something about each of them. Some will be interesting, others difficult to understand. But each Bible book has its own story to tell—and that's why they're all important.

Finally, you will read things in the Bible that flat-out don't make sense. When that happens, make a note of the problem and move on. After all, if you're eating a fish and you come to a bone, you don't stop eating the fish. No, you take out the bone. You set it aside. And you go on with your meal. The same approach works for the Bible.

If you keep running into the same *kind* of problem, however, then you may want to pick up a reference book or two—one that gives you the background necessary to make sense of a difficult text. Once again, you don't *need* any of the books I'm going to mention, but they can help. (What's more, they make wonderful Christmas gifts!)

- *Bible dictionaries.*

   Just what the name implies: a list of words used in the Bible, along with the definitions. If you want to know what a cubit is, the dictionary will tell you. (It's anywhere from 17 1/2 to 20 inches.) I have two bible dictionaries—one liberal, one conservative—and I use them constantly.

   If you don't have *any* Bible reference books, make a good Bible dictionary the first one you get. And no, I don't have recommendations as to which one is best; they're all good. (Just make sure that the one you get matches the Bible translation you're using!)

- *Concordances.*

   Like a Bible dictionary, a concordance is a list of words used in the Bible; unlike a dictionary, it doesn't tell you *what* they mean, but *where* they're found. If you're trying to remember where the Bible talks about a town clerk, for instance, a concordance is the only way to go; in 30 seconds, I found the reference in Acts 19:35.

   In my opinion, a concordance is the *only* reference tool in which computer software is better than a book, but you're free to disagree. Once again, however, you need to make sure that your concordance matches the version of the Bible that you're using.

- *Single-volume and double-volume commentaries.*

   Commentaries offer a text-by-text (or chapter-by-chapter) explanation of what the Bible *meant*—or rather, they offer an explanation of what the commentary author *thought* they meant. They don't tell you what the Bible text means today . . . and to be honest, some commentaries aren't very good at telling you what it meant back then. In fact, even *good* commentaries can be a little "soggy" in spots.

   All this is a long way of saying that a commentary is like a discussion group: It can be helpful, but it shouldn't be the last word (or even the first word) in your study of the Bible.

   If you're bound and determined to get a commentary, however, try to get one that's only one or two volumes—that way, it won't take up so much space on your shelves. For conservative commentaries, I like Zondervan's *NIV Bible Commentary* as well as the *International Bible Commentary* by the same company, and I *really* like InterVarsity Press's *Bible Background Commentary*. If you're looking for a liberal commentary, on the other hand, try the *Harper's Bible Commentary*.

• *Multi-volume commentary sets.*

Like single-volume commentaries, these offer verse-by-verse explanations of the Bible; unlike single-volume commentaries, they're . . . well, they're multi-volume. Most books of the Bible will get a volume of their own in one of these series; some may get two or three.

Sound good?

FlashPoint: Liberals and conservatives

Most of the time, it doesn't make any difference whether a Bible dictionary or commentary was written by a Baptist, an Episcopalian, a Roman Catholic, or a member of the Orthodox Church. Good scholars are good scholars, no matter what their denomination.

But it *does* make a difference whether the author is a liberal or conservative—and once again, the line between these groups crosses all denominational lines.

By and large, liberals stress that the Bible was written by *people,* conservatives that it was inspired by *God.* Liberals focus on the *differences* that exist between the various books of the Bible, conservatives on their *similarities.* Liberals are uncomfortable with the idea of miracles or predictive prophecy, while conservatives defend it. Finally, liberals generally argue that biblical books were written *later* and by different authors than tradition says; conservatives usually argue for traditional dates and authorship.

They can be—but we're talking about some serious money here. Anyone who wants to get all thirty-four volumes of the *New International Commentary* series, for instance, had better be prepared to shell out $1,358—and it's not even complete! It still has twenty-four books of the Bible to go!

Then too, most multi-volume commentary sets have a dirty little secret: they are "uneven" (which is a nice way of saying that some of the volumes can be pretty lame, even in the best of series).

My advice? Don't buy the whole set . . . but if there's one book of the Bible that especially interests you, then just pick up the volume that covers that particular book. (Yes, you can buy them separately.) If you don't have much money, start with books from *The Daily Study Bible*, *The New Century Bible Commentary*, or the *Tyndale Commentary* series—they're good, cheap, and fairly easy to read. If you're feeling ambitious, both the *Word Bible Commentary* and the *New International Commentary* series are thorough, scholarly, and conservative; for liberal commentaries, try the *Anchor Bible Commentary* or the *Hermeneia* series.

Living the Bible

Last of all, you've not finished reading the Bible until you do something about what you have learned. Jesus put it this way:

> "Everyone who hears these words of mine and puts them into practice is like a wise man who built his house on the rock. The rain came down, the streams rose, and the winds blew and beat against that house; yet it did not fall, because it had its foundation on the rock. But everyone who hears these words of mine and does not put them into practice is like a foolish man who built his house on sand. The rain came down, the streams rose, and the winds blew and beat against that house, and it fell with a great crash" (Matthew 7:24-27).

Take what you read in the Bible, in other words, and use it to build the kind of life that lasts forever.

Who Did What When?

These dates are generally accepted by conservative scholars. Keep in mind, however, that all of these dates are tentative and the subject of considerable controversy. All the books of the Bible have been placed into this timeline—either at the period to which their content refers or according to when they were written—even though in some cases it is almost impossible to be very certain about the times given. A question mark following a particular Bible book indicates that it is more difficult than most to pin down to a particular time—and that the date given is really an educated guess.

Biblical Event	Biblical Book
Prehistory	Genesis 1–11
• Adam & Eve	1 Chronicles 1
• Cain & Abel	
• Noah & the Ark	
• The Tower of Babel	

The Patriarchs: c. 1900-1800 B.C.   Job (?)

- Abraham & Sarah   Genesis 12–50
- Isaac & Rebecca   1 Chronicles 2–8
- Jacob/Israel
- Joseph

The Exodus: c. 1445-1405 B.C. **(or 1290-1250** B.C.**)**   Exodus

- Moses, Aaron, & Miriam   Leviticus

                          Numbers

                          Deuteronomy

Israel Enters Canaan: c. 1405 B.C. **(or 1250** B.C.**)**   Joshua

- Joshua & the Battle of Jericho

The Time of the Judges: c. 1405-1050 B.C.   Judges

(or 1250-1050 B.C.**)**   Ruth

- Deborah & Barak   1 Samuel 1–7
- Gideon
- Samson
- Samuel

The United Kingdom of Israel: c. 1050-931 B.C.   1 Samuel 8–31

- Saul   2 Samuel
- David & Solomon   2 Kings 1–12
- Civil War   1 Chronicles 11–29

                          2 Chronicles 1–12

                          Psalms

	Proverbs
	Ecclesiastes
	Song of Solomon
The Divided Kingdoms of Israel & Judah:	1 Kings 12–22
931-722 B.C.	2 Kings 1–17
• Jeroboam I	2 Chronicles 13–28
• Ahab & Elijah	Isaiah 1–39
• Elisha	Hosea
• Uzziah	Joel
• The Destruction of Israel	Amos
	Jonah
	Micah
The Kingdom of Judah: 722-586 B.C.	2 Kings 18–25
• Hezekiah	2 Chronicles 29–36
• Manasseh	Jeremiah
• The Destruction of Judah	Lamentations
	Obadiah
	Nahum
	Habakkuk
	Zephaniah
The Babylonian Capitivity: 586-536 B.C.	Isaiah 40–66
• Nebuchadnezzar	Ezekiel
• The Fall of Babylon	Daniel

Life Under Persian Rule: 539-331 B.C.	Ezra
• The Return to Judah	Nehemiah
• The Temple Rebuilt	Esther
	Haggai
	Zechariah
	Malachi

Life Under Greek Rule: 331-143 B.C.

- Alexander the Great
- Antiochus Epiphanes
- The Maccabean Revolt

The Kingdom of the Maccabees: 143-63 B.C.

Life Under Roman Rule: 63 B.C. onward

The Life of Jesus: c. 4 B.C. – A.D. **31**	Matthew
• Baptism	Mark
• Ministry in Galilee	Luke
• Ministry in Judea	John
• Death & Resurrection	

The Church in Jerusalem: A.D. **31-34**	Acts 1–8
• Pentecost	
• Death of Stephen	
• Persecution by Saul (Paul)	

Paul Converted: A.D. 35	Acts 9
Paul's First Missionary Voyage: A.D. 45-47	Acts 13; 14
• Cyprus	
• Asia Minor	
Jerusalem Council: A.D. 49	Acts 15
	James (?)
Paul's Second Missionary Voyage: A.D. 49-52	Acts 16–18
• Asia Minor	1 & 2 Thessalonians
• Greece	
Paul's Third Missionary Voyage: A.D. 53-58	Acts 18–20
• Asia Minor	1 & 2 Corinthians
• Greece	Galatians
	Romans
Paul's Imprisonment and Journey	Acts 21–28
to Rome: A.D. 58-63 (?)	Ephesians
	Philippians
	Colossians
	Philemon
Paul's Second Imprisonment	1 Timothy (?)
in Rome: A.D. 67 (?)	2 Timothy (?)
	Titus (?)

The Great Jewish War: A.D. 66-70   Hebrews (?)

    • Jerusalem & The Temple Destroyed   1 & 2 Peter

                                     Jude

The Closing Days of the Apostolic Church: 1, 2 & 3 John (?)

    A.D. 70-100   Revelation

QUICKSTART

Old Testament:
The Law

Genesis
God Creates His People

"In the beginning God created the heavens and the earth" (Genesis 1:1).

Highlights

- Adam and Eve's Creation and Fall (Genesis 2; 3).

- Noah and the Ark (Genesis 6–9).

- The Tower of Babel (Genesis 11).

- Sodom and Gomorrah (Genesis 18; 19).

- The Testing of Abraham (Genesis 22).

- Jacob Tricks His Father (Genesis 27).

- The Story of Joseph (Genesis 37; 39–47).

Why was it written?

"Genesis" literally means "beginnings," and the book of Genesis is just what its name implies. It is a book of beginnings; it tells the story of how this world began, as well as the origin of death, languages, and technology.

But Genesis doesn't tell us these things just in order to satisfy our curiosity; it does so in order to give us the context we need to understand another story: the story of the twelve tribes of Israel. In a sense, it's a prologue to the story found in Exodus, Leviticus, Numbers, and Deuteronomy—the great story of how God delivered His people from Egypt and brought them into the Promised Land.

Before God can *deliver* His people, however, He first must *choose* a people. And before He can lead His people *out* of Egypt, they first must go *into* Egypt. The stage must be set, in other words, and the characters introduced before the play can begin.

That's why the book of Genesis provides us with more than just beginnings; it also gives us a sense of continuity. "God's people are not an afterthought," it says. "They have been a part of God's plan, right from the beginning."

In short, Genesis tells us where we've come from so that we can know both where we are now, and where we're likely to go from here.

What you'll learn in Genesis

Genesis is a book about families—in fact, 95 percent of Genesis is the story of families led by just five men: Adam, Noah, Abraham, Isaac, and Jacob.

One of the themes you'll find in these stories is that of "selection by elimination." Genesis begins with the story of Adam, who is the father of all humanity. It moves on to Noah, who is a descendant of Adam through Seth (not Cain or Abel). Abraham is a descendant of Noah through Shem (not Ham or Japheth). And Jacob is a descendant of Abraham through Isaac (not Ishmael). By the time Genesis comes to an end, in other words, its focus has narrowed down to a very small part of humanity.

That's not to say that God's people are a spiritual elite—in fact, another theme of this book is family strife. Adam and Eve's desire to be "like God" leads to their falling out with each other; their descendants go on to commit murder, incest, and rape. All in all, Genesis tells some of the ugliest stories in Scripture.

In doing so, Genesis highlights God's infinite patience. In spite of everything God's people do to each other, He continues to protect them and care for them. And if it seems as though God's people are a long way from Him, it is only a matter of time before God comes looking for them, just as He did Adam and Eve.

GoodWords

- **Abram:** Literally means "the father is exalted." When God promised to make his descendants "as numerous as the stars" (Genesis 22:17), Abram's name was changed to Abraham ("father of multitudes").

- **Adam:** A pun on the Hebrew word for dirt (*adamah*). If Genesis had been written in English, it would have said that "God made man out of mud, then named him 'Clay.' "

- **Coat of many colors:** The experts aren't sure what is meant by this phrase. It may be that Joseph's coat had been made with expensive dyes; it may be that it had long sleeves. (Long sleeves made it impossible for you to work with your hands—anyone who wore such a coat was telling everyone that he didn't have to dirty his hands with manual labor.)

- **Haran:** An ancient city in what is now Syria.

- **Isaac:** Literally means, "he laughed." Today, Abraham might have named his son "Snickers."

- **Jacob:** Literally means, "he who takes by the heel"—in other words, someone who doesn't fight fair. After he wrestled with God, Jacob's name was changed to Israel ("God-fighter").

- **The tree of the knowledge of good and evil:** When Hebrew wants to say "everything," it uses pairs of opposites. "Earth and sky," for instance, means "the whole universe." Likewise, "the knowledge of good and evil" means "knowing everything there is to know." Adam and Eve were told not to eat from this tree lest they became know-it-alls.

- **Ur:** Abraham's original home; it is located in what is now Iraq.

Ten Hebrew words you should know

- **Amen:** "So be it," or "make it so!"

- **Cherubim:** The plural of cherub—thus, to speak of "cherubim*s*" is an exercise in overkill. The Bible speaks of the cherubim as nonhuman intelligent beings that praise God and live in His presence. It does not say what a cherub looks like, though most experts feel the name may come from the Assyrian word, *karubu*—huge, mythical lions or bulls with eagle's wings and human heads, who ran errands for the gods. (You may want to remember this the next time someone says that your children are "little cherubs"!)

- **Chesed:** (pronounced *CHE-sed*, with the *ch* pronounced in the same way as it is in the Scottish word, *loch*). Often translated as "loving-kindness," *chesed* is better translated as "loyalty" or "faithfulness to the treaty that God made with His people."

- **Eleph:** Literally "thousand," but it can also mean "clan," "squad," or "a heavily armed warrior." For instance, when the Bible says "17,268 men attacked," it can mean that 17,268 men attacked . . . or it can mean that 268 men from seventeen different clans attacked . . . or it can mean that seventeen squads with a total of 268 men attacked . . . or it can mean that seventeen heavily armed warriors and 268 lightly armed men attacked.

- **Hallelujah:** Praise God!

- **Holy:** Set aside for God's use.

- **Israel:** "One who fights with God"—the name given Jacob, the youngest son of Isaac and grandson of Abraham. Israel's children became the *nation* of Israel; when Israel split into two countries, the northern kingdom took the name of Israel, while the southern one was known as Judah.

- **Messiah:** "The one anointed," or "the one whom God has chosen and blessed to lead His people." All kings and priests were anointed at their inauguration; when God's people fell on hard times, they began to look for a king who would rule as David had ruled—victoriously and with justice. Their name for this future king was the "messiah"; the Greek word for *messiah* is *Christ.*

- **Seraphim:** Literally "burning ones"—six-winged creatures that live in God's presence, they were seen in vision by Isaiah. Since seraphim is the plural of seraph, to speak of "seraphim*s"* would be like talking about a flock of sheeps.

- **Shalom:** Often translated as "peace," this word carries with it the idea of "the way things ought to be." When the hungry are fed and the naked clothed, when wars shall cease and justice is done, when sickness is no more and sin has been wiped out—then, and only then, will we have true *shalom.*

- **YHWH:** God's personal name. It seems to mean something like "I am." English Bibles usually translate this as Lᴏʀᴅ (with all the letters capitalized).

FlashPoint: Camels

Genesis mentions camels seventeen times, yet there's no archaeological evidence that camels were used as beasts of burden in Canaan and Egypt until the time of the judges (roughly 600 to 700 years later). Some see this as proof that Genesis was composed a long, long time after the events described took place. Others point out that camels may have been domesticated in Arabia as early as the third millennium B.C.; if that's the case, then camels may have been used in Canaan after all. It could be that camels are mentioned in Genesis, not because they were so common, but because they were so rare.

FlashPoint: Dominion

Is the Bible responsible for the environmental crisis? Lynn White suggested it was in his famous essay, "The Historical Roots of Our Ecological Crisis" (*Science,* March 1967). He argued that Genesis 1 has been used by many believers to justify their exploitation of nature. And it's easy to see why commands to "subdue the earth" and "have dominion over the earth" might have that effect.

Other scholars point out, however, that "dominion" implies the idea of "responsible care" rather than "brutal abuse." As Victor Hamilton points out in the *New International Commentary* on Genesis:

"*Exercise dominion* reflects royal language. Man is created to rule. But this rule is to be compassionate and not exploitative. Even in the garden of Eden he who would be lord of all must be servant of all."

FlashPoint: Science and the Bible

Aside from the life of Jesus, nothing in the Bible stirs up more controversy than the first eleven chapters of Genesis. Did God create the world in seven days? Were Adam and Eve real people? Was there a worldwide flood? Do all languages come to us from the Tower of Babel? The more you wrestle with these questions, the more you wish there was some answer other than "yes" or "no"!

By and large, conservatives tend to read these chapters as scientific statements of *fact,* while liberals see them as poetic symbols of *truth*. Many conservatives, for instance, insist that Genesis teaches that God created the world in seven, literal days just a few thousand years ago; they use Creation Science to explain how He did this. Most liberals, on the other hand, say that science provides the "how" of creation and Genesis provides the "why." They believe God used the Big Bang and the process of evolution to create our world.

Actually, trying to do science with Genesis is like trying to swat flies with a violin: it's awkward, and it's not good for the violin. Genesis tells us the story of Creation in the way that God wants us to understand it—and we can't tell this story in any other way without losing something important.

Exodus
God Delivers His People

"Then the LORD said to Moses, 'Go to Pharaoh and say to him, "This is what the LORD, the God of the Hebrews, says: 'Let my people go, so that they may worship me' " ' " (Exodus 9:1).

HighLights

- The Birth of Moses (Exodus 2)

- God Calls Moses (Exodus 3; 4)

- The Plagues of Egypt (Exodus 5–11)

- The Exodus (Exodus 12:31–51; 13:17–14:31)

- The Ten Commandments (Exodus 20)

Why was it written?

Most families have a set of stories that are all their own—family stories, like the one about the time Dad fell off the roof with a bucket of paint. Or just exactly what it was that Mom did after she locked her car keys in the trunk on Christmas Eve. These are the stories we tell over and over again, because they are stories that *define* us. They don't just entertain us; they remind us who we are as a family.

Families aren't the only ones who tell these defining stories; nations do too. Think of *King Arthur and His Knights of the Round Table,* for instance, or *El Cid,* or *The Song of Roland.* These stories help define what it means to be English or Spanish or French, just as you can't understand what it means to be an American without knowing something about the Civil War.

Likewise, Exodus is *the* defining story of Judaism—a story told and retold by the prophets, the psalmists, and the downtrodden of every age. Just how it's told depends upon the person who tells this story. Sometimes it brings hope; sometimes it urges change. But in every case, it is a story about the God who delivered His people from slavery in Egypt.

In other words, the book of Exodus focuses more on story than on history. Though it is based on actual events, it focuses not so much on the *when* and *where* as on the *how* and *why*. It's not a travelogue; it's not a list of the sights and scenes that the Israelites encountered after they left Egypt. Instead, it's a national epic. It's the story that God's people tell whenever they need to remind themselves just who they are.

What you'll learn in Exodus

Reading Exodus is a good way to learn how God solves problems, for Exodus begins with a problem. God had promised Abraham that his descendants would inherit Canaan, yet they'd wound up in Egypt as slaves. So what was God going to do about it?

What God did, of course, was to lead His people out of Egypt—and not in a modest, quiet way. In fact, God seemed to go out of His way to make His job difficult. How else can you explain His choice of a stammering murderer to be the leader of His people? Or the way that He hardened Pharaoh's heart?

The God of Exodus, in other words, is a God who keeps His promises—and then some! He is not just the God who delivers Israel. No, He is the God who delivers Israel in a way that proves He is the God of the whole earth.

GoodWords _____

- **Ark of the covenant:** Every now and then, someone asks me how the Israelites managed to drag that great, big boat through the desert for forty years. So just for the record, let it be noted that the ark of the covenant is *not* the same as Noah's ark. The ark of the covenant was a gold-plated wooden box about four feet long, two and a half feet wide, and two and a half feet deep. On the top was a statue of two winged creatures called *cherubim;* inside were the Ten Commandments, Aaron's rod, and a pot of manna.

- **Cherub:** One of God's nonhuman servants. The Bible doesn't say what a cherub looks like, although experts suggest that their name may come from the Assyrian *karubu*—huge, mythical lions or bulls with eagle's wings and human heads that ran errands for the gods. The plural of cherub is cherubim, by the way, just as the plural of seraph is seraphim. (That's why there are no such things as cherubim*s* and seraphim*s*.)

- **Egypt:** Actually, there are two Egypts: Upper and Lower. Upper Egypt stretches along the Nile for almost 600 miles; it is never more than nine miles wide. Lower Egypt is the delta of the Nile. Beginning at the present-day city of Cairo, it's a hundred miles long and anywhere up to 150 miles wide. The symbol of Upper Egypt is the vulture; the symbol of Lower Egypt is the cobra. (That's why you see both animals on Pharaoh's headdress.)

- **Goshen:** The flat, fertile pastureland near the eastern part of the Nile delta.

- **Hivites:** These may be the same people as the Hurrians—a people from northern Iraq who pushed into Canaan during the second millennium B.C.

- **Jethro:** The father-in-law of Moses, also known as Ruel and Hobab. He is proof, by the way, that the Israelites weren't the only ones who worshiped the Lord at this time.

- **Lord:** Written in capital letters, it stands for YHWH (probably pronounced "Yahweh")—the covenant name of God.

- **Manna:** Literally, it means, "What is it?"—a question that people have been asking ever since. The most popular explanation is that manna is the secretion of a small insect that lives on tamarisk trees, but no hypothesis is too wild to have found its way into print.

- **Moses:** The original "comeback kid." In Exodus, Moses goes from slave to prince, and from exiled murderer to the leader of God's people. And no, despite what you see on Michelangelo's statue, Moses did not have horns. What he did have was "a shining face"—a phrase Jerome mistranslated as "horns" in his Latin Bible.

- **Mount Sinai:** Since we're not sure of the route the Israelites followed out of Egypt, we don't know for sure where God gave the Ten Commandments to Moses. Some traditions point to Jebel Serbal, others to Jebel Musa. Coming up with additional candidates is a favorite leisure activity of many archaeologists.

- **Pharaoh:** None of the pharaohs mentioned in the book of Exodus are named—a fact that annoys a good many people. If you accept a fifteenth-century B. C. date for this book, however, then the pharaoh of the Exodus was probably Amenhotep II; if you favor a thirteenth-century date, then the pharaoh was probably Ramses II.

- **Red Sea:** For the last few decades, the experts have been telling us that the Hebrew words *Yam Suph* did not mean "Red Sea" but "Reed Sea"—a marshy spot somewhere on the Sinai Peninsula. Now it turns out that *Yam Suph* probably does mean "Red Sea" after all. Go figure.

- **Sinai Peninsula:** Had the Isaelites gone directly from Goshen to Canaan, they would have run into a series of coastal forts that were built by the Egyptians to protect their frontiers. By heading inland, the Israelites avoided a direct confrontation . . . but they also made it impossible for us to know just exactly which route they followed.

- **Timbrel:** A hand drum much like a tambourine, but without the jangling metal discs.

- **Urim and thummim:** Literally, "lights and perfection." What these were or how they were used to determine God's will has been a matter of debate.

The Pyramids

No, the Israelites didn't build the Pyramids (and the Bible doesn't say they did). The Pyramids were built during Egypt's Old Kingdom (2686-2160 B.C.); the Israelites didn't enter Egypt until . . . well, figure around 1800 B.C. or so. In other words, by the time the Israelites showed up, the Pyramids were already ancient history.

The twelve tribes

- Reuben

- Simeon

- Levi: the tribe of Moses and all priests.

- Judah: the tribe of both King David and Jesus.

- Dan

- Napthali

- Gad

- Asher

- Issachar

- Zebulon

- Joseph: split into two sub-tribes—Manasseh and Ephraim.

- Benjamin: the tribe of both King Saul and the apostle Paul.

FlashPoint: When did the Exodus take place?

The Exodus obviously takes place during Egypt's New Kingdom (1550-1070 B.C.), but it's difficult to pin down events more precisely than that. Conservatives used to argue for a date of 1445 B.C. and liberals for 1250 B.C., but lately, it's anybody's guess.

FlashPoint: What kind of Exodus?

Outside of the Bible, there is no clear, unambiguous evidence of the Exodus. This doesn't mean that it didn't happen—after all, the Egyptians were not the kind of people who would write about their defeat at the hands of slaves! Then, too, there were a lot of people moving around the Middle East at the time—so many that it's difficult for archaeologists to sort out just who was moving where and why. But even if you believe, as I do, that the Exodus *did* happen, a number of questions remain. By and large, most experts fall into one of these three camps:

* Most conservatives believe that hundreds of thousands—even millions!—of Israelites moved out of Egypt in one big wave. After wandering forty years in the wilderness, they moved into Canaan and displaced many of the local people.

* Many liberals (and some conservatives) believe that a few thousand people moved out of Egypt and into Canaan—either all at once, or in a series of waves. There, they joined up with fellow worshipers of YHWH and formed the nation of Israel.

* A few liberals believe that no such exodus ever took place. Instead, there was a peasant revolt in Canaan; the victors then "adopted" the story of the Exodus in order to explain their success.

Leviticus
Living a Life of Holiness

27 CHAPTERS — READING TIME: 3 HOURS

" 'Speak to the entire assembly of Israel and say to them:
"Be holy because I, the LORD your God, am holy" ' "(Leviticus 19:2).

Highlights

- Foods Clean and Foul (Leviticus 11).

- The Day of Atonement (Leviticus 16).

Why was it written?

God made an agreement with the people of Israel: He would be their God, and they would be His people. He would bless them; in return, they would love and serve Him. That's why He had rescued them from Egypt; that's why they followed Him.

Even though God's people were no longer in Egypt, there were still plenty of things that could threaten their relationship with Him—such things as sickness, sin, and death. So God gave His people a list of the steps they should take in order to protect their relationship with Him—rules about such things as property, marriage, and health.

What's more, God gave them a list of the steps they should take if they ever broke their agreement with Him—rules about sacrifices, offerings, and rituals of purification.

In other words, Leviticus is more than just a book of rituals. It's a book about relationships—a step-by-step manual, as it were, that describes how God and His chosen people should love each other.

What you'll learn in Leviticus

If nothing else, reading through Leviticus will teach you both persistence and patience. Most contemporary readers find it tedious; almost all come away perplexed. What should we do, after all, with a book that contains elaborate laws about baldness?

Behind all these laws, however, several principles remain—principles such as "wrongs must be made right." "Take care of the poor." "Love your neighbor as yourself." These principles remain in force, even if some of the laws that apply these principles do not.

In short, Leviticus tells us that religion must be practical. Our relationship with God doesn't just affect the way we pray or worship. It should also affect our love life, our health habits, and the way we do business.

"If it matters to you," Leviticus tells us, "it matters to God. Live accordingly."

GoodWords

- **Atonement:** The basic idea is one of reconciliation or harmony. Experts disagree as to whether the original meaning of this term was "to cover," "to wipe clean," or "to offer a ransom."

- **Clean:** Think "kosher." Something (or someone) that could be offered to God for His use.

- **Ephod:** A waistcoat or vest.

- **Holy:** Given to God for His use.

- **Leprosy:** A general term that covered all diseases of the skin (including the heartbreak of psoriasis).

- **Urim and thummin:** Literally, "lights and perfection." What they were or how they were used to determine God's will has been the subject of much conjecture.

FAST FACT

Sacrifices and offerings

Strange as it may seem to us, Jewish worship resembled a slaughterhouse more than it did a modern church service. Almost every time an Israelite came to worship God, he brought an animal to be killed. Most sacrifices and offerings fell into one of four groups:

- *Burnt offerings* expressed the worshiper's gratitude and dedication to God; they usually involved the sacrifice of a male lamb or bull or an offering of grain.

- *Sin offerings* asked God's forgiveness for something the worshiper had done wrong; they usually involved the sacrifice of a male lamb or goat. (As was the case with burnt offerings, a worshiper who couldn't afford a lamb or goat could substitute a pigeon.)

- *Guilt offerings* asked forgiveness for a wrong done to another person; they usually involved a ram, or a female lamb or goat.

- *Peace offerings* were a way to give thanks; they could involve any animal or an offering of grain.

Numbers
Travels With God

36 CHAPTERS — READING TIME: 4 HOURS

" 'God is not a man, that he should lie, nor a son of man, that he should change his mind. Does he speak and then not act? Does he promise and not fulfill?' " (Numbers 23:19).

Highlights

- The Spies Report; The People Rebel (Numbers 14).

- Moses Loses His Temper and Fouls Up (Numbers 20).

- Snakes That Bite (Numbers 21).

- The Story of Balaam (Numbers 22–24).

Why was it written?

Many of the most popular stories of our day are built around travel. Think of Huckleberry Finn as he floats down the Mississippi or Jack Kerouac on the road across America or the *U.S.S. Enterprise* as it "boldly goes where no man has gone before."

Each of these are what the movie industry used to call a "road picture." And whether the main character is Huck Finn or Captain Kirk, the basic elements are always the same: The hero has wonderful adventures. He meets interesting people. And in the course of his travels, he learns something important about himself.

The biblical book of Numbers is one of the earliest of all these travel stories. Like them, it's the story of a trip—the trip God's people made from Egypt to the Promised Land of Canaan. Like all good travel stories, Numbers is filled with stories of the events and people encountered along the way. And as in all good travel stories, in Numbers, God's people learn something important about themselves.

Unfortunately, the only thing most of God's people learn is just how stubborn and rebellious they are. Time and again, they rebel against God's leadership along the way. As a result, only two of the people who originally set out from Egypt—Caleb and Joshua—actually complete the journey into Canaan.

Still, those two do make it—and with them, the children of the people who had originally begun the trip. What happens next is taken up in the books of Deuteronomy and Joshua. As far as Numbers is concerned, the story ends when the journey does: at the borders of Canaan.

What you'll learn in Numbers

You can read Numbers as bad news or as good news—the choice is yours.

Chapters 1 through 25 give us the bad news: Following God in the past is no guarantee of following Him today. Everyone who escapes from Egypt falls along the way. The people rebel against God. The Levites rebel against God. Even Moses rebels against God!

But chapters 26 through 36 give us the good news: God always finds a way to fulfill His promises. If one generation rejects God's blessings, then He'll work with the next. In other words, no matter how hard you try, you can't stop God from blessing *somebody*—even if it's not you!

So which message do you most need to hear? Do you need to be reminded of the importance of persistence or do you need to be reassured of God's faithfulness? Either way, you'll find the message you need in Numbers.

GoodWords

- **Anakim:** In addition to being the first name of Darth Vader, this was a Canaanite tribe widely believed to be giants. (They were also known as "Nephilim.") Some experts interpret Genesis 6 as suggesting that the Anakim were the result of angels impregnating humans; others don't.

- **Balaam:** The Canaanite prophet who blessed God's people in spite of himself. Ancient inscriptions referring to Balaam have been found in what is now Jordan; apparently he was quite a popular fellow at the time.

- **City of refuge:** With no police and no formal court system, justice was left to the family of the person who had been injured. Obviously, this could lead to problems. A person who had accidentally killed someone, for instance, might be lynched before he had the chance to explain what had happened.

That's why God designated cities of refuge; they were a place where the accused could get a fair hearing. If it turned out that he was guilty of no more than an accidental death, he would remain there until emotions cooled and he could return home safely.

- **Forty:** Some experts suggest this number may sometimes be used as a symbol for an indefinite period of time—one that is long, but still limited in nature.

- **Levites:** Members of the tribe of Levi. They were in charge of all religious activities. All priests were Levites, but not all Levites were priests. Priestly Levites were descendants of Aaron and could offer sacrifices; the rest were assigned tasks such as carrying and assembling the sanctuary, preparing offerings for sacrifice, and providing music for the worship services.

- **Midianites:** Descendants of Abraham through his wife Keturah. The Midianites were a loose confederacy of traders, shepherds, and raiders who lived in what is now southern Jordan. Their relationship with Israel was ambiguous. In the story of Balaam, they clearly appear as enemies. Then again, Moses was married to a Midianite, and his Midianite father-in-law was a valued friend of Israel.

- **Moabites:** Descendants of Lot through his eldest daughter, and as such, distant relatives of Israel. The Moabites lived in what is now Jordan; they often quarreled with the Israelites.

- **Moses:** Numbers pictures Moses as a man stretched to the breaking point. He is overworked and underappreciated. His leadership is continually challenged. His own family questions his motives and qualifications. And even his relationship with God proves to be problematical; on more than one occasion, Moses has to talk God out of destroying Israel (see Numbers 11 and 14).

  In other words, if you want to know what it's like to be a leader, take a look at Moses. And if you want to know how to handle the stress of leadership, you can learn a lot from Moses.

- **Nazirite:** Literally, a "dedicated one." We're not told why someone might choose to be a Nazirite; apparently it was a means by which anyone (not just a Levite) could devote himself fully to God's service. One of the most famous Nazirites was Samson.

- **Sanctuary/tabernacle:** The tent that served as a center of worship for Israel. Its courtyard was roughly 145 feet long by 72 feet wide, with the tent itself 44 feet long by 15 feet wide.

- **Sheol:** Often translated as "hell," this word means simply "the grave." God's people didn't seem to have any clear notion of life after death until the time of Daniel (c. 600 B.C.); even in the time of Jesus, ideas of the afterlife were still controversial.

FlashPoint: How many Israelites were there?

Taken at face value, the books of Exodus and Numbers suggest that roughly 2.5 million people spent forty years wandering in the Sinai desert.

While "all things are possible with God," the large size of this group troubles some people. They wonder how a desert no bigger than West Virginia could support that many people. Others point out that—according to Numbers 3:43—there were 22,273 firstborn males in Israel, while Numbers 1:46 says there were 603,550 men old enough to fight. If both these numbers are correct, the average Israelite woman must have had twenty-seven sons . . . in addition to whatever daughters she may have had!

One solution to this problem may be that the Hebrew word for "thousand" can also mean "squad," "clan," or "heavily armed warrior." When Numbers says there were 22,273 firstborn males, it may mean there were 273 firstborn males organized into twenty-two squads or it may mean there were twenty-two heavily armed warriors among the 273 firstborn males who were counted or it may mean there were 273 firstborn males among the clans that were counted or . . . well, you get the idea.

Whether you take these numbers "literally" or not, the main point of these census lists remains the same: God had fulfilled His promise to Abraham that He would multiply the people of Israel.

Deuteronomy
Blueprint for Utopia

34 CHAPTERS — READING TIME: 3 HOURS

"Hear, O Israel: the LORD our God, the LORD is one. Love the LORD your God with all your heart and with all your soul and with all your strength" (Deuteronomy 6:4, 5).

Highlights

- The Ten Commandments (Deuteronomy 5).

- The Law of Love (Deuteronomy 6:4–9).

- Blessings and Cursings (Deuteronomy 28).

- The Death of Moses (Deuternomy 34).

Why was it written?

People have always wondered what an ideal society might be like. And from Plato's *Republic* to *The Communist Manifesto,* people have tried to sketch the outlines of such a society—its laws, its customs, its attitudes toward everything from religion to the lending of money.

The book of Deuteronomy is one of the earliest such "blueprints" for an ideal society. Set in the second millennium before Christ, it follows much the same format as any treaty of its day. "God has chosen the people of Israel," Deuteronomy says in effect. "Now Israel may choose to follow God—and it can do so by ordering its society in the way that He has commanded." If the Israelites do this, God will bless them. If they don't . . . well, you don't want to go there.

The society outlined in Deuteronomy had a powerful attraction to many people—so much so that books such as Joshua, Judges, Samuel, and Kings are known as "Deuteronomic histories." Prophets such as Isaiah based much of their messages on its laws and ideals. And when Jesus was asked which was the greatest of God's commands, He quoted from this book.

Even today, both the "religious right" and liberation theologians have drawn much of their agenda from Deuteronomy. Even today, in other words, Deuteronomy is making a difference in the way people look at society.

What you'll learn in Deuteronomy

Ask people about many issues of the day, and you'll often end up with a debate on responsibility versus compassion. Conservatives tend to stress the first; they want to make sure people "reap what they sow." Liberals tend to stress the second; they want to make sure no one ever "slips through the safety net."

Both sides, of course, are quick to see the faults of the other. Conservatives claim liberals lack true compassion; they believe that liberal guarantees of food, shelter, and medical care will encourage laziness and irresponsibility. Liberals, on the other hand, think conservatives are hypocrites; they point out that many of the same conservatives who preach "self-reliance" have benefited from the help of government.

Interestingly, Deuteronomy has managed to combine both virtues—responsibility and compassion. When it comes to bearing consequences, for instance, Deuteronomy 30:15ff warns that anyone who is not obedient will die. At the same time, God lays out a social-welfare program that makes modern welfare policies look downright stingy. Every seven years, all debts must be forgiven. No one is to starve. And no one is to deny the poor by saying, "Well, it's their own fault." As God says in Deuteronomy 15:7ff, "Do not be hardhearted or tightfisted toward your poor brother. . . . Be openhanded toward your brother and toward the poor and needy in your land."

GoodWords _____

- **Anakim:** A tribe of southern Palestine whose people were feared as giants.

- **Ammonites:** Like the Israelites, these were Semitic people who settled in Palestine sometime between 1500 and 1000 B.C. This led to frequent clashes between Israel and the Ammonites—clashes the Israelites often lost, since the Ammonites (who mostly lived in what is now Jordan) often allied themselves with the Philistines (who mostly lived in what is now the Gaza Strip).

- **Baal of Peor:** As god of lightning, rain, and fertility, Baal (or "lord") was worshiped in a way that is now illegal in every state except Nevada. The Moabites (a Semitic people living on the fringes of Palestine) used the obvious attractions of Baal worship in an attempt to co-opt the Israelites. The story of the whole sordid affair is found in Numbers 25.

- **Cities of refuge:** With no police and no courts, justice in ancient Palestine was entirely a family matter. In other words, if you killed someone, you could count on his or her closest male relative (who was known as "the avenger of blood") to come looking for you.

  "But what if it was an accident?" you say.

  Then you had better hope "the avenger of blood" believes you—and that he's the forgiving sort.

  "That's not fair!" you say.

  Well, no. That's why Israel had "cities of refuge"—places where people could get an official ruling of "not guilty" and hang out until tempers cooled.

- **Jeshurun:** Meaning "the upright one," it was a name given God's people to express what they could become.

- **Jordan:** The principal river of Palestine. Israel's passage through the Jordan marked its entrance into the Promised Land of Canaan. (In spite of this, several tribes settled on its eastern side.)

- **Levite:** A member of the tribe of Levi, one of the twelve tribes making up the nation of Israel. Not all Levites were priests, but all priests were Levites. Nonpriestly Levites assisted in certain aspects of ritual and worship and were supported by public offerings.

- **Moses:** Ethnically, Moses was an Israelite. Culturally, he was an Egyptian. Legally, he was a murderer. Spiritually, he became the deliverer of God's people. Few people have managed to cram so many opposites into one life.

- **Tithe:** One-tenth of one's income—an amount many churches suggest should serve as a standard for giving today. (On the other hand, I've heard very few churches suggest that Deuteronomy 14:22-29 should be taken literally.)

- **Utopia:** Coined by Sir Thomas More, the word means both "good place" and "no place." Deuteronomy is "utopian" in both meanings of the word: While provisions such as the forgiveness of all debts every seven years would have been radical in their effect, there is no evidence they were ever implemented.

FlashPoint: Who wrote the books of Moses?

Most conservatives believe the first five books of the Bible were written by Moses; most liberals do not. Instead, liberals follow something called the "Documentary Hypothesis"—the belief that these books were woven together by an unknown editor who used four sources: J, E, D, and P. According to this theory:

- *J* dates to the ninth century B.C.; it's marked by a very personal view of the God who is known as YHWH.

- *E* dates to the eighth century B.C.; it's marked by its lofty and elevated view of the God who is known in Hebrew as *elohim.* Together with *J,* it forms the book of Genesis.

- *D* is the source for Deuteronomy; it dates to 621 B.C. and was added to *J* and *E* in the sixth century B.C.

- *P* is mainly concerned with the laws and rituals of the priesthood; it was not combined with the other sources until 400 B.C. or so.

As you can imagine, this controversy over authorship has led to a great deal of disagreement about the purpose of these books. Conservatives, for instance, believe Deuteronomy records a speech Moses gave just before Israel entered Canaan. As such, it was meant to help God's people make the adjustment from the nomadic life of the Exodus to a settled life in Palestine. But liberals believe Deuteronomy was written at a time when Israel had split into two kingdoms, each plagued by poverty and injustice; as such, it was meant to call people back to "the good old days" of Israel's beginnings.

Myself, I'm always skeptical of any theory that ascribes multiple authors to a single book. It's only a matter of time, after all, before somebody "proves" that the book you're reading right now was actually written by several different people!

QUICKSTART

Old Testament:
History

Joshua
God Keeps His Promise

" 'You know with all your heart and soul that not one of all the good promises the LORD your God gave you has failed. Every promise has been fulfilled; not one has failed' " (Joshua 23:14).

Highlights

- Rahab and the Spies (Joshua 2).

- Israel Crosses the Jordan River (Joshua 3; 4).

- The Battle of Jericho (Joshua 6).

Why was it written?

Remember how hard it was to wait when you were a child? The drive to your grandparents' house took forever; summer vacation seemed as though it would never come. And Christmas! Using the word "slow" to describe the wait for that holiday would have been like saying the Pacific Ocean is "wet."

Remember those feelings, and you'll know how God's people felt just before the events that are described in this book. God had promised the land of Canaan to their ancestor Abraham—and they had waited 400 years for Him to keep His promise! Would the waiting never end?

It did. In either 1400 B.C. (the date favored by conservatives) or 1200 B.C. (a date favored by moderates), the Israelites crossed the Jordan River into Canaan. God had kept His promise. Their years of waiting had come to an end. Now they were home.

What you'll learn in Joshua

The book of Joshua can be divided into two parts. The first twelve chapters form a Book of War; the next twelve form a Book of Peace. The Book of War describes the conquest of Canaan; the Book of Peace tells how the land was divided among the tribes of Israel. Each book is important in its own right, and each book has problems of its own.

Most modern readers, for instance, find the Book of War appalling. Whole cities are destroyed and their inhabitants killed. The idea of a "holy war" to exterminate the inhabitants of Canaan doesn't play well today—not after the Crusades and Auschwitz and September 11, 2001.

The Book of Peace presents a very different problem: it's boring. Little more than a surveyor's plat, it gives us the precise location of each tribal boundary with a passion for detail that is absolutely deadening.

You think I'm exaggerating? Try Joshua 15:1-4.

> The allotment for the tribe of Judah, clan by clan, extended down to the territory of Edom, to the Desert of Zin in the extreme south. Their southern boundary started from the bay at the southern end of the Salt Sea, crossed south of Scorpion Pass, continued on to Zin and went over to the south of Kadesh Barnea. Then it ran past Hezron up to Addar and curved around to Karka. It then pased along to Azmon and joined the Wadi of Egypt, ending at the sea. This is their southern boundary.

And that's just the southern frontier of one tribe!

Alien as the book of Joshua may seem today, its lessons are important. The Book of War, for instance, assures us that nothing can stop God from fulfilling His promises. No river is too deep. No wall is too high. No army is too strong for God. If God says He will do something, He'll do it.

In the Book of Peace, we learn the importance of boundaries. Most of life's decisions, after all, come down to the issue of setting limits, establishing turf, deciding what's mine and what's yours. And most of life's problems come when we don't pay attention to our boundaries. Joshua reminds us how important it is that we know our limits and our boundaries—because if we don't set them, somebody else will.

GoodWords

- **Ai:** Literally "ruins"—an appropriate name for a city that archaeologists say was destroyed somewhere around 2000 B.C., and not rebuilt until 1000 B.C. or so. If that's the case, the battle described in Joshua was a small-scale engagement aimed at a squatter's camp that was built on the site of the old city. (See "thousand" below.) Then again, it may be that archaeologists have the wrong site for Ai.

- **Book of Jashar:** An ancient hymnal, now lost, mentioned in Joshua 10:13 and 2 Samuel 1:18. The Syriac translation of Joshua calls it the "Book of Praises."

- **City of refuge:** A temporary haven for anyone who had killed someone else by accident; the person would wait there until tempers had cooled.

- **Jericho:** One of the world's oldest walled cities and the first to be encountered by the Israelites when they entered Canaan. Back in the 1930s, archaeologist J. Garstang announced he had found evidence of "the walls that came a tumblin' down." Later archaeologists have disputed his findings, but all would agree that the history of Jericho is "extremely complex."

- **The Jordan River:** This river—220 miles in length, with a fall of 600 feet—winds its way from the freshwater Sea of Galilee to the extremely saline Dead Sea. Its average width in the area where the Israelites crossed is between eighty and a hundred feet; its average depth varies from three to ten feet. (Spring floods, however, can make it considerably larger.)

- **Joshua:** His name means "the Lord saves"—an appropriate name for the man who served Moses as military commander. Joshua also went with Moses when he climbed Mt. Sinai (Exodus 24), served as one of the twelve scouts who spied on Canaan (Numbers 13), and took over leadership of the people from Moses after his death.

- **Rephaim:** Frequently translated as "giants." The Rephaim are related in some way to the "Anakim" or "Nephilim." King Og of Bashan was one of the Rephaim; his bed is supposed to have been twelve feet long and six feet wide!

- **The River:** The Euphrates River.

- **Thousand:** While this word can literally mean "one thousand," it can also mean "clan," "squad," or even "a single soldier who has the metal armor and weapons of a heavy infantryman."

Violence in the Bible

True, the Bible has some pretty horrible stuff in it—torture, rape, mutilation, and murder. But it's worth remembering that God doesn't necessarily approve of everything that His people do—even if they do it in His name. Many times, as a matter of fact, the Bible includes these scenes in an attempt to show us what happens when people *don't* follow God.

Then too, most of the laws that seem pretty ghastly to us were actually an attempt to limit bloodshed. Take the famous *lex talonis,* for instance—"an eye for an eye and a tooth for a tooth." In a society where an insult could lead to murder, this was actually a way to calm down things. "Yes, you can give as good as you got," it said in effect, "but no more."

Likewise, anything captured in a "holy war" was *cherem*—it was destroyed as a sign that it had been given to God. Granted, this in itself was pretty terrible . . . but it did prevent people from using religion to justify their own desire for loot.

Judges
God Fights the Gathering Darkness

"Then the Lord raised up judges, who saved them out of the hands of these raiders. . . . for the Lord had compassion on them as they groaned under those who oppressed and afflicted them" (Judges 2:16, 18).

Highlights

- The Story of Deborah (Judges 4).

- The Story of Gideon (Judges 6–8).

- The Story of Samson (Judges 15–16).

- The Ugliest, Nastiest Story in the Bible (Judges 19).

Why was it written?

If the book of Judges was a movie, there's no way you would let your children watch it. Judges contains some of the ugliest stories in Scripture—stories of murder, torture, arson, and rape. Its humor is crude, even scatological. Most shocking of all (at least to its original readers), its heroes routinely break the sacred laws of hospitality—laws that held the host responsible for the safety of his guests.

So what is a book like Judges doing in Scripture?

Simply put, it's a bridge between two stories. The predecessor of Judges, the book of Joshua, closes on a note of triumph. Its successor, the book of Samuel, opens on a scene of disaster. In the book of Joshua, the Israelites conquer the Canaanites. But in the book of Samuel, the Canaanites are once again masters of the land. So what went wrong? The book of Judges provides the answer.

Judges is a collection of stories about life in the land of Israel between the time of Joshua and the time of the prophet Samuel—a collection of stories about a time when Israel was little more than a loose-knit confederation of tribes, and "every man did what was right in his own eyes" (Judges 21:25, KJV). As such, it's not a pretty book, but it is honest. It is a graphic and explicit account of what went wrong with God's people during a critical period in their history.

What you'll learn in Judges

As children, most of us loved stories that ended with the words "and they lived happily ever after." As adults, most of us know that such endings are rarely true; we all know that happy endings can become flawed beginnings.

While they seldom make pleasant reading, stories about things that go wrong can help us avoid a similar fate. That's why hospitals schedule regular meetings to discuss why patients died. That's why business students are given case studies of failed corporations.

And that's why the Bible includes what the experts call "Deuteronomic history." These are books—like Judges, Samuel, and Kings—that spell out in detail the message of Deuteronomy: Follow God, and you will prosper; stray from Him, and you will suffer. In other words, if the stories in this book don't have happy endings, it's not God's fault.

That's not to say the book of Judges is all gloom and doom. In fact, it takes its name from the judges (or "deliverers") God used to rescue His people. And it's worth noting that God didn't send these judges because His people had finally shaped up. No, the Bible says God sent these judges because He was "moved by pity" for their distress.

Still, there is only so much a few judges can do. That's why the book of Judges eventually bcomes the story of Israel's long, slow slide into the abyss. Even the judges become worse as time goes along, while the good they do grows less and less. Actually, by the end of this book, Israel is faced with destruction.

GoodWords _____

- **Angel of the Lord:** Literally, "Yahweh's messenger" (Yahweh being God's personal name). There are times in Judges when this particular messenger seems to be more than just a stand-in for God; some experts suggest this messenger may have been the Second Person of the Trinity.

- **Baal and Astarte:** Canaanite fertility gods. Baal was the lord of rain and lightning; his consort, Astarte (or Asherah), was a kind of Canaanite "Mother Earth."

- **Canaanites:** The original inhabitants of Palestine. The Canaanites were an urban, cultured people who worshiped a multitude of gods; they also believed that poor people should know their place and stay in it.

- **Concubine:** What do you call a woman who has entered into a stable, sexual relationship that lacks the safeguards and strictures of a formal marriage? We fumble with phrases such as "significant other" and "common-law wife." In biblical times, they simply would have called her a "concubine."

- **Ephod and teraphim:** An ephod was the ceremonial robe worn by priests; Middle Easterners also used ephods to clothe their idols. Teraphim were the statues of household gods.

- **Jael:** If you're wondering where she picked up her tent-peg-and-hammer skills, remember that in the Middle East, pitching tents was considered a woman's job. The Kenites, by the way, were nomadic tinkers and smiths; they played much the same role in Israelite society that gypsies did in eighteenth- and nineteenth-century Europe.

- **Joshua:** The military leader who commanded God's people after the death of Moses and brought Israel into the Promised Land of Canaan.

- **Judge:** The job of a judge was to promote justice. In Israelite society, that meant a judge was police, judge, jury, executioner, and military leader all rolled into one.

  Even conservative experts disagree as to just how long Israel was ruled by judges. While all agree that this period began with the Israelite entry into Palestine, some believe that event took place somewhere around 1400 B.C., others around 1200 B.C. But all agree the time of the judges ended somewhere around 1000 B.C. (or slightly later, if you count the prophet Samuel as a judge).

- **Nazirite:** A person who took a vow to serve the Lord in some special way. As a sign of this vow, Nazirites were forbidden to cut their hair, eat anything made of grapes (such as raisins or wine), or touch a corpse. Samson, of course, had already broken that last requirement long before he got his famous haircut.

- **Philistines:** Known by the Egyptians as "the people of the sea," these were Hellenistic warriors who had fled their home islands off the Greek coast and settled in Palestine at roughly the same time that Israel left Egypt.

- **Shibboleth:** A word that literally means both "ear of grain" and "flood of water." Thanks to the incident described in Judges 12:6, a shibboleth came to mean any issue used by a group as a simple means of determining friend from foe. The fact that we've replaced this term with "litmus test" speaks volumes about our declining knowledge of Scripture.

- **Thousand:** This word can also mean "clan," "squad," or "heavily armed warrior." If the Bible says "23,000 people died in battle," it may mean "23,000 people died in battle," or it may mean "two military units with 300 people in them died in battle," or it may mean "two heavy infantrymen and 300 light infantrymen died in battle."

Archaeology and the Bible

Forget Indiana Jones. Most archaeologists do not spend their time searching for the lost ark of the covenant. In fact, a growing number disclaim *any* link between their field and biblical studies.

Still, a basic knowledge of archaeology can help you imagine what life must have been like in biblical times. Archaeology can't tell you *why* God called Abraham (or even *if* He did), but it can give you a pretty good idea of what the people of that time might have eaten, what they wore, and how they may have worshiped.

Interested? Check out the magazine *Biblical Archaeology Review.* It offers a lively (and controversial) look at the field from a popular perspective.

Ruth

Unexpected Love

" 'Where you go I will go, and where you stay I will stay.
Your people will be my people and your God my God' " (Ruth 1:16).

HighLight

- Ruth's Courtship of Boaz (Ruth 3).

Why was it written?

Life would be so much simpler if God's people were the only good people. If that were the case, then Israel could have ignored the surrounding nations with no great loss.

But Israel needed the skills that only the people of other nations could provide. It needed Phoenicians to help build the temple. Philistines to guard the king. And Egyptians to breed the horses that Israel then sold to its northern neighbors.

Israel was forced to deal with foreigners—and that raised a question: How does God deal with foreigners? Does He reject them, simply because they are not Israelites?

Certainly Israel had good reason to be suspicious of its neighbors. By and large, close contact with them had brought disaster. Towards the end of the Exodus, for instance, some Israelite men had taken Moabite wives and worshiped Moabite gods. This had made God angry, and only the death of the offending men had saved Israel from destruction.

77

Clearly foreigners—especially foreign women—were bad news.

Or maybe not.

Ruth was a foreigner, after all, and a Moabite woman at that! But even though she was a foreigner, Ruth had chosen to follow God. She had shown the "loving kindness" that God desires.

If you're wondering about ultimate results of this "mixed marriage," all you need to know is that Ruth's great-grandson was David, the greatest king of Israel. (And David, you'll remember, was the ancestor of Jesus.)

The book of Ruth, in other words, is a gentle reminder that God's people shouldn't be too exclusive. God loves all people—even foreigners. And even foreigners can love God. And the foreigner who loves God should be welcomed and cared for the same as any other follower of God.

Even if that "foreigner" is a Moabite woman.

What you'll learn in Ruth

At first glance, God seems to be very active in the book of Ruth. His name comes up continually. People repeatedly ask God to bless or care for one another.

Yet a careful reader will notice that God seems strangely distant in this book. There are no dramatic miracles, no sensational answers to prayer. Indeed, it is by "chance" that Ruth "happens" to glean in the field of her near-kinsman Boaz.

In other words, the world of Ruth is much like the world of today. It is a world in which God's followers suffer from hardship and famine and death. It is a world seemingly ruled by chance and accident. It is a world in which God may seem to be very far away, even from His faithful followers.

Yet the book of Ruth tells us that God is *not* distant—far from it! It was not by "chance" alone that Ruth met the man who would answer Naomi's prayer. Neither is it Naomi's plans alone that lead to Ruth's marriage. And Ruth's child is not the natural result of her union with Boaz; no, it is "the Lord that gave her conception."

God is always with us even though He may use "natural" events and "human" plans. Behind everything we do and through everything that happens to us, God reigns supreme.

And whenever people treat each other with "loving kindness," the book of Ruth tells us that God is hard at work.

GoodWords

- **Ephah:** A little more than half a bushel. In one day, Ruth gathered enough to feed her family for a month!

- **Loving kindness:** This is one way to translate the Hebrew word *chesed* (pronounced *CHE-sed,* with the *ch* pronounced the same way it is in the Scottish word *loch*). *Chesed* basically means "loyalty" or "faithfulness to the treaty that God made with His people," but it also carries the ideas of "mercy," "kindness," and "love."

- **Moab:** The high plateau immediately to the west of the Dead Sea. Most Moabites were herders; they worshiped gods such as Chemosh and Baal, and were frequently at war with the Israelites.

- **Near-kinsmen:** This is one way to translate the Hebrew word *goel* (pronounced *go-ALE*). A *goel* was your nearest male relative—the one to whom you turned in times of trouble. If you were in debt, for instance, he bailed you out. If you'd been murdered, it was his job to see to it that justice was done and that your family was provided for. And if this meant that he had to marry your widow so that your family line would continue . . . well, it wasn't always easy being a *goel!*

FlashPoint: Is the Bible sexist?

"Once upon a time," or so the story goes, "everybody worshiped the Great Mother Goddess. It was a time when everyone lived at peace and everyone was equal.

"But then somebody came up with the idea of worshipping a *male* god, and things have gone downhill ever since. Wars broke out. Inequality reigned. Women groaned under the iron heel of patriarchy. And that's why the Bible is such an evil book."

As attractive as this story may be to some, it's not true. For one thing, there's no evidence that anyone *ever* worshiped a Great Mother Goddess unless they worshiped a lot of other gods as well—both male and female. What's more, there's no evidence that people who worship a *lot* of gods are nicer than people who believe in one god. (Think of Alexander the Great, after all. Or Julius Caesar. Or Genghis Khan.)

Finally, the Bible's attitude towards women is . . . well, it's complicated. There's no question that it's set in a society in which men run the show. Yet it's also clear that women are created in God's image, that God values them, and that God has work for them to do.

And no, God's ideal for women is not that they be barefoot and pregnant. Anyone who thinks this needs to re-read the stories of Deborah, Ruth, and Esther.

1 & 2 Samuel

God Looks for a Leader

55 CHAPTERS — READING TIME: 6 HOURS

" 'Does the Lord delight in burnt offerings and sacrifices as much as in obeying the voice of the Lord? To obey is better than sacrifice, and to heed is better than the fat of rams' " (1 Samuel 15:22).

Highlights

- The Birth of Samuel (1 Samuel 1).

- Adventures of the Ark (1 Samuel 5; 6).

- Saul Becomes King (1 Samuel 8–10).

- David Is Chosen as King (1 Samuel 16).

- David and Goliath (1 Samuel 17).

- David and Bathsheba (2 Samuel 11; 12).

- The Revolt of David's Son (2 Samuel 13–19).

Why was it written?

How do you pick a good leader? How can you make sure a good leader stays good? And is leadership always a good thing, or does it come at a price?

We're not the only ones who struggle with these questions; ancient Israel did too. In fact, the experts agree it was during a particularly bad stretch of leaders that someone sat down and wrote the collection of case studies we know today as the books of Samuel.

Had the author of Samuel been a Greek, he would have tried to answer those questions philosophically—and the result might have been similar to Plato's *Republic* or Aristotle's *Politics*. But as a Hebrew, the author dealt with these issues by telling stories about some of the leaders Israel knew. The result is a series of profiles that explore the topic of leadership, both good and bad.

By the way, nobody knows when Samuel was written. Educated guesses range from the time of Solomon—around 950 B.C.—to sometime just after the Babylonian exile, perhaps 530 B.C. or so. And yes, Samuel is just one book; the only reason it's been split into two books is because it was too large to fit onto one scroll.

What you'll learn in 1 and 2 Samuel

The book of Samuel tells us that security always comes at a price. When the Israelites asked for a king to protect them from the Philistines, for instance, Samuel reminded them what else this king would do:

> "He will take your sons . . . [and] your daughters. . . . He will take the best of your fields and vineyards and olive groves. . . . Your menservants and maidservants and the best of your cattle and donkeys he will take for his own use. He will take a tenth of your flocks, and you yourselves will become his slaves. When that day comes, you will cry out for relief from the king you have chosen, and the LORD will not answer you in that day" (1 Samuel 8:11-18).

The stories in the books of Samuel all bear out the truth of that prediction.

Fortunately, Samuel also proves that God can deal with any setback. When Israel rejects God's leadership, for instance, He has a backup plan. When they lose to the Philistines, He goes it alone. Even when David stumbles and falls, God is not dumbfounded. He's always in charge—and it's a wise leader who keeps this in mind.

If you want to be a good leader, then follow the One who's really in charge. That's the message of Samuel.

GoodWords

- **Amalekites:** A nomadic people who lived on the fringes of Israelite society. David made up for Saul's failure to destroy them all.

- **Ammon, Edom, Moab:** Kingdoms on the eastern border of Israel. The stories in the books of Samuel took place when the "great powers" of Egypt and Assyria were temporarily in decline. This gave Israel a brief "window of opportunity" to expand and flourish. Unfortunately, it gave these other local powers a chance to do so as well.

- **Anoint:** Literally, to pour oil over someone's head—a sign that God had chosen that person for a special purpose. The Hebrew word for someone who's been anointed is *messiah;* the Greek word is *christ.*

- **Aram:** A hostile state to the north of Israel. Some Bibles translate this name as Syria.

- **Ark of the covenant:** A gold-plated wooden box that symbolized God's presence. Samuel often uses the ark to point out that people are always trying to help God, but God doesn't need anybody's help.

- **Baal:** The Canaanite god of thunder, rain, and fertility. His consort was the fertility goddess Astarte.

- **Book of Jashar:** A collection of heroic songs that the author of Samuel used as a source for his book. Experts speculate that the author may have also drawn from other books to write Samuel—perhaps one containing the "adventures of the ark," or another listing the battles of Saul and David. Clearly, divine inspiration isn't just a matter of dreams and visions; it can also involve the use of written sources.

- **David:** King of the tribe of Judah from roughly 1011 to 1004 B.C. and king over all of Israel from 1004 to around 971 B.C. David was chosen to lead Israel against its foreign foes; in the end, the greatest threat to David's kingdom came from within.

- **Dagon:** A Canaanite god of fertility, roughly equivalent to Baal. The Philistines adopted him as their chief deity when they moved to Palestine. Older Bibles often have illustrations that picture him as looking like a fish; most experts today suspect this wasn't the case.

- **Ephod:** A robe worn by priests; ephods were also used to "dress" idols. Exactly how an ephod could determine God's will is not clear.

- **Goliath:** A Philistine warrior. If you'd like to know more about the way Goliath might have fought and thought, read Homer's *Iliad*—it's the story of what the Philistines' northern cousins were doing at roughly the time of the events described in Samuel.

- **Philistines:** Originally from the islands off the Greek coast, these people migrated to Palestine sometime around 1200 B.C. When the book of Samuel begins, the Philistines already control the coast; their drive inland forms the background for most of the book. David won fame by killing the Philistine warrior Goliath; curiously, most of David's bodyguards (also known as Cherethites and Pelethites) were Philistines.

- **Samuel:** Priest, judge, and prophet. In the person of Samuel was combined every aspect of leadership that Israel would ever need. If he had a failing, it was that he didn't prepare his own sons to serve as leaders after him.

- **Saul:** King (or better yet, warlord) of all Israel from 1050 to about 1011 B.C. Though a big man physically, Saul comes across as something of a child; he is continually reacting to what someone else has done.

- **Shiloh:** A town approximately thirty miles north-northeast of Jerusalem. It served as Israel's religious center until the ark was captured by the Philistines.

- **Thousand:** This term can mean the literal number 1,000. It can also mean a squad, a clan, or a heavily armed warrior.

- **Urim and thummim:** Devices used to determine God's will, apparently in connection with an ephod.

- **The witch of Endor:** Necromancy was an important part of Canaanite religion; the woman referred to in 1 Samuel 28 was evidently one of the few priestesses who had survived Saul's reign. Exactly who (or what) she summoned is a matter of some dispute; if it was really Samuel who appeared, then why had he obeyed the command of a pagan medium? And why was Saul (a wicked man) told that he'd be spending the afterlife in the same place as Samuel (a righteous man)?

Why two Samuels?

Actually, there's only one book of Samuel—like the books of Kings and Chronicles, it was split simply because it was too big for one scroll!

The *other* religions of the Middle East

If you've seen *Star Wars,* then you have a pretty good idea of the gods worshiped by most people in the Middle East in ancient times. Yes, the specific name of each god might vary from place to place—the goddess of love, for instance, was known by some as "Ishtar" and others as "Astarte"—but the *role* played by each god stayed pretty much the same.

The chief of all the other gods, for instance, was usually old, wise, and pretty much out of the picture (think Obi-Wan Kenobi). Most of the heavy lifting was actually done by a young, virile male god (think Luke Skywalker). Add a young, fertile goddess of love and war (Princess Leia), an evil god of death (Darth Vader), and . . . well, you get the picture.

The dead also played an important role in Canaanite religion. Food and drink offerings were left on the graves; in return, "the ancestors" looked after their descendants. The "witch of Endor" seems to have been a specialist in this sort of thing; given the results of her interview with Saul, it's no wonder that the Israelites were told to leave the dead alone!

1 & 2 Kings
The Road to Exile

" 'As for you, if you will walk before me in integrity of heart and uprightness, as David your father did, and do all I command and observe my decrees and laws, I will establish your royal throne over Israel forever, as I promised David your father' " (1 Kings 9:4, 5).

Highlights

- Solomon Splits a Baby (1 Kings 3:16-28).

- Dedication of the New Temple in Jerusalem (1 Kings 8).

- Revolt of the Northern Tribes (1 Kings 12).

- Stories of Elijah the Prophet (1 Kings 17–19; 21; 2 Kings 1; 2).

- Stories of Elisha the Prophet (2 Kings 2–8; 13).

- The Fall of Israel (2 Kings 17).

- Stories of Good King Hezekiah (2 Kings 18–20).

- The Fall of Judah (2 Kings 24; 25).

Why was it written?

"You go your way, and I'll go mine."

More than one relationship has ended with these words. Sometimes an entire nation has been split by them—split because its people decided that whatever divided them was more important than what they had in common.

The two biblical books of Kings tell the story of one such nation—the nation of Israel. Sometime around 1011 B.C., David had united its twelve tribes into one kingdom. But the high taxes of Solomon, combined with the foolishness of Rehoboam, led to civil war, and David's kingdom was divided. The northern nation—by far the largest and richest of the two—kept the old name of Israel, while the southern nation of Judah kept little more than Jerusalem, the old capital city.

But division didn't mean the end of problems. Israel was plagued by political infighting and religious apostasy, and Judah was no stranger to these things either. Unable to resolve their problems and unable to present a common front, the two nations became easy prey for their enemies.

As a result, the two nations experienced similar fates. Israel was invaded by Assyria in 722 B.C.; its capital city of Samaria was destroyed and its people carried into exile. Judah was invaded by Babylon in 586 B.C. Its capital city of Jerusalem was also destroyed, and its people carried into exile.

Once in exile, Judah took a long, hard look at its history. There's no indication that the northern kingdom of Israel ever did this; perhaps that's why it vanished from history. But Judah's people eventually came to a clear understanding of just where they had gone wrong and what they needed to do about it.

One result of this long, hard look was that Judah managed to retain its identity as a people and eventually managed to return from exile. Another result was the book we know as Kings. Drawn together by an unknown editor during the Babylonian exile—somewhere around 570 B.C.—Kings is a series of case studies in failure.

What you'll learn in 1 and 2 Kings

Think of 1 and 2 Kings as a commentary on the book of Deuteronomy. Deuteronomy tells us "what goes around, comes around." If you need some examples of this principle in action, then all you need to do is read the stories found in Kings.

Fortunately, Kings does more than just warn us of God's justice; it assures us of His mercy as well. Think of the patience that God showed, for instance, in putting up with Israel's sins for almost 200 years. Think of His faithfulness to David—a faithfulness that led Him to keep an heir of David on the throne of Judah. Most of all, think of Solomon's prayer—a prayer that brought comfort to God's people when they were exiled in Babylon:

> "If they turn back to you with all their heart and soul in the land
> of their enemies who took them captive, and pray to you toward
> the land you gave their fathers, toward the city you have chosen
> and the temple I have built for your Name; then from heaven,
> your dwelling place, hear their prayer and their plea, and uphold
> their cause. And forgive your people, who have sinned against
> you; forgive all the offenses they have committed against you, and
> cause their conquerors to show them mercy; for they are your
> people and your inheritance, whom you brought out of Egypt,
> out of that iron-smelting furnace" (1 Kings 8:48-50).

GoodWords

- **Aram:** A hostile state to the north of Israel; some Bibles translate this word as "Syria." Capital city: Damascus.

- **Assyria:** An empire known for its cruelty and aggression. Preoccupied with internal politics, Assyria, which was based in what is now northern Iraq, posed little threat to Israel during the reigns of David and Solomon. But from 911 to 609 B.C., Assyria was the number one power of the Middle East.

- **Baal:** The Canaanite god of thunder, rain, and fertility. His consort was the fertility goddess Astarte or Asherah. The name "Baalzebub" ("lord of the flies") is an Israelite pun on one of his titles: "Baalzebul" ("lord of lords").

- **Babylon:** Once no more than a province of Assyria located in what is now southern Iraq, Babylon became an empire in its own right following Nabopolassar's revolt of 626 B.C. Believing that "the enemy of my enemy is my friend," Judah supported Babylon's revolt. Babylon's triumph, however, left Judah scrambling for some means of protecting itself against its old ally.

- **Egypt:** Most of the events in Kings took place when Egypt was under foreign rule—first by the Libyans (from 950 to 750 B.C.) and then by the Ethiopians (from 750 to 663 B.C.). But when Egypt regained its independence under Psamtik I, it once again became an active player in world affairs. Judah tried to use Egypt as a counterweight against Assyria and Babylon; the results were disastrous.

- **Elijah:** Active in the northern kingdom of Israel during the reign of King Ahab (c. 874 to 853 B.C.), he was the greatest prophet in the Hebrew Bible. Despite this, he lost his nerve at least once; this suggests that God can use someone without him or her being perfect.

- **Elisha:** Often confused with his master and predecessor Elijah, Elisha was active in Israel during the reigns of kings Joram, Jehu, Jehoahaz, and Jehoash (c. 850 to 800 B.C.).

- **Israel:** An independent nation from 931 to 722 B.C., Israel was made up of the ten northern tribes that had been loyal to Saul during David's rebellion. No one knows what became of Israel after it was captured by Assyria; the best guess is that its people intermarried with the surrounding nations and gradually lost their identity.

- **Judah:** An independent nation from 931 to 586 B.C., Judah largely consisted of the land that had belonged to David's tribe.

- **Ophir:** Possibly southern Arabia or Somalia.

- **Phoenicians:** Famous for their skill as merchants and sailors, these people lived in a cluster of cities just north of Israel. Hiram of Tyre, a Phoenician, made an important contribution to Israelite religion when he oversaw the construction of the temple in Jerusalem. Jezebel of Sidon, also a Phoenician, made a very different kind of contribution when she promoted the worship of Baal in Israel.

Why two books of Kings?

Like Samuel and Chronicles, Kings is really one book. It was divided only because it was too big to fit onto one scroll.

The kings of Israel and Judah

The chart on the next page offers a conservative view of when these kings (and one queen) reigned over Judah and Israel. Since some kings shared the throne with their heirs, some dates overlap (and all the dates are B.C., of course.) In the list, a change in dynasty is indicated by a change in the typeface.

The United Kingdom of Israel
Saul (1050-1011)
David (1011-971)
Solomon (971-931)

Judah	Israel
Rehoboam (931-913)	Jeroboam (931-910)
Abijam (913-911)	
Asa (911-869)	Nadab (910-909)
	Baasha (909-886)
	Elah (886-885)
	Zimri (885)
	Omri (885-874)
Jehoshaphat (872-848)	*Ahab (874-853)*
Jehoram (854-841)	*Ahaziah (853-852)*
Ahaziah (841)	*Joram (852-841)*
Athaliah (841-835)	Jehu (841-814)
Joash (835-796)	Jehoahaz (814-798)
Jehoash (798-782)	
Amaziah (796-767)	Jeroboam II (793-753)
Azariah/Uzziah (790-739)	Zachariah (753-752)
	Shallum (752)
Jotham (750-731)	Menahem (752-742)
	Pekahiah (742-740)
Ahaz (735-715)	Pekah (740-732)
Hezekiah (729-686)	*Hoshea (732-722)*
Manasseh (697-642)	
Amon (642-640)	
Josiah (640-609)	
Jehoahaz (609)	
Jehoiakim (609-598)	
Jehoiachin (598-597)	
Zedekiah (597-586)	

The Queen of Sheba

Experts agree that Sheba was located at the southern tip of the Arabian peninsula. Now known as the countries of Yemen and Aden, the kingdom of "Seba" controlled the trade in frankincense and myrrh; together with its fertile land and extensive irrigation works, this made the Sabeans both wealthy and powerful.

Whatever gifts the Queen of Sheba may gave given Solomon, legend has it that he gave one to her—a son. The kings of Ethiopia traced their ancestry to this child, and Rastafarians use this to justify their belief that the Emperor Haile Selassie was the "Black Lion of Judah." Be that as it may, the Sabeans did colonize Ethiopia, and Ethiopian Jews (or "Falasha") continued to live in that country until they immigrated to Israel in the 1970s.

1 & 2 Chronicles
Requiem for a Nation

" 'If my people, who are called by my name, will humble themselves and pray and seek my face and turn from their wicked ways, then will I hear from heaven and will forgive their sin and will heal their land' " (2 Chronicles 7:14).

Highlights

- The Death of Saul (1 Chronicles 10).

- The Defeat of Sennacherib (2 Chronicles 32).

- Stories of Bad King Manasseh (2 Chronicles 33).

- Judah Rediscovers God's Law (2 Chronicles 34).

Why was it written?

Think of Chronicles as an accident report, much like the one you fill out when you have a fender-bender. For this book describes a wreck—the wreck of an entire nation.

Once upon a time, God's people had been united and strong. David's kingdom had stretched from Sinai almost to the Euphrates. And nations such as Edom, Moab, and Ammon had offered tribute to Israel—so much so that "silver and gold [were] as common in Jerusalem as stones" (2 Chronicles 1:15).

But then it all fell apart. David's kingdom split during the reign of his grandson, Rehoboam. Tributary states revolted. Wealth was squandered in useless wars and fruitless bribes to untrustworthy allies.

The end came for the northern kingdom of Israel in 722 B.C., when the Assyrians conquered, leveled its cities, and deported its people. The southern kingdom of Judah managed to survive until 586 B.C., when it was invaded by the Babylonians. The Babylonians destroyed Jerusalem, demolished the temple, and led God's people into captivity.

Unlike Israel, however, Judah managed to retain its religious identity. And eventually, some of its people managed to return to Jerusalem. They rebuilt that city—at least in part—and they also rebuilt the temple.

As busy as they were, these "returnees" still had questions. Like all disaster victims, they wanted to know what had happened, why it had happened, and what they could do to keep it from happening again.

That's why Chronicles was written; it was meant to help a battered group of survivors make sense of their experience. That's why it doesn't say anything about the northern kingdom of Israel; "those people" had disappeared many centuries ago. Instead, it focuses on the rise and fall of God's people in Judah, from the time of Adam up to the destruction of Jerusalem.

What you'll learn in 1 and 2 Chronicles

Chronicles takes its theme from Deuteronomy. "As you sow," it says, "so shall you reap." In other words, God's people suffered, because their kings were evil. But if their kings chose to follow God, they would prosper.

If all this sounds a little simplistic, you're right. A quick comparison with Samuel, for instance, will show that the author of Chronicles had to "clean up" David's career in an apparent attempt to explain David's success. Then too, the tragic end of good King Josiah provides a *big* exception to Deuteronomy's rule.

In fact, Chronicles gives two important exceptions to this rule—exceptions that were meant to give God's people a reason for hope. The first was the power of repentance: Even a king as evil as Manasseh could avoid the consequences of his acts if he turned back to God. The second exception was God's promise to David:

" 'When your days are over and you go to be with your fathers, I will raise up your offspring to succeed you, one of your own sons, and I will establish his kingdom. He is the one who will build a house for me, and I will establish his throne forever. I will be his father, and he will be my son. I will never take my love away from him, as I took it away from your predecessor. I will set him over my house and my kingdom forever; his throne will be established forever' " (1 Chronicles 17:11-14).

In other words, no matter how bad God's people may be, He will not abandon them. He will see to it that a good king will come—a king who will reign forever.

GoodWords

- **Asherah:** A Phoenician fertility goddess; the wife of Baal. She was often symbolized by a wooden pole or tree trunk.

- **Baal:** Literally "lord"—the Canaanite god of rain and fertility.

- **High place:** An open-air place of worship located on a hilltop.

- **Pass through the fire [to Molech]:** Most experts think this means that the person in question offered a human sacrifice to the god Melek (or "king"). Melek may have been similar to Nergal—the Assyrian god of the underworld.

- **Thousand:** The word can mean literally "1,000," but it can also mean "clan" or "heavily armed warrior." If a text says there were 17,200 troops, for instance, it may mean that there were seventeen heavily armed and two hundred lightly armed warriors.

 FAST FACT ### Why two Chronicles?

Actually, there is only one book of Chronicles—like Samuel and Kings, it was divided because it was too big for one scroll.

Sources of Chronicles

The author of Chronicles makes it clear that he did quite a bit of research before writing his book. Among the works cited are:

- *The Chronicles of King David.*

- *The Book of Nathan the Prophet.*

- *The Book of Gad the Seer.*

- *The Prophecy of Ahijah the Shilonite.*

- *The Visions of Iddo the Seer Against Jeroboam the Son of Nebat.*

- *The Book of Shemaiah the Prophet.*

- *The Book of Jehu the Son of Hanani.*

- *The Sayings of the Seers.*

Unfortunately, the originals of these books have been lost.

Then again, books such as *The Acts of Uzziah,* by the prophet Isaiah, may be part of the biblical book that bears his name.

Ezra
God Purifies His People

" 'Though we are slaves, God has not deserted us in our bondage. He has shown us kindness in the sight of the kings of Persia: He has granted us new life to rebuild the house of our God and repair its ruins, and he has given us a wall of protection in Judah and Jerusalem' " (Ezra 9:9).

HighLights

- Rebuilding the Temple (Ezra 3–6).

- Ezra's Prayer and Reform (Ezra 9; 10).

Why was it written?

Like Chronicles, Ezra tries to make sense of Judah's history in the light of recent disasters. The two books are so closely linked, as a matter of fact, that some experts feel that Chronicles and Ezra were both written or edited by the same person.

Ezra and Chronicles differ greatly in purpose, however. The author of Chronicles needed to explain why Judah was destroyed; he saw Jerusalem's destruction by the Babylonians as God's judgment upon the sins of Judah's kings. But Ezra has a much more difficult task: He has to explain why Judah was restored!

After all, if Judah deserved God's punishment, then why does it now deserve His mercy? Not because of the temple—it had been destroyed. Not because of the priests—they had been ritually defiled by their time in Babylon. In other words, there was no *ritual* way to deal with Judah's sins. So why should God bring His people back?

Indeed, some may have questioned whether God actually was involved in the return from exile. The return from Babylon was not a repeat of the Exodus, after all. There were no spectacular miracles. No Moses. Not even a glorious entrance into the Promised Land. No, all that it involved was a few thousand survivors straggling back to their old homes as the result of some bureaucrat's decision.

In short, the author of Ezra was struggling with the same question that we struggle with today—the question of providence. How can we say that God is in control when He's apparently nowhere to be seen?

What you'll learn in Ezra

It's hard to appreciate Ezra's insistence on national purity. What could be more ugly, after all, then Ezra's insistence that Jewish men must divorce their non-Jewish wives?

If Ezra is quick to defend Judah's honor, however, it's only because that honor had been questioned. When it came to "mixed marriages," for example, Ezra points out that the problem was limited to 111 families out of a possible 30,000. What's more, Ezra's interminable lists of names demonstrates the people's desire to strengthen their ties with the past. "In spite of everything," Ezra says, "the Jews had retained their identity as God's chosen people."

At the core of Ezra is the idea of the remnant—the idea that God will always have a group of people who worship Him, no matter what. And in our time, which is much like Ezra's day—a time without miracles, a time when it seems impossible that God's people could survive another generation—it is good to remember Ezra's words: "God has not deserted us in our bondage."

GoodWords

- **Ahasuerus:** Probably Xerxes—Persia's "king of kings" (which is the literal meaning of "Ahasuerus") from 486 to 465 B.C.

- **Ahava:** An otherwise unknown irrigation canal in Babylon.

- **Aramaic:** Like most of the Hebrew Bible, the book of Ezra is written in Hebrew—except for Ezra 4:7–6:18 and Ezra 7:12-26. These chapters are written in Aramaic—the common language of diplomacy and commerce in that day.

- **Artaxerxes:** Third son and successor of Xerxes; he reigned from 465 to 423 B.C.

- **Ashurbanipal:** Assyria's last great king; he ruled from 668 to 626 B.C. (Some translations refer to him as "Osnappar.")

- **Beyond the River:** The Persian province that included Judah.

- **Cyrus:** Known for his tolerance and wisdom, he founded the Persian Empire c. 559 B.C. and reigned for almost thirty years.

- **Darius:** Probably not the man mentioned in Daniel 5:31. Ezra's Darius ruled Persia from 522 to 486 B.C. His attempt to conquer Greece was foiled at the Battle of Marathon in 490 B.C.; millions of long-distance runners have cursed his name ever since.

- **Ecbatana:** Thanks to its cool, mountain climate, it was the summer capital of Persia.

- **Esarhaddon:** King of Assyria from 681 to 669 B.C.

- **Ezra:** A priest and an official in the Persian court. His title today would be something like "Undersecretary for Jewish Affairs." Experts disagree as to when Ezra visited Judah. The traditional date is 458 B.C., but others have suggested 428 B.C. or even 398 B.C.

- **Feast of Booths:** Also known as the Feast of Tabernacles, this seven-day fall festival was a celebration of the grape and olive harvest, as well as a reminder of how God had cared for the Israelites while they traveled through the desert during the Exodus.

- **Feast of Unleavened Bread:** A seven-day spring festival connected with the Passover. It was a celebration of the grain harvest, as well as a reminder of how God delivered the Israelites from Egypt.

- **Jeshua:** The high priest who returned with Zerubbabel from Babylon; Haggai and Zechariah know him as Joshua.

- **Levites:** No, not people who wore blue denim jeans, but members of the tribe of Levi. They served as the temple's "support staff"—maintaining the building, keeping the books, singing in the choir, and providing security.

- **Persia:** Stretching from Egypt to Afghanistan, the Persian Empire lasted almost 200 years until its destruction by Alexander the Great in 331 B.C. Though tolerant of all beliefs, the empire's official religion was Zoroastrianism—a highly ethical faith whose adherents worshiped the god of light, Ahura Mazda.

(And, yes, a Japanese carmaker really did name his product after this particular god. Why, he did that, I don't know.)

- **Satrap:** A ruler of one of the twenty satrapies into which the Persian Empire was divided.

- **Salt of the Palace:** The officials so named were bound by some sort of loyalty oath or treaty.

- **Sons of Asaph:** Levites who provided vocal and instrumental music for the temple's services.

- **Steadfast love:** The Hebrew word *chesed* signifies God's faithfulness to the covenant He had made with Israel—that He would be their God, and they would be His people.

- **Urim and thummim:** Literally meaning "lights and perfection." Attached to the breastplate worn by the high priest, they were used to determine God's will . . . though how they did this is a matter of conjecture by the experts.

- **Zerubbabel:** A descendant of King David. In 537 B.C. the Persians made him the first governor to serve in Judah after its people returned from exile. He served in this post for at least twenty years and may be the same man as the "Sheshbazzar" named in Ezra 1:8. His name means "offspring of Babylon."

The Jewish calendar

Like our own, the Jewish calendar had twelve months and roughly 3651/4 days. Aside from that, everything was different.

The months, for instance, were *lunar* months, with a new month starting every new moon. Since a lunar month is roughly 291/2 days, this meant that there were only 354 or so days in a year. The Jews dealt with this by adding an extra month every two or three years—a month called "Second Adar."

If that weren't bad enough, the Jewish calendar also had *two* New Years—a "religious" New Year in the spring and a "political" New Year in the fall.

As a result, you need to be *very* careful when you're working out dates in the Bible. For instance, if the Bible says that something took place in "the first month," does it mean the first month of the religious calendar or the first month of the political calendar?

Hebrew month	Rough equivalent	Festivals
Nisan	March/April	Passover, Unleavened Bread, First Fruits
Iyyar	April/May	
Sivan	May/June	Pentecost
Tammuz	June/July	

Ab	July/August	
Elul	August/September	
Tishri	September/October	Feast of Trumpets, Day of Atonement, Feast of Tabernacles
Marchesvan	October/November	
Chislev	November/December	Hanukkah
Tebeth	December/January	
Shebat	January/February	
Adar	February/March	Purim

Nehemiah
The Street-Smart Saint

"Remember me with favor, O my God, for all I have done for these people" (Nehemiah 5:19).

Highlights

- Nehemiah Takes On the Job of Rebuilding Jerusalem (Nehemiah 1; 2).

- Nehemiah Overcomes Opposition to His Work (Nehemiah 4–6).

- Nehemiah Begins a Series of Religious Reforms (Nehemiah 13).

Why was it written?

Like the book of Ezra, Nehemiah is a story of return and restoration. Both are set in the fifth century B.C.—a time when Judah was a part of the Persian Empire and the Jews were returning home from exile in Babylon. Both Ezra and Nehemiah make it clear that God's people faced a number of obstacles upon their return. And both give almost the same amount of space—four chapters in Ezra, three in Nehemiah—to the work of Ezra, the priest who reformed the religion of Judah.

So close is the connection between the two books, as a matter of fact, that Ezra and Nehemiah were counted as a single book in the Hebrew Bible. And most experts agree that chapters 8 through 10 of Nehemiah (if not the whole book) were written by the same person who wrote (or edited) the book of Ezra.

But the tone of Nehemiah is a good deal more secular than that of Ezra. Nehemiah was a government official, after all, not a religious scholar like Ezra. What's more, his mission had been to rebuild the walls of Jerusalem—not to restore the fortunes of the temple.

Then too, Nehemiah's book is not meant to inspire faith so much as it is to defend the reputation of its author! In other words, Nehemiah is an apology—an attempt by an extremely controversial official to "set the record straight." And like many such attempts, it gives us a fascinating (if one-sided) view of what was going on behind the scenes during one of the most critical periods in Judah's history.

What you'll learn in Nehemiah

It's a fact that religious people have a reputation for being pretty bland. Passive. Unassuming. Nice people, to be sure, but definitely lacking in "street smarts."

That's why Nehemiah comes as such a shock. He's definitely not a "nice" person! No, he's a street-fighter—tough, shrewd, and wise to the ways of bureaucratic infighting. He's a leader who's not above pulling hair and cracking heads if that's what it takes to get something done. And though he's intensely religious, Nehemiah is nobody's fool. "We prayed to our God," he notes in Nehemiah 4:9, "and posted a guard day and night to meet this threat."

Nehemiah is a reminder that you don't have to be a wimp in order to follow God. He's a reminder that good things don't just happen; they happen when somebody *makes* them happen. And he's an example of what Jesus meant when He told us to be, not just "harmless as doves," but also "wise as serpents" (see Matthew 10:16).

GoodWords _____

- **Ammonites:** Descendants of Lot—and traditional enemies of Judah.

- **Artaxerxes:** King of Persia from 465 to 423 B.C.

- **Ashdodite:** Ashdod was one of the five cities of the Philistines.

- **Beyond the River:** The Persian province (or "satrapy") that included Judah.

- **City of David:** The ancient fortress that was occupied by David. It measured only 100 yards by 500 yards and later served as the cemetery for Judah's kings.

- **Cupbearer:** The court official who saw to the safety of the emperor's private quarters and made sure that his drink was not poisoned. Not a butler, in other words, but a security chief.

- **Darius:** Not the king mentioned in Daniel 5:31. Nehemiah's Darius ruled Persia from 522 to 486 B.C. His attempt to conquer Greece was foiled at the Battle of Marathon in 490 B.C.

- **Eliashib:** Grandson of Joshua, who as high priest had restored the temple in the time of Zerubabbel, Zechariah, and Haggai.

- **Ezra:** A priest *and* an official in the Persian court. His title today would be something like "Undersecretary for Jewish Affairs." Experts disagree as to when he visited Judah. The traditional date is 458 B.C., but others have suggested 428 B.C. or even 398 B.C.

- **Feast of Booths:** Also known as the Feast of Tabernacles. This seven-day fall festival celebrated the grape and olive harvests and reminded Israel how God had cared for their ancestors when they traveled through the desert during the Exodus.

- **Geshem:** An Arab, probably the same man as the "King of Kedar" mentioned in an inscription that archaeologists found in northwestern Arabia.

- **Horonite:** A native of either Beth-horon or Horonaim—both of which are cities located to the east of Judah. Nehemiah obviously meant to insult Sanballat by calling him this, but why this would be offensive is not clear.

- **Levite:** Members of the tribe of Levi; they served as "support staff" for the temple.

- **Nehemiah:** Chief of household security for the Persian emperor Artaxerxes and governor of Judah from 444 to 433 B.C. Following his term in office, Nehemiah briefly returned to Persia, then went back to Judah. Experts disagree as to whether his position in the Persian court indicates that he was a eunuch.

- **Persia:** Stretching from Egypt to Afghanistan, the Persian Empire lasted almost 200 years until it was destroyed by Alexander the Great in 331 B.C. Though tolerant of all beliefs, the empire's official religion was Zoroastrianism—a highly ethical faith whose believers worshiped the god of light, Ahura Mazda. (There are still Zoroastrians living in India today where they are known as "Parsis" or "Persians.")

- **Samaria:** The Persian province that included the area of the old northern kingdom of Israel.

- **Sanballat:** Governor of Samaria and opponent of Nehemiah. Letters written by Jews in Egypt at this time (the Elephantine papyri) indicate that some Jews looked to him for leadership.

- **Sons of Asaph:** Levites who provided music for worship.

- **Steadfast love:** The Hebrew word *chesed* stands for God's faithfulness to His promises.

- **Susa:** One of Persia's three capitals (the other two being Babylon and Ecbatana).

- **Tobiah:** An Ammonite noble who was probably half Jewish; his opposition to Nehemiah's plans was made all the easier by his family ties to Judah's elite. His name, oddly enough, means "the LORD is good."

- **Urim and thummim:** Literally meaning "lights and perfection" and used as a means of determining God's will.

- **Zerubabbel:** A descendant of King David, he served as the Persian governor of Judah from 537 to 507 B.C.

The Samaritans

In 722 B.C., the Assyrians conquered the northern kingdom of Israel and forced all of its people into exile.

Or did they?

When the Jews returned from Babylon, they found a number of local people who claimed to be the descendants of Judeans who'd been left behind, as well as some who claimed to be members of the "ten lost tribes." The Jews rejected these people as ritually impure—the product of "mixed marriages" with foreigners.

In spite of this, a number of these "Samaritans" continued to worship the God of Israel. In fact, there are still several thousand Samaritans living in Israel today. Their Bible is the "Samaritan Pentateuch"—an extremely old version of the five Books of Moses. They still worship as they did in the time of Nehemiah. And they still conduct animal sacrifices. In fact, I'm told that the sacrifice of their Passover lamb is open to the public; it's supposed to be quite a show!

Esther
God's Unseen Hand in History

" 'And who knows but that you have come to royal position for such a time as this?' " (Esther 4:14).

Highlights

- Esther Is Made Queen (Esther 2).

- Haman's Plot Is Foiled by Esther (Esther 3–7).

Why was it written?

To be honest, the experts have always had a hard time understanding why this book found a home in the Bible. Sure, it's a wonderful story—a rags-to-riches tale about a beautiful woman, chock-full of intrigue and danger, with more plot twists than you'll find in the collected works of O. Henry. And yes, it explains the origins of Purim—that rowdy winter festival so beloved by the Jews.

But it's not a very religious story. None of its characters are shown taking part in any kind of Jewish ritual (with the possible exception of fasting); it doesn't even mention God's name. That in itself was reason enough to make many religious people uneasy. In fact, the rabbis were still arguing about its place in Scripture as late as the third century A.D. (and possibly even into the fourth).

Then too, many question its historicity; there are too many details that don't seem to add up. For instance, Mordecai was supposed to have left Jerusalem in the time of Jeconiah, which would make him at least 115 years old by the time of

Xerxes. The Greek historian Herodotus says Xerxes was married to Amestris (not Vashti or Esther). What's more, a Persian king could marry only another Persian. (Esther was Jewish, remember?)

But over the years, experts have come to appreciate just how accurate a picture Esther gives us of the Persian Empire. Scheming officials, drunken feasts, a speedy postal system, and a king who is suspicious to the point of paranoia—whoever wrote Esther knew the setting well.

Even its chronology shows an intimate knowledge of Persian affairs: Vashti is deposed in the third year of Xerxes's reign; Esther is named queen in his seventh year. Why the wait? Herodotus gives us a clue: It was during this interval that Xerxes attempted his invasion of Greece.

History has also given meaning to the story of Esther—a story of God's unseen care in a time of danger. Whether it be the death camps of Hitler or the gulags of Stalin, God's people have repeatedly found themselves faced by the same peril as did Esther. And over the years, God's people have drawn both courage from her example and hope from her success.

What you'll learn in Esther

It's a familiar cartoon figure: the guru on his mountaintop, eyes closed in contemplation. The reason it's so common, of course, is that it embodies our idea of what a truly spiritual person is like: he's withdrawn, detached, cut off from the cares and the affairs of this world.

Life on a mountaintop isn't possible for most of us, however. Even if we wanted to pull away from society, we couldn't. We have bills to pay and families who need our care.

That's why Esther is so valuable: It's a story about people who *can* follow God *because* they live in the real world. Esther and Mordecai aren't naifs, after all. No, they're players—powerbrokers—in a society that made *L. A. Law* look like *Rebecca of Sunnybrook Farm*. And they succeed on the basis of three very "worldly" virtues—guts, heart, and brains.

Not that everything depends on human effort, of course. Esther's success (and Haman's defeat) hinge upon what some might call "coincidence," and others "providence." And if the line between the two is not clear in this story, then that's the way it is in our world too.

In other words, Esther is more than just a story about hope and happy endings. It's a story about what it's like to follow God in the real world.

GoodWords

- **Ahasuerus:** A Hebrew transliteration of the Persian title, *Khshayarsha* (which means "king of kings"). You're probably more familiar with the Greeks' attempt to pronounce his name: Xerxes. (And yes, this is the same Xerxes who ruled Persia from 486 to 465 B.C. and whose invasion of Greece was thwarted at the battles of Thermopylae and Salamis in 480 B.C.)

- **Banquets:** Most of the action in this story takes place at banquets—and much of the action is a good deal more understandable when you remember that Persians were famous for the heavy drinking that took place at their banquets.

- **Gallows:** The Persians executed people by impaling them on a long pole; the height of Haman's "gallows" indicates he wanted everyone to see what he planned to do to Mordecai.

- **Haman the Agagite:** The first-century Jewish historian Josephus says that Haman was an Amalekite—a member of the nomadic tribe that roamed the Sinai from the time of Moses to that of David. (Agag, after all, was the name or title of two Amalekite kings mentioned in the Bible.) Since the Amalekites were always at odds with the Israelites, this would be enough to explain Haman's animosity.

  Most contemporary scholars, however, believe that "Agag" refers to an otherwise unknown part of the Persian Empire. If that's the case, Haman's hatred of Mordecai speaks volumes about the kind of maneuvering and intrigue that went on in the Persian court.

- **Mordecai:** According to the *International Standard Bible Encyclopedia,* a clay tablet has been found that names "Marduka" as an official of Xerxes's court. Could this be the same "Mordecai" who has such a prominent role in the book of Esther?

- **Persia:** Stretching from Egypt to Afghanistan, the Persian Empire lasted almost 200 years until its destruction by Alexander the Great in 331 B.C. Though tolerant of all beliefs, the empire's official religion was Zoroastrianism—a highly ethical faith whose adherents worshiped the god of light, Ahura Mazda.

  Satrap: The Persian Empire was divided into twenty *satrapies,* more or less; each one was governed by a satrap.

- **Susa:** One of the three capitals of the Persian Empire (the other two being Ecbatana and Babylon).

Purim

One of the most beloved of all Jewish festivals, it celebrates the survival of the Jewish people in the face of persecution.

On the 14th of Adar (sometime in February or March), Jews will gather in synagogues to hear the book of Esther read out loud. During this reading, the audience is supposed to cheer every time Mordecai's name is mentioned—and boo every time Haman's name comes up! Many worshipers bring noisemakers—even firecrackers!—and most write "Haman" (or "Hitler") on the soles of their shoes and stamp their feet at appropriate times during the service.

Drinking is also common during this festival—in fact, the *Midrash* (a Jewish Bible commentary) commands worshipers to get so drunk during Purim that they can't tell the difference between someone saying "Blessed be Mordecai" and "Cursed be Haman"!

Believe it or not, this may be the festival referred to in John 5:1.

FlashPoint: Catholic and Protestant Esthers

The version of Esther found in Catholic Bibles is based on the text found in the Septuagint (LXX)—a Greek translation of the Old Testament that dates to 250 B.C. or so. The version found in Protestant Bibles is based upon Hebrew manuscripts collectively known as the Masoretic text (MT). That's why the "Catholic" book of Esther is roughly a hundred verses longer than the "Protestant" version; it's longer because it's based upon a different source.

So why does the LXX differ from the MT? Catholic scholars believe the LXX preserves an early version of the story—one that's just as good as the version that was eventually preserved in the MT. Protestant scholars, on the other hand, believe the MT represents the "original" version, while the LXX reflects the efforts of commentators anxious to tidy up loose ends.

My advice? Read them both, and make up your own mind.

QUICKSTART

Old Testament:
Writings

Job

The Good News About the Bad News

*" 'The Almighty is beyond our reach and exalted in power;
in his justice and great righteousness, he does not oppress' " (Job 37:23).*

HighLights

- Satan Makes a Bet With God (Job 1; 2).

- Job Complains (Job 3).

- God Questions Job (Job 38–41).

- Job Repents and Is Restored (Job 42).

Why was it written?

Job wasn't written to answer the question of why bad things happen to good people. Rather, it was written to affirm the fact that bad things do happen to good people.

And that's good news.

You see, biblical books such as Deuteronomy tell us that God will bless the nation that follows Him and curse the nation that doesn't. If you want secure borders and good harvests, then follow God. But turn away from Him, and your crops will fail, your businesses will go bankrupt, and your land will be invaded by foreigners.

"Good things come to those who do good"—that's the message of Deuteronomy. And for the most part, we would agree. "Cheaters never prosper," we like to say. "Truth will out. Honesty is always the best policy."

The problem comes when people take these beliefs and push them too far. "Good things *always* happen to *every* good person," they end up saying. "Evil comes *only* to those who've done wrong. You deserve what you get, in other words—no exceptions."

Of course, if life is going your way, you might agree with this. "I'm living right," you tell yourself, "and I've earned my happiness."

If your luck turns bad, however, you can end up feeling pretty guilty. What's more, this philosophy makes God little more than a cosmic vending machine— put some good behavior into the slot, and you've bought yourself some pleasure; put in some bad behavior, and you've bought yourself some pain.

If that's the case, then why did Job suffer? Unlike us, after all, Job is a perfectly righteous man. Yet still, he suffers. And contrary to the conventional wisdom offered by his friends, Job's suffering is wholly undeserved. He suffers, in fact, precisely *because* he is a righteous man.

In short, Job was written to raise questions—not provide answers. It was written to a people who were absolutely, positively sure that bad things *always* happened to bad people.

It was Job's task to prove them wrong.

What you'll learn in Job

Job's last speech ends with a declaration of ignorance: " 'Surely I spoke of things I did not understand, things too wonderful for me to know' " (Job 42:3).

And any explanation of evil must begin where Job ended. Too often, after all, we take the place of Job's friends; we offer pat answers that only make things worse. But Job reminds us that we lack the wisdom needed to make sense of evil. We don't know why bad things happen to good people. And we don't know what purpose is served by human suffering.

Nevertheless, Job does lay down some ground rules—some guidelines, if you will. They do not solve the problem of evil, but they can keep us from losing our way as we deal with it.

The first is that God is in control. Nothing happens without His say so. And while this doesn't solve the problem of evil—in some ways, as a matter of fact, it makes it worse—it does tell us that everything happens for a reason. Even if we don't know what that reason might be, we can still take comfort from the fact that we are not just victims of chaos.

Then, too, Job makes it clear that God is not the author of evil. To be sure, it offers no real explanation of Satan—who he is, where he came from, and why God takes his taunts so seriously. But Job makes it clear that Satan—not God—is the one who bullies Job.

What's more, Job tells us that faith is not the same thing as unquestioning obedience. It's Job's friends who defend God; Job himself is sure that God has done him wrong. Yet in the end, God says to Job's friends, " 'You have not spoken of me what is right, as my servant Job has' " (Job 42:7).

Finally, Job tells us that the only real answer to suffering is God. Job never does get straight answers to his questions; he never does learn why he has suffered so much. But in the end, he is content. Job has seen God, and that is enough for him.

GoodWords

- **Behemoth:** Literally, this word means "a beast." Some feel the monster described in Job 40:15-24 is really a hippopotamus! The apocryphal book of 2 Esdras, however, makes Behemoth the "husband" of Leviathan.

- **Job:** Pronounced so that it rhymes with "robe."

- **Leviathan:** A large sea monster. While Job 41 seems to refer to a crocodile, most experts link this word to the ancient myth of a "chaos dragon" who opposes everything good.

- **Redeemer:** A *goel* (pronounced *go-ALE*)—literally, "the one who buys back." Sometimes translated as "near kinsman," a *goel* was your nearest male relative—the one to whom you turned in times of trouble. If you were in debt, for instance, he bailed you out. And if you'd been murdered, he would track down the culprit, see to it that justice was done, and provide for your family.

- **Sheol:** Older versions of the Bible translate this word as "hell." A better translation is "the grave."

- **Uz:** Somewhere east of Palestine, possibly a part of the Arabian Desert.

Satan

One of the officials in the Persian Empire was a kind of "official snoop." His job was to keep an eye on all the other government officials and make sure they were doing their job. If they were, well and good. If they weren't, he would rat on them to the emperor.

Today, we'd call this kind of official an "inspector general"; in the Persian Empire, he was known as "the Satan"—a word meaning "the one who opposes at law," or "the adversary."

In other words, "the Satan" is not a name, it is a job title. In Job, "the Satan" functions as a prosecuting attorney who checks on the loyalty of God's creatures. Other parts of the Bible flesh out this role; by the New Testament, "the Satan" has become the angel who opposes God at every turn.

Psalms
Songs of Life With God

150 CHAPTERS — READING TIME: 8 HOURS

"Sing to the Lord a new song, his praise in the assembly of the saints.
Let Israel rejoice in their Maker; let the people of Zion be glad in their King" (Psalm 149:1, 2).

Highlights

- God's Power as Creator Is Compared With His Concern for My Life (Psalm 19).

- A Song for Those Times When You're as Low as You Can Go (Psalm 22).

- The Shepherd's Psalm (Psalm 23).

- Take Your Frustration and Point It Toward God (Psalm 42).

- The Basis for Luther's Hymn, *A Mighty Fortress* (Psalm 46).

- God Loves Me and Forgives Me When I've Done Wrong (Psalm 51).

- A Song for the Times When I'm Jealous of Others (Psalm 73).

- God Will Help Me in Times of Danger (Psalm 91).

- God Cares for All of His Creatures (Psalm 147).

Why were they written?

It would be simple to say that the book of Psalms is a collection of hymns—songs used in the worship services of ancient Israel.

And by and large, this simple answer would be correct. Most of the psalms were originally written for a trained, professional choir that would sing them while sacrifices were made and festivals took place at the temple in Jerusalem.

But that simple answer leaves out what happened to the psalms after they were written. It leaves out the way God's people took the psalms and made them their own.

With time, you see, songs meant to be performed in public became personal prayers. Hymns meant to be sung as a part of ritual became statements of individual guilt and remorse. And lyrics describing the glory of the reigning king came to symbolize the promise of the Messiah who would come.

Perhaps the closest modern example of the way the psalms were used is the way we use television today. Like the original setting of the psalms, what we see on television is a performance by trained professionals. We are watching what other people do.

Yet most of us take what we see on television and "personalize" it. We adapt it. We take it out of its original context and make it our own.

For instance, think of how often you've repeated a catch phrase that you first heard on television. (In fact, you've probably heard whole conversations that were made up of little more than catch phrases!) Think of the number of times you've compared something that was going on in your life with something you saw on television. And think of the number of times you've behaved in a certain way because that's the way a character on TV had acted.

For many of us today, television provides the mold into which we pour reality. For better or for worse, it shapes our language, our thoughts, and our lives.

And just as television does this for us today, likewise the psalms did this for ancient Israel. What began as scripts to be sung became the thoughts of a people. And in the process, God's people became more like Him.

The same thing can happen today, if you take the psalms and make them a part of your own life.

What you'll learn in Psalms

No one can read the psalms without being amazed at the sheer number of troubles that can befall a human being. The psalms describe people who are threatened by war, troubled by doubt, afflicted with illness, plagued by guilt, distressed by poverty, and angered by the success of their enemies.

Even the beloved twenty-third psalm—the "Shepherd's Psalm"—talks about walking through "the valley of the shadow of death"!

In each case, however, the psalm's author concludes that God is good, God is in control, and God is able to deal with the problem—whatever the problem may be.

Not every ending is a happy one, to be sure. Many of the psalms end with the author still waiting for God's deliverance.

Likewise, not every psalm is a pleasant one. Some of them, for instance, conclude with the hope that God will kill all of the bad guys who trouble God's people! (Imagine what it would be like to sing that in church!)

But the central message of the psalms is clear: God can deal with any human problem. Nothing is beyond Him. And anything—anything!—that troubles us can be brought to Him.

GoodWords _____

- **Hosts, Host of Heaven:** Refers either to the stars or to a personification of the stars as an army of spiritual warriors.

- **Lord:** If this word has only the first letter capitalized, it means exactly what you think it does. However, if all the letters are capitalized, then you need to read the next entry.

- **LORD:** Literally YHWH (pronounced "Yahweh")—the name God uses when He wants to remind Israel of His special relationship with them. YHWH would probably be better translated as "I am," but the Israelites regarded God's name as too sacred to pronounce and substituted the word *adonai* (or "Lord") for it whenever they read the Bible aloud. Most English Bibles preserve this custom, though some may use "Jehovah" (which is a combination of the words YHWH and *adonai*).

- **Nehiloth:** To be sung with flute music.

- **Sons of Asaph:** Temple musicians.

- **Zion:** The hill on which the temple was built—a symbol that stands for all of Israel.

How to sing the psalms

A number of the psalms are prefaced with instructions on how they are to be sung or the name of the tune to which they should be sung. Unfortunately, we don't know what any of these instructions mean. If any of these terms look familiar to you, let me know: *Alamoth, Al-Taschith Do Not Destroy, Gittith, Jonath-Elem-Rechokim, Dove on Far-off Terebinths, Lilies, Maskil, Sheminith, Shiggaion,* and *Testimony.*

Another word that pops up often in the psalms is *selah.* Even though it appears over seventy times in the psalms, nobody knows what it means. Scholarly guesses have ranged from "amen" to "stop for a moment and let the orchestra play." Some even think it may mean "turn up the volume"!

Hebrew poetry

No, it doesn't rhyme—not in English, and not in Hebrew either.

Instead, most Hebrew poetry gets its power from repetition; it takes an idea or phrase, changes it, then repeats it. In the process, you learn more about its meaning.

Psalm 77 is a good example of this: "I cried out to God for help." [That's the basic idea.] "I cried out to God to hear me." [There it is again.]

Sometimes, the psalmist uses repetition to narrow and focus the message of the psalm. Take a look at Psalm 93, for instance: "The Lord reigns," [there's the idea]. "He is robed in majesty" [we've repeated the idea that God is like a king], "and armed with strength." [Aha! We're not going to talk about God's wisdom or glory; we're going to talk about His *power.*]

Finally, there are times when the psalmist uses repetition to startle listeners with a new idea. Take a look at Psalm 149, for instance. Having said that God "crowns the humble with salvation," the psalmist then says, "Let the saints rejoice in this honor" [basic idea] "and sing for joy on their beds" [repetition]. "May the praise of God be in their mouths" [repetition again], "and a doubled-edge sword in their hands" [whoa!] "to inflict vengeance on the nations and punishment on the peoples, to bind their kings with fetters, their nobles with shackles of iron, to carry out the sentence written against them."

Talk about repetition! The same idea is repeated four times—but what does this have to do with praising God? Take a look at the way the psalm ends: "This is the glory of all his saints!" If you want to praise God, in other words, then singing is not enough; you've got to do something about all the bad guys in the world.

Proverbs
Wisdom for Everyday Living

31 CHAPTERS — READING TIME: 3 HOURS

"The fear of the LORD is the beginning of knowledge" (Proverbs 1:7).

HighLights

- A Hymn to Lady Wisdom (Proverbs 8; 9).

- Portrait of a Wise Woman (Proverbs 31).

Why was it written?

Long before there were Young Urban Professionals, there were ambitious people who wanted to get ahead in life. There were also wise old men—or *elders*—who were willing to teach them how to get ahead . . . for a price.

In fact, "schools for ambitious young men" were very popular in the ancient Middle East. There were at least a dozen in Egypt, for instance, during the time when the Pyramids were being built! They were so popular, as a matter of fact, that experts have a special name for the curricula of these schools: They call it "Wisdom Literature."

Proverbs is a good example of this "Wisdom Literature." It's a collection of simple rules and sound advice that dates back to the time of Solomon—nearly 3,000 years ago. And it was written, as Proverbs 1:2-4 says,

. . . for attaining wisdom and discipline; for understanding words
of insight; for acquiring a disciplined and prudent life, doing
what is right and just and fair; for giving prudence to the simple,
knowledge and discretion to the young.

What you'll learn in Proverbs

The life advocated by the book of Proverbs may seem dull to some. And it's true
that you won't find many of the heroic virtues in Proverbs—not courage, for
instance, nor physical strength, nor cunning with the weapons of war.

But Proverbs does praise the virtues that anyone can practice. It recommends
honesty, generosity, and hard work. It praises the person who is humble, frugal,
loyal, devout, and discreet. And it repeatedly urges us to remember the poor—to
have compassion on them, to be kind to them, and not to close our ears to their
needs.

In short, the book of Proverbs reminds us that we don't have to be specially gifted
in order to be a success. In the long run, it is often the quiet virtues that make the
difference—the quiet virtues that Proverbs sums up with the single word of
wisdom.

GoodWords

- **Fool:** Not the same as "stupid." Sometimes, it describes a person who makes bad choices out of
  stubbornness; sometimes, it describes someone who makes bad choices because he is too lazy to make
  good ones. And sometimes, it describes someone who is so bad-tempered and rude that he can't help
  but make bad choices. A good concordance (such as Young's or *Strong's*) will tell you which meaning is
  intended.

- **Sheol:** Though some older Bibles translate this word as "hell," a better translation would be "the grave."

- **Wisdom:** More than just knowledge, this word carries with it the idea of shrewdness, skill, or even
  "street smarts." In some verses, wisdom is personified in such as way as to almost make you think that
  wisdom is the same thing as God.

Wisdom literature

The invention of writing created a new kind of person: "the knowledge worker" or scribe. He (and it was always he) was someone who could read and write. As such, he was a valuable person to have around the royal palace. Scribes were the lawyers and the bookkeepers, the teachers and clerks, the court recorders and counselors of their day. As such, they were public intellectuals—a cross between college professors and secretaries.

Obviously, anyone with that kind of job description would get frustrated at times, and scribes were no exception. At times, it seemed to them as though life was a hopeless muddle. Anything that could go wrong, would go wrong—and there was nothing you could do about it. At other times, the scribes were more optimistic. Life seemed to be an orderly affair, with simple rules that guaranteed success.

The "Wisdom Literature" composed by these scribes reflects both points of view. The book of Ecclesiastes, for instance, takes a dark and pessimistic view of human nature; the book of Proverbs is more optimistic. Obviously, there's truth in both views—and that's why both books are in the Bible.

FlashPoint: Lady Wisdom

Proverbs 1, 3, and 9 speak of "Lady Wisdom" as the means by which God created the earth, and reveals Himself to humanity.

Many experts have noticed the parallel between this and the statement in John's Gospel that Jesus was "the Word" by which God created the world and revealed Himself to humanity. Some have taken this to mean that Jesus *was* God's wisdom—and that as such, He is a created being. Others have made "Lady Wisdom" to be the feminine counterpart of Jesus; if Jesus was the male revelation of God, in other words, then Lady Wisdom is God's female revelation.

Myself, I think that people who take metaphors literally should stick to football.

Ecclesiastes
When Self-Help Doesn't Help

"Don't be over righteous, neither be over wise—why destroy yourself? Do not be over wicked, and do not be a fool—why die before your time? It is good to grasp the one and not let go of the other. The man who fears God will avoid all extremes" (Ecclesiastes 7:16–18).

Highlights

- Lifestyles of the Rich and Hopeless (Ecclesiastes 1; 2).

- There's a Time and a Place for Everything (Ecclesiastes 3)

- Make the Best of Life While You Can (Ecclesiastes 9).

Why was it written?

Check any bookstore, and you'll probably find that the biggest section is labeled "self-help." That's where you'll find all those wonderful books that tell you how to lose weight, impress your boss, and straighten out your relationship with your mother-in-law in only ten days.

There's nothing new about "self-help" books. Long before *Thin Thighs in Thirty Days* came along, ancient experts were writing their own tips for better living. We know one such collection of helpful hints as the biblical book of Proverbs, but every culture—Egypt and Mesopotamia in particular—made its own contribution to what the experts now call "Wisdom Literature."

Unlike modern experts, however, the ancients knew two very important things. First, they knew their advice didn't always work. They knew you could read all the right books, listen to all the right advice, do all the right things, and still fail miserably. And second, they knew that everyone—even those who succeed—still must face the fact that they will die.

"So what's the use of living the good life," you might ask, "if I'm still going to die?"

Good question. In fact, that's the central question of Ecclesiastes. It's a book for people who know *what* they should do, but want to know *why* they should bother. It's a book that picks up where most other self-help books end.

What you'll learn in Ecclesiastes

Saintliness, scholarship, or sumptuous living—ask most people what makes for a good life, and they'll point to one of these three things. "Be good," some will say. "Be wise," others will reply. "Eat, drink, and be merry," will be the reply of others.

Which of the three is best? Most of us lack the time, money, or courage to try them all—but not the author of Ecclesiastes. Like a scientist in a laboratory, he tried each of these alternatives in his effort to determine their worth.

His conclusion?

None of the above . . . and all of the above.

"None of the above," because none of these lifestyles comes with any guarantees. Easy-living becomes boring with time. Wisdom doesn't ensure happiness. In fact, fools seem to do about as well as anyone else. And when it comes to religion . . . well, we all know people who've gone off the deep end there.

That's why Ecclesiastes urges us to hedge our bets—to live lives that combine all three aspects of the good life: saintliness, scholarship, and sumptuous living. Work at a job you enjoy, spend time with your family, and take each day as it comes; anything else is useless.

This may seem strange advice, coming from the Bible. And in truth, it is not the only advice Scripture gives on this subject. There are plenty of other passages that challenge us to dare great things for God.

But for people at the end of their rope—people who've given up trying to find any meaning in life—Ecclesiastes is like the knot that helps them hang on.

"Don't sweat the big stuff just now," Ecclesiastes says to people in crisis. "You don't have to find the ultimate meaning of everything right this minute. Easy does it; one day at a time. Keep living that way, and, step by step, you'll build yourself a satisfying life."

Saintliness, scholarship, or sumptuous living? Other books of the Bible will tell you which is best. Ecclesiastes tells you how to live while you're waiting for the answer.

GoodWords

- **Almond tree blossoms:** A metaphor for the white hair of old age. The people of Canaan, after all, saw these blossoms more often than the snow we use as a symbol for age.

- **Ecclesiastes:** Sometimes taken to mean "teacher." Nobody knows for sure.

- **Sheol:** Sometimes translated as "hell," this word actually refers to nothing more than the grave.

- **The son of David, king in Jerusalem:** Ecclesiastes 1:1 suggests this book was written by King Solomon. Some suggest that Solomon wrote the Song of Solomon in his youth, the book of Proverbs when he was middle-aged, and Ecclesiastes when he was a querulous old man.

- **Vanity:** The word literally means "vapor" or "breath." It carries with it the idea of something that lacks substance and permanence. One version of the Bible translates this phrase as "soap bubbles." While that seems a bit whimsical, it does convey the essential meaning.

- **Wisdom:** The Hebrew word is *chochma* (with both *ch's* pronounced like the *ch* in *loch*). It means more than just information or even human wisdom. "To have wisdom" means to see the world as God sees it. Even today, Jewish mystics speak of wisdom in much the same way that Christians do of Providence or even the Holy Spirit.

The Bible hits the Top 40

No study of Ecclesiastes would be complete without listening to *The Byrds* sing "For Every Thing (Turn, Turn, Turn)"—a song based on Ecclesiastes 3:1-8. Call the request line of your local "Classic Rock" radio station, and ask them to play it for you.

FlashPoint: When was it written?

Conservatives believe Ecclesiastes was written roughly 900 years before Christ. Most liberals think it was written during the time of the Persian Empire—perhaps 450 B.C. or so. In my opinion, it doesn't matter; the message of this book is timeless.

FlashPoint: The words of the what?

Ecclesiastes begins with the statement that we are about to read "the words of the *qohelet*." If you want to start a fight, ask the experts what the Hebrew word *qohelet* really means. Most would say it's related to *qahal* ("assembly"), but there the agreement ends.

Some say *qohelet* is a title or nickname that means, "someone who gathers people together"—an assemblyman or a teacher, in other words.

Others say it refers, not to a person, but to the book itself. Ecclesiastes is an "assembly" of wise sayings.

Still others say *qohelet* has nothing to do with *qahal*. They link it with the Hebrew word *qehillah,* which means "harangue" or "argumentative speech." If that's the case, then Ecclesiastes 1:1 might be translated, "The words of someone who will try to change your mind"—an appropriate beginning for a very contrary book.

Song of Solomon
Love Songs for the Unashamed

8 CHAPTERS — READING TIME: 30 MINUTES

"He has taken me to the banquet hall, and his banner over me is love" (Song of Solomon 2:4).

HighLight

- "Your teeth are like . . . sheep"? (Song of Solomon 4:2).

Why was it written?

If it appeared anywhere other than the Bible, you'd know why the Song of Solomon was written: It's a love poem. An erotic love poem. An erotic love poem that describes the physical joys of love in graphic detail. (Trust me—they're doing stuff in the Song of Solomon that is still illegal in the state of Idaho!)

What has puzzled experts for thousands of years, however, is the fact that the Song of Solomon is in the *Bible*. In the pages of sacred Scripture, after all, the events described in this book seem as out of place as a French-kiss during a Communion service.

That's why the experts have come up with at least three explanations for why the Song of Solomon was written—three theories, each of which has its own way of interpreting this book.

One of the oldest explanations is that the Song of Solomon is an allegory of God's love for His people. In other words, everything in this book stands for something else. Solomon stands for God. The woman stands for Israel (or the church or the soul). Her teeth represent pure doctrine. Her breasts symbolize the Old and New Testaments, etc., etc., etc.

Though it's still popular, this approach seems a little strained to some. It's true that God's love for us is like that of a man for his wife . . . but to push the book's symbolism beyond that leads to interpretations that are just plain silly.

That's why some experts say that the book is not an allegory, but a drama. They'd say that the book has three main characters: a humble shepherd, his beautiful Shulammite lover, and a wicked king who tries to seduce her. Read this way, the book is a powerful argument for monogamy (and a powerful indictment of Solomon—a king who was famous for his many wives and concubines).

Other experts disagree. They point out that drama was unknown in ancient Israel. What's more, the book lacks many of the elements you'd expect to find in a play—such as a plot, for example.

That's why the consensus of most experts today is that the Song of Solomon is nothing more than what it appears to be: a love song. (Or even a collection of love songs—perhaps as many as thirty.) Parts of it may have been sung during spring festivals, such as Passover and the Feast of Tabernacles. Others may have been sung at weddings.

But always, the intent was to praise the love of a man and a woman for each other—the love that is "as strong as death" (Song of Solomon 8:6).

What you'll learn in the Song of Solomon

Somehow the idea has gotten around that God's people should be a grim and cheerless lot. Strict. Austere. Even priggish. And that God is vexed whenever someone, somewhere, somehow manages to enjoy the physical pleasures of life.

Nonsense.

As the Song of Solomon reminds us, God created our bodies; God created sex. And God knew what He was doing when He made it possible for us to enjoy the physical act of love.

And the Song of Solomon portrays this enjoyment in ways that can only be described as lush and exotic. No, it is not a book for modest people. It is not a book for prudes. Instead, it is a book that looks back to the time before sin, when "the man and his wife were both naked, and they felt no shame" (Genesis 2:25).

To be sure, the Song of Solomon makes it clear that love alone is not enough. Love will not remove every difficulty or prevent every misunderstanding.

Then too, the love it describes is a love based on commitment. It is not promiscuous. It is not based on a whim. No, it is a love that lasts—a love that expresses itself in dedication, devotion, and faithfulness to one another.

But once these conditions have been met, says the Song of Solomon, then almost anything goes . . . just as God intended.

GoodWords

- **Aloes:** A perfume, probably from the eaglewood tree of southeast Asia.

- **Amana:** The Anti-Lebanon mountains of present-day Syria, famous for their alabaster.

- **Bath-rabbim:** A gate in the city of Heshbon.

- **Calamus:** A sweet-smelling reed or grass—possibly gingergrass or sweet sedge.

- **En-gedi:** An oasis on the western shore of the Dead Sea that is fed by a hot spring.

- **Gilead:** Located across the Jordan River from Jerusalem, this mountainous region was heavily wooded and used for grazing cattle.

- **Hennah:** A tropical shrub used to make a reddish-brown cosmetic dye.

- **Heshbon:** A city whose location allowed it to control the lower part of the Jordan River valley.

- **Hermon:** The southern part of the Anti-Lebanon mountains in Syria.

- **Kedar:** A nomadic people of the Syrian desert, famous for their flocks.

- **Lattice:** Since window glass did not exist, windows were covered with a wooden grill.

- **Mandrakes:** The fruit of this plant looked like a cross between a tomato and an apple; it was believed to be an aphrodisiac.

- **Myrrh:** Resin from the tree *Balsomodendron myrrha;* it was used as an ingredient in some perfumes.

- **Nard (or spikenard):** An incredibly expensive perfume that was imported from the Himalayas.

- **Palanquin:** A chair or bed that was carried by poles on the shoulders of two or more men.

- **Saffron:** Probably the saffron crocus—a source of perfume.

- **Senir:** Another name for Hermon.

- **Sharon:** Most likely the gently rolling plain near the northern coast of Israel.

- **Shulammite:** A native of Shulem (also known as Shunem), a town about fifty miles north of Jerusalem.

- **Solomon:** David's son and king of Israel. He was famous for his wisdom, his wealth, and his many wives and concubines. The high taxes needed to support his policies, however, made many people unhappy and led to the breakup of his kingdom after his death.

- **The Song of Solomon:** Also known as the Song of Songs and the Canticle of Canticles.

- **Tirzah:** Famous for its beauty, this city is located about twenty-five miles north of Jerusalem. When Solomon died and Israel split into two kingdoms, Tirzah served for a time as the capital of the northern kingdom.

Just exactly what is going on here?

Many of the words that appear in the Song of Solomon appear no place else in Scripture and only once in this book. (The technical phrase that experts use for this kind of word is *hapax legomenon*.) It appears that many of these words refer to places, plants, or animals, but it's difficult to be more precise than that.

Then too, it appears that many of the phrases in this book are . . . uh, "euphemisms" for the act of love—a fact that makes it even more difficult to puzzle out the meaning of this book.

If you're feeling brave (and you have the cash), get a copy of Marvin Pope's *Song of Songs* in the Anchor Bible Commentary Series. It's an eye-opening explanation of the parallels between Solomon's book and the other love poems of his day. It's a great Bible commentary, but it's definitely one that you'll want to keep on the top shelf, where your kids can't find it!

QUICKSTART

Old Testament:
The Major Prophets

Isaiah

The LORD Is Salvation

" 'Come now, let us reason together,' says the LORD. 'Though your sins are like scarlet, they shall be as white as snow; though they are red like crimson, they shall be like wool' " (Isaiah 1:18).

Highlights

- Song of the Vineyard (Isaiah 5).

- Description of the Messiah (Isaiah 8).

- Sennacherib Takes on God—and Loses (Isaiah 36; 37).

- The Suffering Servant (Isaiah 53).

- God's Free Offer of Salvation (Isaiah 55).

- What True Worship Is All About (Isaiah 58).

- God's New Heaven and New Earth (Isaiah 65).

Why was it written?

Isaiah is actually an anthology—a carefully arranged collection of the poems, prophecies, and historical writings attributed to the prophet Isaiah.

I say "attributed" because experts from Luther and Calvin on have noticed that Isaiah divides neatly into two parts. The first part is made up of chapters 1 to 39; it deals with the political situation in Palestine during the eighth century before Christ. In these chapters, Assyria is the main threat to Judah, with an anti-Assyrian alliance of Syria and Israel posing a secondary threat. Babylon is only a minor power—a power that is viewed by some as a potential ally of Judah.

The second part (chapters 40 to 66) deals with the political situation in Palestine during the sixth century before Christ. By this time, Assyria is long gone. So is the kingdom of Israel. Judah has already been defeated by Babylon; its temple has been destroyed, its people carried into exile. In this section of Isaiah, Judah looks for help from Persia, not Egypt.

Clearly, these two parts of Isaiah speak to very different situations—and clearly, it's improbable that the prophet Isaiah lived the 150 years or so it would take to span these two periods of time. That's why liberals believe that Isaiah combines two books—one written by the prophet himself, and another written some time later by his followers.

Conservatives disagree; they point to the large number of similarities in the language of these two books. They also think it's unlikely that a "school" of Isaiah's followers could survive such long periods of war and exile, yet still remain untouched by the messages of Jeremiah and Ezekiel. That's why they argue for the traditional view that Isaiah is responsible for both sections—the first as a commentary on current events, the second as a prophecy of the future.

Whichever view you hold, this much is certain: Isaiah was written for troubled times. And it's in troubled times that it is most appreciated, even today.

What you'll learn in Isaiah

Don't confuse God with motherhood, apple pie, and the flag—that's the essential message of Isaiah 1 to 39, a message intended for a nation that tended to take God for granted. Like many Americans today, the people of Judah thought God would always bless them; they thought God would always bring them good luck, just so long as they kept Him happy with the proper rituals.

"Not so," says the prophet. "God is not going to protect you; in fact, God is going to bring judgment upon you, because God is not interested in your petty little rituals. No, what God really wants from you is justice, truth, and mercy."

These are harsh words—all the more so because God was the One who had instituted these rituals! But as he warned Judah of her sins, Isaiah also warns us against the kind of religion that makes God little more than a campaign promise.

Although Isaiah afflicts the comfortable, he also comforts the afflicted. Chapters 40 to 66 are for those people who've already suffered God's wrath; these chapters promise forgiveness, restoration, and hope. And in some of the most moving words of Scripture, they promise that God will bring about our salvation by means of His "suffering servant"—a promise that Christians believe was fulfilled by Jesus.

Isaiah calls Him "a man of sorrows, and familiar with suffering." He goes on to say of Him that like one from whom men hide their faces He was despised, and we esteemed Him not. Surely He took up our infirmities and carried our sorrows, yet we considered Him stricken by God, smitten by Him and afflicted. But He was pierced for our transgressions, He was crushed for our iniquities; the punishment that brought us peace was upon Him, and by His wounds we are healed (see Isaiah 53:3-5).

It is the promise of this healing that has sustained God's people over the ages.

GoodWords

- **Ahaz:** Son of Jotham and king of Judah from 735 to 715 B.C. He was pro-Assyrian in his foreign policy and pro-idolatry when it came to religion.

- **Assyria:** The Nazis of the Middle East. Their reign of terror lasted from 911 to 609 B.C. Capital cities: Asshur, Calah, and Nineveh—all in what is now northern Iraq.

- **Babylon:** A restless vassal of Assyria, Babylon achieved independence (and finally dominance) during the reign of Nebuchadnezzar II (605 to 562 B.C.).

- **Cyrus:** emperor of Persia. His armies defeated Babylon in 539 B.C. Cyrus was famous for his tolerance; he was the one who allowed the Jewish exiles to return to Jerusalem.

- **Hezekiah:** Son of Ahaz and king of Judah from 727 to 698 B.C. Hezekiah is remembered as a good king, but his anti-Assyrian policies linked him closely to the Babylonians—more so than later generations might have wished.

- **Isaiah:** A Judean prophet active between 740 and 701 B.C. Legend has it his father Amoz was the brother of the Judean king Amaziah. We do know he was married to a woman known only as "the prophetess" and that he fathered two sons with the improbable names of Shearjashub ("a remnant shall return") and Maher-shalal-hashbaz ("the loot speeds; the prey hastens"). Isaiah's own name means "the LORD is salvation."

- **Israel:** David's kingdom split during the reign of his grandson; the term Israel can refer either to the unified kingdom before this division or to the northern portion of the nation, which became a kingdom in its own right (924 to 721 B.C.). Capital city of the latter: Samaria.

- **Jotham:** Son of Uzziah and king of Judah from 750 to 734 B.C. Though his name means "the LORD is perfect," he was a pretty mediocre king.

- **Judah:** When David's kingdom split, the northern part got most of the people and land, while the southern part (Judah) got the capital city of Jerusalem. Politically speaking, Judah was always on the knife-edge of disaster; it was finally destroyed by the Babylonians in 586 B.C. After decades of captivity, however, Judah came back from its defeat; the more powerful kingdom of Israel never did.

- **Lilith:** Sometimes translated as "night hag" or "screech owl," this word apparently refers to a feminine demon who was believed to live in deserts.

- **Merodach-Baladan:** No, not a character in *The Lord of the Rings*, but the Hebrew name for Marduk-apla-iddina II, a man who, between the years 721 and 710 B.C., was twice king of Babylon.

- **Rabshakah:** A title, not a name; a rough equivalent in our language might be "commander in chief" or "chief of the king's security detail." The Rabshakah's ability to speak Hebrew has led some to suggest he had an Israelite background.

- **Sennacherib:** Son of Sargon II and king of Assyria between 705 and 681 B.C. Some have suggested his siege of Jerusalem was broken by an outbreak of bubonic plague.

- **Sheol:** The grave.

- **Syria:** Not to be confused with Assyria, Syria was the kingdom just north of Israel. Its anti-Assyrian foreign policy made it the ally of Israel (and the enemy of Judah) in the eighth century B.C. Capital city: Damascus.

- **Terebinth:** *Pistachia* terebinthus—a low, spreading tree thought by some to be sacred.

- **Uzziah:** Also known as Azariah, he was the son of Amaziah, and king of Judah from 791 to 740 B.C. Though one of Judah's best kings, he presumed to burn incense in the temple—a job that was reserved for priests—and contracted leprosy as the result. His reign overlaps that of his son because they ruled as co-regents, for ten years or so.

The age of prophets

A "prophet" literally means "a spokesman"—and while God has had many spokesman and spokeswomen over the years, most of the Bible's major and minor prophets lived and preached during a period of just 200 years. What's more, most of them were concerned with just two events: the fall of the northern kingdom of Israel to Assyria in 722 B.C. and the fall of the southern kingdom of Judah to Babylon in 587 B.C.

Chronologically, the first prophet with a biblical book of his own is Joel, who preached from somewhere around 810 to 750 B.C. The end of his ministry overlapped those of Jonah (c. 760 B.C.), Amos (c. 760 B.C.), and Hosea (who preached until 722 B.C.). Joel was quickly followed by the prophets Isaiah (c. 740-700 B.C.) and Micah (c. 742-698 B.C.).

A sixty-five-year gap followed the end of Micah's ministry, broken only by Nahum and Zephaniah, both of whom *may* have preached sometime around 640 B.C.

With the preaching of Jeremiah (c. 621-580 B.C.), prophecy began in earnest once more. His ministry overlapped that of Habakkuk (c. 605 B.C.), Ezekiel (c. 604-570 B.C.), Obadiah (c. 587 B.C.), and Daniel (604-535 B.C.).

A fifteen-year gap followed the close of Daniel's ministry; then two prophets began to preach almost simultaneously: Haggai and Zechariah (c. 520 B.C.). With that, prophecy all but came to an end; only Malachi (c. 460 B.C.) would find a home for his prophecies in the Bible.

Jeremiah
The God Who Won't be Taken for Granted

52 CHAPTERS — READING TIME: 5 HOURS

" 'This is the covenant I will make with the house of Israel after that time,' declares the Lord. 'I will put my law in their minds and write it on their hearts. I will be their God, and they will be my people' " (Jeremiah 31:33).

Highlights

- The Parable of the Potter (Jeremiah 18).

- Jeremiah Takes on the False Prophets (Jeremiah 26–28).

- God Promises to Write His Law on the Hearts of His People (Jeremiah 31:33).

- Jeremiah Takes on the Kings of Judah (Jeremiah 34–38).

- The Babylonian Conquest and Its Aftermath (Jeremiah 39–43).

Why was it written?

The Assyrians had ruled the Middle East for 300 years, but now their empire was dying. Many hoped they could turn the Assyrians' misfortune to their own advantage—and one who did so was Josiah, king of Judah. Allied with Babylon, Josiah may have reestablished a Jewish presence in Samaria; he certainly did his best to rid Judah of foreign religious practices.

But Josiah died in his attempt to keep Egypt from coming to the aid of Assyria. Naturally, this confused many of God's people. Why had someone who had done so much for God been allowed to die?

Josiah's death ushered in an era of political confusion as well. Much of the royal court was pro-Egyptian, but the pro-Babylonian faction was strong as well—not least because Babylon's King Nebuchadnezzar showed up every few years to punish his enemies. Then too, for twelve years Judah had two kings: Jehoiachin (who was kept as a hostage in Babylon) and Zedekiah (who reigned in Jerusalem).

Faced with this confusion, many took comfort from the words of "court prophets"—religious professionals who claimed to know God's will. They claimed that God had made a binding contract with Judah—a contract that could not be broken. And under the terms of the contract, Judah could only prosper, no matter what it did.

Emboldened by these guarantees of God's blessing, Judah revolted against Babylon. The result was a disaster. Babylon destroyed Jerusalem, took its leaders captive, and left the survivors wondering what good was a God who failed to keep His promises.

What you'll learn in Jeremiah

All too often, God is pictured as a sort of "heavenly bulldozer"—a God who moves straight toward His objective, no matter what gets in the way. In other words, if God says something will happen, then it will happen.

Granted, this notion has some basis in Scripture, but taken to extremes, it leads to fatalism—the idea that "God is going to do what God is going to do, so it doesn't matter what I do."

That's why we need to remember Jeremiah's picture of God—a picture that portrays God, not as a bulldozer, but as a potter. As such, He works with circumstances as they happen. God may *intend* to make a vase, for instance, but events may alter His plans and cause Him to make a cereal bowl instead. Likewise, as God tells Jeremiah:

"If at any time I announce that a nation or kingdom is to be uprooted, torn down and destroyed, and if that nation I warned repents of its evil, then I will relent and not inflict on it the disaster I had planned. And if at another time I announce that a nation or kingdom is to be built up and planted, and if it does evil in my sight and does not obey me, then I will reconsider the good I had intended to do for it" (Jeremiah 18:7-10).

This doesn't mean that God doesn't keep His promises. He does. But He expects us to keep our promises, as well. That's why God's promises are not unconditional. They depend (at least, to some extent) upon our response.

GoodWords _____

- **Assyria:** Judah's old nemesis carried the northern kingdom of Israel into captivity in 722 B.C. Around 609 B.C., however, the Assyrians themselves were destroyed by their old subjects, the Babylonians.

- **Baal:** Literally, "lord." Baal was the Canaanite god of thunder, rain, and fertility.

- **Babylon:** In 626 B.C., Nabopolassar declared himself king of Babylon and led a revolt against the Assyrians; it succeeded. He was followed by the extraordinarily successful Nebuchadnezzar II, who reigned from 605 to 562 B.C.

- **Egypt:** Assyria's decline was Egypt's opportunity; the Saite pharaohs had attempted to expand their kingdom into Palestine and Asia during the seventh century B.C. But Egypt's dreams of empire vanished in 605 B.C., with the defeat of Pharaoh Necho by crown prince Nebuchadnezzar of Babylon at Carchemish.

- **Enemies from the north:** Whether this refers to the Scythians (a nomadic people from southern Russia) or the Babylonians is a matter of some debate.

- **Israel:** From 1050 to 931 B.C., Israel was the united kingdom ruled by Saul, David, and then Solomon. From 931 to 722 B.C., "Israel" referred only to the northern part of David's old kingdom; the southern part took the name of Judah. If that isn't confusing enough, Jeremiah refers to the people of Judah as "Israel" although the northern kingdom was long gone by his time.

- **Jeremiah:** Prophet of God from 626 to 586 B.C.; his sayings, speeches, and visions were collected (in no particular order) in the book that bears his name.

- **Queen of heaven:** Probably Ishtar—the Assyro-Babylonian goddess of fertility. She was also known in Palestine as Astarte, or Ashtoreth.

- **Shaphan:** Secretary to King Josiah and a religious reformer in his own right. His sons were also on the side of the angels—Ahikam played an important part in Josiah's restoration of the temple and protected Jeremiah from his enemies, Elasah delivered an important letter for Jeremiah, and Gemariah urged King Jehoiakim to obey Jeremiah's message. Ahikam's son Gedaliah was made governor of Judah by the Babylonians, only to be assassinated by his fellow Jews.

Jerusalem may have had as many as 30,000 inhabitants during the time of Jeremiah.

FAST FACT

Important dates in Jeremiah

- **639 B.C.**—Josiah assumes the throne of Judah.

- **608 B.C.**—King Josiah is killed by Egyptians; Jehoahaz (his second son) is proclaimed king by the people and reigns three months. King Jehoahaz is then deposed by Egyptians and dies in exile; Jehoiakim (who is pro-Egyptian and Josiah's eldest son) assumes the throne.

- **598 B.C.**—King Jehoiakim is deposed by Babylonians and dies in captivity. Jehoiachin (Jehoiakim's son) assumes the throne and reigns three months; he is then replaced by his uncle Zedekiah. (After surviving thirty-seven years of captivity in Babylon, Jehoiachin was finally released.)

- **586 B.C.**—After a thirty-month siege, Jerusalem is captured by the Babylonians. Zedekiah is transported to Babylon, where he dies. The Jewish nobleman Gedaliah, son of Ahikam, is made governor by the Babylonians; two months later, he is assassinated by fellow Jews at the behest of Baalis, king of neighboring Ammon.

Lamentations

Mourning the People of God

"Yet this I call to mind and therefore I have hope: because of the LORD's great love we are not consumed, for his compassions never fail" (Lamentations 3:21, 22).

HighLight

- God Cares, Even in Tough Times (Lamentations 3).

Why was it written?

The glory days of Judah were over. In the time of Solomon, Judah had stretched from Egypt to the Euphrates River. Now it was a shrunken remnant of its former self— little more than the land immediately surrounding its capital city of Jerusalem. And even that wasn't really its own, for Judah had sworn allegiance to the king of Babylon.

But still its people dreamed of glory. To be sure, the prophet Jeremiah had warned Judah not to break its treaties with Babylon. And twice before, Judah's attempts to win freedom had been crushed—once in 605 B.C., when King Nebuchadnezzar of Babylon had defeated its Egyptian allies, and again in 598 B.C., when King Jehoiachin had been forced into exile. But dreams die hard, and the very king the Babylonians had put in Jehoiachin's place—Zedekiah—would lead Judah's third and final revolt.

Judah didn't have a chance. On January 15, 588 B.C., Nebuchadnezzar's forces began their siege of Jerusalem. Thirty months of bloodshed and starvation followed. And on August 15, 586 B.C., the capital city was captured and destroyed by fire.

As a nation, Judah was no more. Its leaders were in chains; its people dead or demoralized. And the temple—the building that symbolized God's special relationship with Judah—was now a smoldering ruin.

With everything gone, two tasks remained: The dead had to be mourned, and the living comforted. God's people needed a reason for the disaster that had come upon them. And they needed the assurance that God had not completely abandoned them.

Experts disagree as to who wrote Lamentations. Tradition has it that it was composed by the prophet Jeremiah—and 2 Chronicles 35:25 does say that he wrote a "lament" at least once. Others point to differences in style and wording between this book and that of Jeremiah—differences that they cite as proof that Lamentations was written by someone else.

But all agree that Lamentations was written to meet the needs of Judah's people when they were reeling in shock from the destruction of Jerusalem.

What you'll learn in Lamentations

Anyone who has ever asked God to punish the wicked should read this book. It's an eloquent and moving account of the human price exacted by God's judgments. And the knowledge that Judah's people thoroughly deserved what happened to them did not ease the pain. As Lamentations 1:18 says,

> "The LORD is righteous, yet I rebelled against his command.
> Listen, all you peoples; look upon my suffering. My young
> men and maidens have gone into exile. I called to my allies but
> they betrayed me. My priests and my elders perished in the
> city while they searched for food to keep themselves alive"
> (Lamentations 1:18, 19).

Some of this pain is expressed as anger. The author hopes that God will deal with His enemies in the same way that He has dealt with Judah—an interesting twist on the Golden Rule! And Edom is warned not to rejoice over Zion's misfortune, for Judah will recover, but Edom, when it is punished, will not.

And though this book is titled "Lamentations," at its heart is a message of hope. The fact that God was too good to allow Judah's sin to go unpunished means that He is too good *not* to forgive it. Judah will eventually be restored, the author believes, if its people repent.

"The LORD is good to those whose hope is in him, to the one who seeks him; it is good to wait quietly for the salvation of the LORD" (Lamentations 3:25, 26).

GoodWords

- **Assyria:** Assyria had carried the northern kingdom of Israel into captivity in 722 B.C. Around 609 B.C., however, it was itself utterly destroyed by one of its subjects: Babylon.

- **Babylon:** In 626 B.C., Nabopolassar declared himself king of Babylon and led a revolt against the Assyrians; it succeeded. The Assyrian Empire was then divided between the Babylonians and their allies, the Medes.

- **Edom:** Subject to Judah until it broke away sometime around 850 B.C., Edom is the dry, mountainous country just south of the Dead Sea.

- **Egypt:** Assyria's decline was Egypt's opportunity; the Saite pharaohs had attempted to expand their kingdom into Palestine and Asia during the seventh century B.C. Egypt's dreams of empire ended in 605 B.C., however, with the defeat of Pharaoh Necho by crown prince Nebuchadnezzar of Babylon at Carchemish.

- **Israel:** God gave this name to Jacob, the son of Abraham. From 1050 to 931 B.C., "Israel" referred to the united kingdom of Saul, David, and Solomon. When David's kingdom split in 931 B.C., the northern kingdom took the name of Israel; the southern kingdom took the name of Judah. If that isn't confusing enough, Lamentations refers to Judah as "Israel"—perhaps because the northern kingdom was long gone.

Reading Lamentations

Read this book as you would any other collection of poems, for what it is: five poems about the destruction of Jerusalem.

To be sure, you won't find many rhymes in the book of Lamentations—Hebrew poetry depended more on structure than sound. One common feature, for instance, was parallelism: adding to a thought by comparison or contrast. One example of this is Lamentations 3:17.

I have been deprived of peace;

I have forgotten what prosperity is . . .

As you read Lamentations, you'll notice each chapter has either twenty-two verses or sixty-six (which is three times twenty-two). That's because there are twenty-two letters in the Hebrew alphabet. Lamentations is an acrostic—the first verse of the first chapter begins with the first letter of the Hebrew alphabet, the second verse begins with the second letter, and on it goes until the end of the alphabet is reached. (There are two exceptions to this pattern: each letter gets three verses in chapter 3. And while chapter 5 has twenty-two verses, it's not an acrostic. Nobody knows why.)

Most experts agree that chapters 1, 2, 4, and 5 are "corporate laments"—in them, the speaker represents the entire nation of Judah. But chapter 3 is more personal; it is also the most hopeful of the five.

The King James Version of the Bible that is generally used in Protestant churches has:

- *66 books that are divided into*
- *1,189 chapters, which are sub-divided into*
- *41,173 verses, that are made up of*
- *774,746 words, comprised of*
- *3,566,480 letters.*

In the King James Version:

- *The middle chapter is Job 39.*
- *The middle verse is 2 Chronicles 20:17.*
- *The longest verse is Esther 8:9.*
- *The shortest verse is John 11:35 ("Jesus wept.")*

Ezekiel
God's Word in Confusing Times

48 CHAPTERS — READING TIME: 4 HOURS

" ' "As surely as I live, declares the Sovereign Lord, I take no pleasure in the death of the wicked, but rather that they turn from their ways and live" ' " (Ezekiel 33:11).

Highlights

- Ezekiel's Wheels (Ezekiel 1).

- God Leaves the Temple (Ezekiel 10).

- God Does Not Punish Us for the Sins of Our Ancestors (Ezekiel 18).

- The Death of Ezekiel's Wife (Ezekiel 24:15-27).

- The Valley of Dry Bones (Ezekiel 37).

- The Prophecy of Gog and Magog (Ezekiel 38; 39).

- God Restores the Land of Judah (Ezekiel 47:1-12).

Why was it written?

Even in the best of times, politics in the Middle East resembles nothing so much as the plot of a soap opera. But Ezekiel was written during especially trying times—times in which the question of "Who's going with whom?" was especially difficult to answer.

144

For over 300 years, you see, the one constant in Judah's history had been the enmity of the Assyrian Empire. But when the Assyrian king Ashurbanipal died in 669 B.C., his empire crumbled. In its place rose the reborn empires of Babylon and Egypt—and right between the two of them was Judah.

Believing in the proverb that "the enemy of my enemy is my friend," Judah's king Josiah had fought against the Egyptians when they had tried to help the Assyrians fight against Babylon. But Josiah was killed, and the Egyptians replaced his heir with another of his sons—the pro-Egyptian king Jehoiakim.

Babylon's power grew, however, and Jehoiakim was forced to switch his allegiance from the Egyptians to the Babylonians. Two years later, Jehoiakim switched again and reestablished his alliance with Egypt. As a result, Babylon invaded Judah. Jehoiakim did the best thing he could have done under the circumstances: he died. It was his son—Jehoiachin—who surrendered to the Babylonian armies of King Nebuchadnezzar II in 597 B.C.

Nebuchadnezzar brought Jehoiachin to Babylon, where he could keep an eye on him; Nebuchadnezzar also carried off large numbers of court and temple officials to Babylon—among them was the prophet Ezekiel. Jehoiachin's uncle, Zedekiah, was put in charge of Judah, and that was that . . .

Until Zedekiah switched sides and made Judah an ally of the Egyptians. This was no more successful than any previous alliance with Egypt had ever been, however, so Zedekiah was forced to switch sides again and ally himself once more with Babylon.

It should come as no surprise that, with the help of Pharaoh Hophra of Egypt, Judah switched sides yet *again* and rebelled against Babylon. The result? Nebuchadnezzar II captured Jerusalem in 586 B.C. The Babylonians then put out the eyes of Zedekiah, killed his sons, and removed most of his subjects to Babylon.

(And just in case you're wondering, Nebuchadnezzar appointed a Jewish nobleman named Gedaliah to govern the few Jews who remained behind in Jerusalem. But Gedaliah was soon murdered by Jews who favored closer ties with Egypt.)

In short, God's people were divided, bewildered, and beset on every side. False prophets abounded. And with the destruction of the temple in 586 B.C., it seemed as though all contact with God had been lost.

What you'll learn in Ezekiel

Draw a line between Ezekiel chapters 32 and 33. Everything before that line was written before Jerusalem fell to the Babylonians. Everything after that line was written afterwards. Understand this, and you have the key needed to unlock the book of Ezekiel.

Before Jerusalem's fall, Ezekiel's message is a gloomy one. Judah is doomed. Her sins demand punishment. And anyone who opposes God's chosen instrument (i.e. Babylon) will be destroyed.

After the fall, however, Ezekiel's message changes to one of hope. Judah will be restored, not because she is righteous, but because God is good. The temple will be rebuilt more gloriously than before. And the new name of Jerusalem will be "the LORD is there."

Ezekiel gives the right message for the right time, in other words. As the saying goes, he "afflicts the comfortable, and comforts the afflicted."

GoodWords

- **Babylon:** The name of both a city and an empire. Babylon became independent of Assyria in 626 B.C. With the defeat of the Egyptians at Carchemish in 605 B.C., Babylon became the dominant power in the Middle East. It conquered Judah in 586 B.C.; in turn, it was conquered by the Persians on 29 October 539 B.C.

- **Chaldea:** Another name for Babylon.

- **Chebar:** An irrigation canal that branched off the Euphrates River near the city of Babylon in what is now southeast Iraq.

- **Cherubim:** Plural of cherub—thus, to speak of "cherubims" is an exercise in overkill. The Bible does not say what a cherub looks like, though most experts feel the name may come from the Assyrian *karubu*—huge, mythical lions or bulls with eagle's wings and human heads, who ran errands for the gods. (You may want to remember this the next time someone says that your children are "little cherubs"!)

- **Daniel:** Most experts agree that the man spoken of in Ezekiel 14 is not the biblical prophet Daniel; if nothing else, their names are spelled differently in Hebrew. Instead, Ezekiel is probably referring to "Dan'el"—a legendary king known for his goodness and wisdom.

- **Ezekiel:** A priest who was deported to Babylon in 597 B.C.—perhaps when he was not more than twenty-five years old. Five years later, he was called to become a prophet; he functioned as one at roughly the same time as Jeremiah and Daniel. He was married, though his wife died nine years after his move to Babylon. His name means "God will strengthen."

- **Gog and Magog:** Ezekiel 38 and 39 picture these two as making war against God's people at the end of time. Some experts identify them as the Gagaia—a tribe who may have lived north of the Black Sea. Others believe "magog" is a cipher for Babylon. Then again, Ezekiel may not have meant for this phrase to refer to a literal people.

- **Oholah:** A symbolic name for Samaria—the capital of the northern kingdom of Israel. It means either "her tent" or "she has pitched a tent."

- **Oholibah:** A symbolic name for Jerusalem—the capital of the southern kingdom of Judah. It means either "tent" or "my tent is in her."

- **Tammuz:** God of pastures and flocks, and husband of Ishtar—the goddess of love. His annual death and resurrection was thought to cause the seasons.

FlashPoint: Ezekiel R-rated for content?

The vision of God presented in chapters 1–3 caused so much speculation that some rabbis thought Ezekiel should not be read by anyone under the age of thirty. And the difference between the services described in Ezekiel 33–48 and those described in the Pentateuch led some rabbis to believe that Ezekiel should not be in the Bible!

Money in the Bible

It's almost impossible to calculate precisely how much a specific coin might have been worth in biblical times; the price of precious metals bounced around as much back then as it does today.

If you're willing to settle for "good enough," however, keep in mind that a *shekel* was a half-ounce silver coin about the size of a quarter. One shekel bought roughly 250 pounds of grain, 150 shekels bought a horse, and 600 shekels bought you a chariot.

If you got tired of carrying around all those shekels, you could exchange fifteen silver shekels for one gold shekel. Either that, or you could use sixty silver shekels to buy one *mina,* and sixty *minas* (or 3,600 silver shekels) to buy a *talent*.

Daniel

Following God, No Matter What

12 CHAPTERS — READING TIME: 1 HOUR

" 'If we are thrown into the blazing furnace, the God we serve is able to save us from it, and he will rescue us from your hand, O king. But even if he does not, we want you to know, O king, that we will not serve your gods or worship the image of gold you have set up' " (Daniel 3:17, 18).

Highlights

- Daniel Interprets the Dream of Nebuchadnezzar (Daniel 2).

- Daniel's Three Friends in the Fiery Furnace (Daniel 3).

- Belshazzar's Feast, and the Writing on the Wall (Daniel 5).

- Daniel in the Lions' Den (Daniel 6).

Why was it written?

Everyone agrees that Daniel was meant to give comfort and hope to people going through tough times. And everyone agrees that it does so by drawing on stories from one of the most brutal periods in the history of God's people: the Babylonian captivity.

"If God could get His people through seventy years of exile, persecution, and bigotry," says the book of Daniel, "He should be able to help us in our current situation."

149

The problem is that the experts don't agree as to just what situation Daniel was meant to address. Conservative scholars generally believe Daniel's original audience was made up of Jews living in Babylon during the sixth century B.C. Therefore they believe that Daniel should be read as a series of incredibly accurate prophecies about the future—prophecies meant to comfort Jews who were living far from their homeland under Babylonian or Persian rule.

But liberal (and even some conservative) scholars believe that Daniel was written sometime between 167 and 164 B.C. If so, then Daniel was written to encourage the Palestinian Jews who were being pressured by the Hellenistic king Antiochus IV to accept Greek culture and ways. These experts think Daniel is not a prophecy of the future, in other words, so much as it is a commentary on current events.

I agree with those who believe that Daniel is a prophetic book, written during the sixth century before Christ.

Whichever view you pick, however, one thing is clear: Daniel was meant for people who were going through tough times for a good cause. If that sounds like your situation, then Daniel was meant for you.

What you'll learn in Daniel

A kick in the pants or a pat on the back—sometimes people who are going through tough times need the first of these; sometimes they need the second. Fortunately, Daniel delivers both.

In its first six chapters, you'll find story after story that stresses the importance of obedience. What's more, these chapters make it clear that obedience isn't always easy or its results guaranteed. "Like the three Jews who risked a fiery death," says the book of Daniel, "you need to be loyal to God—even if you're not sure what the outcome will be."

The last six chapters of Daniel, on the other hand, are filled with hope. "God's people have a glorious destiny," these chapters promise. And in the end,

"Multitudes who sleep in the dust of the earth will awake: some to everlasting life, others to shame and everlasting contempt. Those who are wise will shine like the brightness of the heavens, and those who lead many to righteousness like the stars for ever and ever" (Daniel 12:2, 3).

The need to endure and the promise of deliverance—you'll find both in Daniel.

GoodWords

- **The Ancient of Days:** God.

- **Babylon:** Located in what is now southern Iraq, this province of Assyria became an empire in its own right following Nabopolassar's revolt of 626 B.C. It was overcome in its turn by the Persians under Cyrus the Great in 539 B.C.

- **Belshazzar:** Eldest son of Nabonidus. He ruled Babylon from 556 to 539 B.C.

- **Chaldea:** A region of Babylon famous for its magicians and astrologers.

- **Cyrus of Persia:** Known for his tolerance and wisdom, Cyrus founded the Persian Empire and conquered Babylon in 539 B.C.

- **Daniel:** Carried into Babylonian exile sometime around 605 B.C., he served in the Babylonian and Persian courts until 530 B.C. or so.

- **Darius the Mede:** No historical figure by that name is known, though some experts have tentatively identified him with Cambyses or Darius Hystaspes—both successors of Cyrus.

- **Seventy weeks:** Generally understood to represent 490 years.

- **Gabriel:** The angel who is identified in the New Testament as announcing the birth of both Jesus and John the Baptist.

- **Horn:** A symbol of a king or kingdom in Bible prophecy.

- **King of the north:** Generally identified (even by conservative scholars) as representing the Seleucid kings who ruled Syria and Mesopotamia in the second century B.C.

- **King of the south:** Generally identified (even by conservative scholars) as representing the Ptolemaic kings who ruled Egypt in the second century B.C.

- **Kittim:** Originally Cyprus, but eventually used for any anti-Jewish power that comes from the west, such as Greece or Rome.

- **Little horn:** Together with the fourth beast of Daniel 7, the "little horn" of Daniel 8 is generally identified as the antichrist.

- **Michael:** The angel given charge of God's people. Some have identified Michael with Jesus before His incarnation. So long as one doesn't use this as "proof" that Jesus was a created being, the idea seems harmless enough.

- **Nebuchadnezzar:** King of Babylon from 605 to 562 B.C., he was known for his ferocity in battle and for his efforts in city-planning.

- **Satrap:** An official roughly equivalent to our governor. The Persian Empire was divided into twenty districts (or satrapies), each administered by a satrap.

- **Son of Man:** While the phrase can mean simply a "human," it quickly took on the meaning of "messiah"—the person whom God will use to redeem His people. Christ often called Himself the "Son of Man."

- **Time, times, and half a time:** Three and a half years, or 1,260 days.

- **Trigon:** A triangular guitar with four strings.

The king's food

In Daniel 1, Daniel and his friends probably refused to eat the king's food because it was not *kosher* — that is, it had not been prepared according to the laws outlined in Leviticus 11.

The language of Daniel

Just like most of the rest of the Old Testament, Daniel is written in Hebrew—except for Daniel 2:4 (last half) through the end of chapter 7. For some reason, this section is written in Aramaic, a language similar to Hebrew. Aramaic was the language of diplomacy and trade in the Middle East at this time, but nobody knows why the author chose to use it for this section of Daniel.

FlashPoint: The abomination that causes desolation

Daniel twice refers to the enemy of God's people as "the abomination of desolation" (Daniel 11:31; 12:11); he also speaks of "a little horn" that spoke boastfully against God (Daniel 7:8). Most scholars believe these three prophecies all refer to the same individual—but there the agreement ends.

Liberal scholars and some conservatives (as well as all of the Jews in the time of the Maccabees) agree that these verses refer to Antiochus IV, the Seleucid king who tried to turn all of the Jews into Greeks in 175 B.C. If this is the case, then "the abomination" has already taken place; it is past.

Protestant Reformers, such as Martin Luther, linked these verses with New Testament prophecies of the antichrist, and applied them to the church leadership of their day; they said "the abomination" was now present and active in Christianity.

But some conservatives believe that the "abomination" or antichrist will briefly rule the world at the end of time; these verses, in other words, refer to the future.

Interestingly, most early Christians felt free to apply these verses to the events of their time. Many saw them as fulfilled in the Roman siege of Jerusalem (see Luke 21:2-24). Writing well after that event, however, the apostle John applied this concept to the *spiritual* enemies of the church. "Every spirit which does not confess Jesus is not of God," he wrote in 1 John 4:3. "This is the spirit of antichrist, of which you heard that it was coming, and now it is already in the world."

The Prophecies of Daniel

	Preterism
Who believes it?	Liberals & some conservatives.
What does it teach?	Daniel was written 167-164 B.C.; it deals with the crisis caused by the attempts of Antiochus IV to Hellenize the Jews.
Chapter 2: Nebuchad-nezzar dreams of a statue.	Babylon; Medes/Persia; Greece; Hellenistic states.
Chapter 7: four beasts; 11th horn reigns 3 1/2 years.	Babylon; Medes/Persia; Greece; Antiochus IV "Epiphanes" rules Judah from 167-164 B.C.
Chapter 8: ram & goat battle; temple restored in 2,300 evenings & mornings.	Persia vs. Greece; Maccabees cleanse temple roughly 1,150 days after Greeks dedicate it to Zeus.
Chapter 9: Jerusalem to be restored in 490 years; "anointed one" cut off.	Maccabees cleanse temple in 164 B.C. following the murder of the high priest Onias III in 170 B.C.
Chapter 11: kings of north & south do battle; northern king dies without allies.	Northern Seleucids battle southern Ptolemies; Antiochus IV dies in 163 B.C., though not as predicted.
Chapter 12: prophecy will be fulfilled in 1,260 days; time prophecies of 1,290 1,335 days are also given.	The author expected God's kingdom to follow soon upon the restoration of the temple; it didn't happen.

Futurism/Dispensationalism	Historicism
Conservative Protestants.	Primarily Seventh-day Adventists.
Written in the 6th-century B.C., its prophecies of the "latter days" will be fulfilled during a seven-year period at the end of time.	Written in the 6th-century B.C., it provides an overview of history that stretches from Daniel's day to the end of time.
Babylon; Persia; Greece; Rome; revived Roman Empire.	Babylon; Persia; Greece; Rome; divided Europe.
Babylon; Persia; Greece; Rome; revived Roman Empire, with the antichrist reigning 3 1/2 years.	Babylon; Persia; Greece; Rome; Christian Europe, with the Roman Church supreme from A.D. 538 to A.D. 1789.
Persia vs. Greece; Maccabees cleanse temple roughly 1,150 days after Greeks profane it.	Persia vs. Greece; heavenly "day of of atonement" begins in 1844, 2,300 years after 490-day prophecy begins.
Jesus begins ministry 483 years after Ezra's return in 457 B.C.; last seven years usher in the end of time.	Jesus begins ministry 483 years after Ezra's return in 457 B.C.; last seven years end with the stoning of Stephen.
Northern Seleucids battle southern Ptolemies; verses 36-45 speak of the antichrist to come.	Northern Seleucids battle southern Ptolemies; verses 36-45 may refer to France, papal Rome, Turkey, Russia, or . . . ?
After reigning 3 1/2 years, antichrist is destroyed at Armageddon; the 1,260, 1,290, & 1,335 days end when God establishes His kingdom.	The 1,260 & 1,290 days both mark the end of the church's secular power in 1798; the 1,335-day prophecy ends in 1843 with the establishment of the Advent movement.

QUICKSTART

Old Testament:
The Minor Prophets

Hosea

God As a Wounded Lover

14 CHAPTERS — READING TIME: 45 MINUTES

" 'Yet the Israelites will be like the sand on the seashore, which cannot be measured or counted. In the place where it was said to them, "You are not my people," they will be called "sons of the living God" ' " (Hosea 1:10).

Highlights

- Hosea Is Told to Take a Wife Who Is Unfaithful (Hosea 1).

- Hosea Forgives and Redeems His Wife (Hosea 3).

Why was it written?

Think of Israel in 750 B.C. as a banana that's covered with brown spots. Sweet, yes—but not destined to last very long.

On the surface, life in Israel had never been better than it was during the reign of Jeroboam II. Business was good. Israel's enemies were in decline. Her armies were always victorious—so much so, that Jeroboam's kingdom was beginning to rival that of David's in size.

But to the keen observer, the signs of rot were evident. Wealth was concentrated in the hands of a few, while the majority suffered in desperate poverty. People were turning from Israel's God to worship local deities. And political instability was growing; during his twenty-five-year career as a prophet, Hosea would see seven monarchs come and go.

Add to this the growing menace of Assyria. Israel's success had largely been due to Assyria's preoccupation with internal affairs; in fact, the Assyrian Empire had been in retreat since the death of Shalmaneser III in 824 B.C. But now Assyria was beginning to stir again. With the accession of Tiglath-pileser III to the throne in 744 B.C., Assyria would once again be a major player in the Middle East.

In other words, if things didn't turn around soon, Israel would be in serious trouble. That's why God sent Hosea; he was God's last, desperate attempt to save this straying nation.

What you'll learn in Hosea

It's amazing how many people think of God as a traffic cop—a God who is always on the lookout for someone who has done wrong and who is always looking for an excuse to punish someone.

It's true that Hosea's message was one of judgment. God could not overlook wrongdoing (and neither should we). Israel had sinned and would soon pay the price.

Shining through these words, however, is a God who is deeply in love with His people. No less than Hosea, God knows what it's like to be betrayed by someone He cares about. And no less than Hosea, God is willing to pick up the relationship and begin again . . . if only His people will let Him do so. God will punish if He must, but He will go to almost any length to avoid doing so. As God says to Israel in Hosea 11:8, 9,

> "How can I give you up, Ephraim?
>
> > How can I hand you over, Israel? . . .
>
> My heart is changed within me;
>
> > All my compassion is aroused.
>
> I will not carry out my fierce anger,

Nor will I turn and devastate Ephraim.

For I am God, and not man—

The Holy One among you."

That was God's message in the time of Hosea, and it is His message to us today. No matter what we've done, no matter how much we've hurt Him, God is willing and eager to forgive us. All He asks is that we accept His offer of love.

GoodWords

- **Admah:** Located at the southern end of the Dead Sea, this city was destroyed along with Sodom, Gomorrah, and Zeboiim.

- **Ahaz:** King of Judah from 735 to 715 B.C.

- **Assyria:** The reigning power in the Middle East from 911 to 609 B.C. It pioneered the worst aspects of police states everywhere: mass executions, rampant nationalism, and the forced relocation of subject peoples.

- **Baal:** Literally "lord" or "master"—the name given the Canaanite god of lightning, rain, and fertility. Hosea 2:16 plays upon the meaning of this word by stating God's desire to be, not our "master," but our spouse. Certain trees apparently were dedicated to Baal and his consort, Asherah. Sacred pillars may also have been used in their worship.

- **Ephod and teraphim:** Ritual objects used in worship. Ephods were garments worn by priests and used to dress idols. Teraphim were the statues or figurines of household gods.

- **Hezekiah:** King of Judah from 729 to 686 B.C.

- **Hosea:** Prophet to the northern kingdom of Israel from 750 to 725 B.C. or so. With the possible exception of Jonah, Hosea is the only northern prophet to have his own book of the Bible. (While the prophet Amos preached in the northern kingdom of Israel just before the time of Hosea, he was actually from Judah in the south.)

- **Israel:** Also referred to in Hosea as "Ephraim" or "Jacob." When David's kingdom split around 924 B.C., the northern kingdom kept the name of Israel. Israel had most of the good farmland and was ideally located for trade. As a result, Israel was soon much wealthier than the southern kingdom of Judah.

  Unfortunately, Israel was also quicker to stray from God. As a result, Assyria invaded Israel in 722/721 B.C., destroyed its cities, and took its people into an exile from which they never returned.

- **Jeroboam II:** An enormously successful, powerful, and corrupt king of Israel. He reigned from 786 to 746 B.C.

- **Jothan:** King of Judah from 750 to 731 B.C.

- **New moons and sabbaths:** Regular monthly and weekly festivals in both Israel and Judah.

- **Shechem:** A Canaanite royal city that briefly served Jeroboam I as capital of Israel.

- **Uzziah (also known as Azariah):** King of Judah from 790 to 739 B.C.

FlashPoint: Gomer

Hosea's wife has been a source of frustration to more than just the prophet himself. Experts have argued for centuries questions such as:

- Is her name (which means "perfection") symbolic? (Probably not.)

- Is she the same woman who is ransomed by Hosea in chapter 3? (Maybe.)

- Why would God command Hosea to marry a prostitute? (Who can say?)

Marriage in ancient times

In biblical times, marriage was a family affair. Parents arranged the match and negotiated the "bride price"—the price that the groom's family must pay to that of the bride. When all arrangements had been made, "betrothal" followed; the couple was legally bound to each other, but not yet allowed to live together.

The wedding itself was a public parade for the bride as she moved to her new house. An enormous party followed—one that involved the whole village and might last as long as two weeks!

Most people married at an early age—the women in their early teens, the men in their late teens. Men were allowed to have more than one wife at a time, but rarely did—they simply couldn't afford it.

Joel
The Day God Steps In and Takes Charge

3 CHAPTERS — READING TIME: 20 MINUTES

" 'Mulitudes, multitudes in the valley of decision! For the day of the LORD is near in the valley of decision. The sun and moon will be darkened, and the stars no longer shine. The LORD will roar from Zion and thunder from Jerusalem; the earth and the sky will tremble. But the LORD will be a refuge for his people, a stronghold for the people of Israel' " (Joel 3:14-16).

HighLight

- The Day of the LORD (Joel 2).

Why was it written?

Suppose that it all collapsed. I mean *everything* collapsed—banks and insurance companies, grocery stores and government programs, even churches and charities. All of it gone. Kaput. Finished.

What would you do then?

What *could* you do then?

That's the situation God's people faced in the time of the prophet Joel. They were threatened by famine, economic collapse, the shutdown of services in the temple . . . and all because of an insect less than two inches long.

Now a plague of locusts may not seem like much of a threat to us today; it may even seem humorous. That's because most of us don't make our living on the land. Even those of us who farm have grown accustomed to the protection afforded by insecticides and government pest-control programs.

But remember that a swarm of locusts can cover up to 2,000 square miles. It can cover the sky and turn day to night. It can cover the land with literally tens of billions of hopping, chewing, devouring insects that eat everything green, right down to the bark on trees.

And when the swarm moves on, all it leaves behind is a desert—a desert with a lot of hungry people. No food, no sacrifices for the temple. No way to feed a family, no way to make things right with God. In short, utter and complete disaster.

So now you understand the size of the calamity facing God's people. It was the Third World debt crisis, the Ethiopian famine, and even the TV evangelist scandals, all wrapped up into one six-legged problem.

So what would you do about it?

What Joel does is to place it in context. He assures his people that God has not forgotten them, that He does indeed hear them, and that He will bless them again if they return to Him.

In fact, says Joel, what is happening now is a kind of trial run for what will happen at the end of time. Then, too, God's people will be in danger—terrible danger. But then, too, God will rescue them and favor them with every imaginable gift . . . just as He will now, if we trust Him.

What you'll learn in Joel

Joel isn't afraid to look at the bad things that happen in life. Almost half of his book, as a matter of fact, is a detailed description of the enemy horde that is invading the land of God's people. Verse after verse describes their destructive power and their unstoppable might.

Yet Joel can paint such a dark picture of the threat because he knows that God is even more powerful. Joel is not afraid of anything that might threaten God's people, because Joel knows that God can deliver them from any threat.

Joel's God, in other words, is big enough to handle anything that comes along. He is the God who cannot be coerced—even the prayers of His own people, says Joel, cannot force Him to act. God is never at a loss, never without a plan, never lacking in the ability to care for the needs of His people. In short, He is the God who is in control.

GoodWords

- **Cereal and drink offerings:** Sacrifices made at the temple—given either to express thanks or to ask for forgiveness from sin.

- **Egypt, Edom, Tyre, and Sidon:** Traditional enemies of God's people. Egypt lay to the south, Edom to the east, and Tyre and Sidon both lay to the north.

- **Sabeans:** The people of Sheba, or southern Arabia.

- **The day of the Lord:** A phrase referring to the time when God will punish His enemies and save His people.

- **The early and the latter rain**: Palestine has basically two seasons—a dry, hot summer, and a cool, wet winter. Because of this, crops are planted in the fall so that they get the water they need to grow. So when God promises to send "the early and the latter rain," He's promising that the rainy season will last long enough to ensure an adequate harvest.

- **The valley of Jehoshaphat:** Jehoshaphat means "Yahweh [God] judges." No literal valley by that name exists, though a number of people who should know better have identified it with the Kidron Valley, between Jerusalem and the Mount of Olives.

  Most experts feel that "the valley of Jehoshaphat" is a metaphor for God's judgment of the wicked, much like Ezekiel's "invasion of Gog and Magog," or the "battle of Armageddon" in the book of Revelation.

- **Zion:** The hill on which the Jerusalem temple was built. It is used as a symbol for the land of Judah or Israel.

 Joel was the first prophet to have a book of his own in our Bible.

Locusts

Locusts are what happened when a grasshopper gets crowded: he gets restless, edgy, and very, very hungry. At a distance, a swarm of locusts on the move looks like a cloud of dust; close up, it resembles a vision of hell. Since a swarm may move as much as thirty miles in a day, you can literally wake up to find that all your crops disappeared overnight.

On the other hand, locusts can be roasted and eaten. People who've done so tell me that they're nutritious and satisfying, with a delicious nut-like taste that goes well with salsa or barbecue sauce.

I'll take their word for it.

Amos

The God Who Couldn't Be Bribed

" 'Let justice roll on like a river, righteousness like a never-failing stream!' " (Amos 5:24).

Highlights

- God Weeps Over Israel (Amos 5).

- God Promises Salvation to All Peoples (Amos 9).

Why was it written?

If you had to pick the time when the northern kingdom of Israel was at its peak, you could do worse than to choose the middle of the eighth century B.C.—around 760 B.C. or so. Jeroboam II had been the king for more than twenty years; Israel's political stability had led to economic prosperity. Her neighbor Syria had been humbled by the Assyrian destruction of her capital, Damascus, in 802 B.C. And the Assyrians themselves were too preoccupied with their own internal revolts to bother their neighbors.

Not that Israel was at peace, you understand. Indeed, the weakness of her neighbors had led Israel (along with her allies, Egypt and Edom) into a number of aggressive wars against Syria, Moab, and Ammon. And though the wars had gone well—especially for the rich, who enjoyed the spoils of victory—they'd bankrupted the poor. Most of Israel's prosperity, as a matter of fact, had come at the expense of the peasant farmers, who made up the majority of her people.

But if you were rich, times had never been better. At least, not until Amos came along.

What you'll learn in Amos

You can't bribe God. That was the essential message of Amos—a message made essential by a religious revival!

The Israelites believed their prosperity was the result of the tremendous sacrifices they had been offering God: bulls and sheep, goats and wheat, wine and incense. To be sure, the money for those sacrifices had been wrung from the lives of the suffering poor. But God had no choice but to bless the rich, they thought, so long as they kept worshiping Him—right?

Wrong.

Ritual is no good without a relationship. Religion is no excuse for wrongdoing. And a faith that ignores the everyday needs of God's "little people" is more than just ineffectual; it is an actual affront to God.

> "I hate, I despise your religious feasts," [says God,]; "I cannot
> stand your assemblies. Even though you bring me burnt offerings
> and grain offerings, I will not accept them. . . . But let justice roll
> down like a river, righteousness like a never-failing stream!"
> (Amos 5:21-24).

All the warnings of Amos came true, by the way, roughly thirty years later. The people who used their "everlasting covenant" with God as an excuse to do wrong? They disappeared along with everyone else, when the Assyrians invaded Israel in 723/22 B.C.

It's something to think about.

GoodWords _____

- **Ammon:** The land to the northeast of the Dead Sea, traditionally thought to be inhabited by the descendants of Lot. Ammon was an enemy of Israel. Capital city: Rabbah. Chief gods: Milcom (Molech) and Chemosh.

- **Amorite:** A synonym for "Canaanite"—one of the peoples who inhabited Palestine before the Israelites.

- **Amos:** A common laborer from Judah, called to prophesy in the northern kingdom of Israel from 760 to 750 B.C. or so. If Joel was the first prophet to have his writings collected into a book, Amos was the second.

- **Arabah:** The wide valley that stretches from the Sea of Galilee to the Gulf of Aqabah. It's also used in a general sense for "wilderness."

- **Assyria:** Synonymous with cruelty, Assyria was the world's most powerful nation for 300 years. During the time of Amos, it was preoccupied with its own internal problems, but with the accession of Tiglath-pileser III in 745 B.C., the evil empire came back with a vengeance.

- **Bashan:** The thickly-populated highlands to the northwest of the Jordan River. Karnaim was one of its cities.

- **Beersheba:** The southernmost city of Judah. The phrase "from Dan to Beersheba" meant roughly the same thing to the Israelites as "from coast to coast" does to us today.

- **Bethel:** Site of Jacob's dream about a stairway to heaven. It became a place of idolatry after the northern kingdom of Israel broke off from Judah.

- **Carmel:** A range of hills in northwest Israel and the site of Elijah's confrontation with the prophets of Baal.

- **Edom:** The mountainous land to the southeast of the Dead Sea, traditionally thought to be inhabited by the descendants of Esau, the brother of Israel's father, Jacob. Capital: Sela (later named Petra). Chief gods: Eloah and Qaus.

- **Gilgal:** The site of Israel's first camp after it crossed the Jordan River and the place where Saul offered sacrifices. By the time of Amos, Gilgal had become a center of idolatry.

- **Hameth:** A city-state in central Syria captured by Jeroboam II. Chief god: Ashimah.

- **Israel:** The name taken by the ten northern tribes that broke away from Judah in 931 B.C. Israel was a wealthy and powerful state until its utter destruction by the Assyrians in 723/22 B.C. Capital: Samaria.

- **Jeroboam II:** King of Israel from approximately 782 to 753 B.C.

- **Kaiwan:** A Babylonian god and the Babylonian name for the planet Saturn.

- **Lodebar:** A place about eight miles south of the Sea of Galilee.

- **Moab:** The land east of the Dead Sea, traditionally thought to be inhabited by descendants of Lot. Capital city: Heshbon. Chief god: Chemosh.

- **Nazirite:** The term literally means "one who is devoted [to God]." Nazirites abstained from haircuts, as well as from anything made from grapes (see Numbers 6). Famous Nazirites include both Samson and John the Baptist.

- **Philistines:** Inhabitants of the five coastal cities (Ashdod, Ashkelon, Ekron, Gath, and Gaza) settled by the "sea peoples" during the second millennium B.C.

- **Phoenicia:** A narrow coastal strip bordering Israel, famous for its traders and sailors. Chief cities: Byblos, Sidon, and Tyre. Chief goddess and god: Astarte and Baal.

- **Prophet:** Literally, "one who speaks [for God]."

- **Sakkuth:** Traditionally translated as "the Feast of Tabernacles." Experts now think "Sakkuth" may be a reference to the Babylonian god "Sakkut" or Saturn!

- **Sheol:** The grave.

- **Shepherd:** Someone who herds sheep—a job that had about as much prestige in biblical times as being a parking-lot attendant does today.

- **Sycamore:** An evergreen tree bearing a fruit similar to that of a fig (albeit a rather small and nasty fig) that was eaten by the poor.

- **Syria:** The land to the immediate north of Israel and a traditional enemy of its people. The Syrians were said to have come to their present land from Kir, but nobody knows where that was. Capital: Damascus. Chief god: Baal (a.k.a. Hadad).

- **Tekoa:** Located about twelve miles south of Jerusalem in the kingdom of Judah, this town was known for the wisdom and bravery of its people.

- **Uzziah:** King of Judah from 767 to 740/39 B.C.

 **Prophets**

Professional oracles seem to have been common in the time of Amos. All that you needed in order to set yourself up as a prophet, after all, was a glib tongue and the willingness to tell your customers what they wanted to hear.

So when Amos said that he was not a prophet, he was actually saying that he was not *that* kind of prophet!

Food

Most people lived pretty far down the food chain in biblical times. Roughly 80 percent of their calories would have come from plants—mostly grain (wheat for the rich, and barley for the poor).

The staple was bread, served with a garnish of whatever might be available: olives or olive oil, cheese, dried fish, figs, raisins, melons, almonds, or honey. Red meat was reserved for special occasions—a festival, perhaps, or a wedding—and most of it would be considered tough by our standards, since they didn't "finish off" cattle in feedlots back then. Everything would be washed down with wine or "strong drink" (which was another name for beer); most drinks were heavily diluted with water.

Many of the foods we take for granted were unknown: turkey, tomatoes, potatoes, chocolate, coffee, tea, and sugar. Pork and shellfish were known, but not eaten since they were considered "unclean" for religious reasons. And though the King James Version speaks of "corn," this was just the British word for "any kind of small grain" (such as wheat or barley). The plant that Americans call "corn" (and the British call "maize") did not appear in the Old World until the Spanish brought it back from Mexico in the 1500s.

Obadiah
The God Who Doesn't Gloat

1 CHAPTER — READING TIME: 5 MINUTES

*" 'As you have done, it will be done to you;
your deeds will return upon your own head' " (Obadiah 15).*

HighLight

- Don't Look Down on People in Trouble (Obadiah 12-14).

Why was it written?

Obadiah is the book of Job with a twist. It doesn't explain why bad things happen to good people. Instead, it deals with the question of why good things happen to bad people!

When Obadiah was written, things were going well for the nation of Edom. Caravans involved in the incense trade had to pass through Edom, and provided regular revenues to that nation. And the kingdom of Judah—Edom's neighbor, rival, and sometimes ruler—had suffered military defeat.

It's hard to say just what this defeat may have been. Or what part Edom may have played in it. Most experts believe Obadiah was written immediately after the Babylonian destruction of Jerusalem in 586 B.C. Others point out that Edom plundered Jerusalem as many as four times during Judah's 300-year history as an independent kingdom, and that bad blood existed between the two nations until Edom's final destruction in A.D. 70.

Still, it's clear there was a whole lot of unholy rejoicing going on in Edom at the time this book was written—and that presented Judah's prophets with something of a problem.

For Judah had deserved defeat. Its people had sinned. God had punished them for their sins. And Judah had no right to complain about the way it had been treated by Edom.

Still, the fact that Edom had benefited from Judah's punishment just didn't seem right. Edom was no more righteous than Judah, after all. Its people were idolaters. And the vicious joy that Edom had shown at Judah's fall was obviously wrong.

In short, the prophet Obadiah must have felt much as we do when we hear that one gang member has knocked off another and taken over his territory. The one who was killed may have deserved his fate. But we hate to see another "low life" benefit as a result.

What you'll learn in Obadiah

Even if we don't know the word *Schadenfreude,* most of us know the joy we feel at another's misfortune. A business rival goes bankrupt, and we smile. A neighbor sues for divorce, and we spread the news. A TV evangelist goes to jail, and we laugh at the jokes that Letterman or Leno make at his expense.

If God's judgment on Edom is any guide, however, this attitude can get us in trouble. True, the person who fell may have deserved his or her fate. (Judah certainly did.) But we are not to gloat—and we are not to take advantage of his or her misfortune. Even bad guys—even bunglers, criminals, and fools—deserve to be treated with dignity, charity, and love.

And if we learn that *we* are the bad guy, then Obadiah offers hope as well. Judah richly deserved every bit of bad news that had come its way, after all. Yet God did not forget His people. Even though they did not deserve it, as a matter of fact, God would restore the people of Judah. He would raise them far higher than they had ever been before . . . just as He will do for us, if we ask.

GoodWords _____

- **Edom:** The mountainous land located to the south of the Dead Sea. Edomites were known for their wisdom (see Obadiah 8); both Job and his friends may have been Edomites. Capital: Sela (later known as Petra and familiar to fans of Indiana Jones as the final resting place of the Grail). Gods: various fertility figures, among whom were Qaus and Eloah.

- **Ephraim:** The second son of Joseph. Prophets sometimes used his name as a symbol for the ten tribes that made up the northern kingdom of Israel.

- **Esau:** By tradition, the father of all Edomites. He was the brother of Jacob, who was the father of all Israelites.

- **Gilead:** A thickly forested land located to the northeast of the Dead Sea and inhabited by Israelites.

- **Halah:** The land just to the north of Nineveh (in what is now Iraq) in which Assyria settled Israel's people following the destruction of the northern kingdom in 722 B.C.

- **Jerusalem:** Capital of the united kingdom of Israel from c.1000 to 931 B.C., and capital of the southern kingdom of Judah until its destruction in 586 B.C. Its size is difficult to estimate, but Jerusalem may have had as many as 30,000 inhabitants during the seventh century B.C.

- **Mighty men:** Warriors.

- **Negeb:** The desert south of Judah.

- **Philistines:** Inhabitants of the five coastal cities of Ashdod, Ashkelon, Ekron, Gath, and Gaza. They were the traditional enemies of Israel.

- **Phoenicia:** A narrow coastal strip bordering Israel, famous for its traders and sailors. Chief cities: Byblos, Sidon, and Tyre. Chief goddess and god: Astarte and Baal.

- **Samaria:** Capital of the northern kingdom of Israel from c. 885 to 722 B.C., and a symbol of that kingdom. The Assyrians destroyed it after a three-year siege; 30,000 citizens were then carried away as captives.

- **Shephelah:** The rolling country between Palestine's central mountain range and its coastal plain.

- **Teman:** Probably a district in northern Edom.

- **Zarephath:** A Phoenician town, about fourteen miles north of Tyre. This is the place where a poor widow cared for the prophet Elijah during a famine.

Warfare in biblical times

Until the French Revolution, most armies were small. That's because traditional societies simply didn't have the food to feed a large standing army. At most, a few thousand "professionals" would carry the armor and sword of a heavy infantryman; a few dozen nobles might zip around the battlefield in horse-drawn chariots. Any peasants who were pressed into battle did so with little more than the weapons they had at home: a sickle, perhaps, or a sling and some rocks. The professionals would fight the battles; the peasants would finish off the dead. And in the fall, everybody would go back to the serious business of raising enough food for the coming year.

Jonah

The God Beyond Hatred

" 'But Ninevah has more than a hundred and twenty thousand people who cannot tell their right hand from their left, and many cattle as well. Should I not be concerned about that great city?' " (Jonah 4:11).

Highlight

- Go ahead—read all four chapters. You'll be glad you did!

Why was it written?

Forget the whale—it was never more than a bit player, anyway. No, if you're going to understand why this book was written, you'll have to deal with an issue much more difficult than the question of just what it was that swallowed Jonah. You must confront the seductive power of hatred.

Right from the start, after all, God had been driving home the message that the Israelites were different. They were special. Unique among the nations, they were His chosen people. Needless to say, this didn't encourage a "live and let live" attitude toward other nations!

Any temptation towards tolerance, however, was squashed by the behavior of Israel's neighbors. They really were as everyone said they were—in fact, they were worse! Their governments were corrupt; their gods cruel and decadent. And throughout its history, Israel suffered from the unrelenting hostility of its neighbors.

So is it any wonder that Israel was often tempted to hate its neighbors?

176

And is it any wonder that Israel was often tempted to believe that God hated Israel's neighbors just as much as Israel did?

We all know how exhilarating it is to hate someone who deserves it. Someone without a speck of goodness in them. Someone who, having shown no mercy, deserves no mercy in return. It's fun to hate someone like that!

It's also dangerous. Because when you hate someone that much, the day will come—it always does—when you discover that you're not that different yourself. And if you thought that *they* deserved no mercy, then what will you do with yourself?

What you'll learn in Jonah

The Assyrians were the Nazis of the Middle East. If anyone deserved death, it was them.

Yet God was merciful to Assyria—not just once, but twice. He sent Jonah to warn them of the punishment that was coming their way, and He called off that punishment when Assyria gave up its wicked ways.

In doing this, God showed that you don't have to be good in order for Him to love you. Or to turn that around, you can never be so bad that God can't possibly love you. God's mercy is always undeserved; God loves people because He chooses to do so—not because they've earned it.

Is this good news? Not always. Even though Jonah himself had rebelled against God—and even though it was only by the grace of God that Jonah himself had been saved from death by drowning—Jonah didn't want God to forgive those "undeserving" Assyrians.

And that's the second lesson of Jonah—the fact that God's love can find a home, even in the most unlikely place. The pagan sailors turn out to be more merciful than the prophet of God. The capital of the evil empire turns to God, while His prophet sulks on the outskirts of town. You just never know how people will respond to God, do you?

All you can do is give them a chance to do so.

GoodWords

- **A great fish:** The Hebrew word means simply "fish"; ancient Greek translations of this passage used the word that means "sea monster."

- **Jonah:** A prophet of the northern kingdom of Israel during the reign of Jeroboam II (c. 793 to c. 753 B.C.); he is also mentioned in 2 Kings 14:25.

- **Joppa:** Present day Jaffa—a coastal city about thirty-one miles northwest of Jerusalem and the only port of any significance within Jewish territory.

- **Nineveh:** An ancient city of the Assyrians, located in what is now Iraq. Technically, Nineveh was only a regional capital—the official capital was Asshur, about fifty miles to the south. But Shalmaneser I (c. 1274 to c.1244 B.C.) built a palace in Nineveh, and subsequent kings spent a great deal of their time there. Nineveh became the undisputed capital of Assyria during the reign of Sennacherib (705-681 B.C.).

- **Sheol:** The grave.

- **Steadfast love:** God's faithfulness to His promises.

- **Tarshish:** A Phoenician city in southeastern Spain, famous as a source of tin. In other words, when asked to go to Nineveh, Jonah responded by fleeing as far as possible in the opposite direction.

How big was Ninevah?

Archaeologists tell us that the walled city of Nineveh took in roughly 1,640 acres—not quite three square miles. But Jonah tells us that Ninevah was "a great city of three days' journey." So what's going on here?

Some scholars believe this phrase indicates it took Jonah three days to walk up and down every street in the city. Others think that it may refer to the administrative district of which Nineveh was the center.

A more recent suggestion is that a pecking order existed for ancient cities. Important cities required a long stay by official delegations; unimportant ones got a short visit. (You see much the same thing during presidential elections—Chicago gets a weekend visit by the candidates, while Bismarck, North Dakota gets a fifteen-minute stopover at the airport.) If this suggestion is correct, then "three days' journey" is a statement about protocol rather than geography.

FlashPoint: The great fish

So just exactly what was it that swallowed Jonah?

We don't know. The Bible says only that it was made by God, it was big, and it lived in the sea.

Some have speculated that Jonah may have been swallowed by a sperm whale—and to prove this, they've pointed to stories of sailors who have survived being swallowed by those creatures. Unfortunately, such stories turn out to have been just that: stories. No one has ever been able to track down reliable evidence that such an incident actually took place.

Does that mean Jonah *was not* swallowed by . . . well, by something big that lived in the sea? Of course not! God can do anything He wants. But don't try to "prove" that Jonah was swallowed by a whale with stories that aren't true.

Ninevah's reform

Unlikely as the story of Jonah may seem, history does record a number of religious reforms that took place in Nineveh during the reign of Adad-nirari III (810-782 B.C.). And Jonah's message may have found a receptive audience because Nineveh had endured a plague in 765 B.C., an eclipse in 763 B.C., and another plague in 759 B.C.

Equal time for anti-Assyrians

If you'd like a radically different perspective on Assyria, read the books of Nahum and Zephaniah.

Micah
The Dangers of Contentment

7 CHAPTERS — READING TIME: 30 MINUTES

"He has showed you, O man, what is good. And what does the LORD require of you? To act justly and to love mercy and to walk humbly with your God" (Micah 6:8).

Highlights

- Micah's Vision of Peace (Micah 4).

- Micah's Hope of Mercy (Micah 7).

Why was it written?

Where I live, the best time of year comes in early autumn. The days are warm. The nights are cool. And the absence of swarming insects (as well as school-aged children) makes this the perfect time of year to enjoy life out-of-doors.

Likewise, God's people must have been tempted to enjoy life during the last half of the eighth-century B.C. Assyria had wiped out most of Judah's economic rivals, and God's people were prospering as a result. Life was good, and the living was easy . . . if you were rich.

But the poor were having a tough time of it. Greedy landlords were squeezing them off the land. Dishonest merchants were robbing them blind. And the very people who should have been the first to defend their interests—the priest and prophets? They weren't lifting a finger to help the poor.

Most of the priests and prophets, as a matter of fact, were very careful not to disturb the status quo. "Everything is fine," they said. "Everything is wonderful. God will see to it that the wonderful times we're now enjoying will continue forever."

But the good times were already coming to an end. Assyria was beginning to stir again, and Judah couldn't count on God's protection—not if it didn't hold up its end of the bargain.

For God's promise of protection depended on Judah's promise of obedience. And Judah was falling short. Its prosperity was making it greedy, dishonest, and even superstitious. If Judah did not change its ways, it was doomed.

"You are so busy enjoying the fine weather we've been having," Micah tells his people, "that you've ignored the signs of a soon-coming winter. Get prepared now, while there's still time."

What you'll learn in Micah

Like Hosea and Isaiah—both of whom were writing at this time—Micah must walk a fine line. He must convince his people of their need to change. But he must do so without discouraging them so badly that they give up. Bad as they've been, in other words, Micah must convince his people that there is still hope.

This "split focus" accounts for Micah's dual messages. On the one hand, he blasts his audience for all the things they've done wrong—especially the way they've treated the poor. "But as much as you deserve punishment," Micah says, "God is great enough to rescue you . . . if you will turn to Him." And turning to God, says Micah, isn't just a matter of going to church. No, it affects your entire life. "He has showed you, O man, what is good," says Micah in a famous passage. "And what does the LORD require of you? To act justly and to love mercy and to walk humbly with your God" (Micah 6:8).

GoodWords _____

- **Asherim:** Images of the Phoenician goddess Ashera. She was the wife of Baal—the god who made all things grow.

- **Assyrians:** From 933 to 612 B.C., they were the champion bad guys of the Middle East. Cultured, cruel, and ambitious, their empire was based in modern-day Iraq and Syria, but stretched all the way from Turkey to Egypt.

- **Moresheth-gath:** Micah's hometown, located twenty miles southwest of Jerusalem.

- **Samaria:** In 931 B.C., God's people split their land into two kingdoms: Israel (with its capital of Samaria) to the north, and Judah to the south. Samaria was destroyed by the Assyrians in 722 B.C.—while Micah was a prophet, as a matter of fact.

FlashPoint: To walk humby

Though it is one of the most famous phrases in the Bible, no one is quite sure how to translate this phrase from Micah 6:8. The basic idea is that we should follow God with the same caution and care as would a tightrope walker who is crossing Niagara Falls on a clothesline.

Taunt songs

Trying to "psych out" your enemy is as old as the Bible and as new as the Gulf War. During Operation Desert Storm, for instance, Saudi and Iraqi radio stations would broadcast insults in the form of poetry at each other.

"Your mother wears army boots," these poems would say in effect, "and we will dance on her grave."

Many books in the Bible record similar taunt songs—Micah among them. They don't make for pleasant reading, but they shouldn't be taken too literally. In a sense, they're a form of psychological warfare.

Nahum

The God of Wrath and Justice

3 CHAPTERS — READING TIME: 15 MINUTES

"The LORD is slow to anger and great in power;
the LORD will not leave the guilty unpunished" (Nahum 1:3).

HighLight

- Nahum's Poetic Description of the Assyrian's Evil Empire (Nahum 3).

Why was it written?

Just when you think you've got it licked, it's back—and it's worse than ever.

You've heard stories like that, haven't you? The hero is faced with something evil: a pack of wolves, perhaps. He (and it's usually a "he") drives them off. But no sooner is he "safe" than back come the wolves—and this time, they're meaner and madder than ever before.

Sound familiar?

Then you know what it was like to live in the time of Nahum.

Everyone had breathed a sigh of relief when Shalmaneser III died in 824 B.C. He was king of the Assyrians—and under his leadership, they had hacked, killed, and looted their way across the Middle East. But Shalmaneser III's death had made Assyria turn inward; for the next eighty years, the evil empire was preoccupied with its own, internal revolts.

183

Now, however, the Assyrians were back, and under the leadership of Tiglath-pileser III (744-627 B.C.), they'd taken over most of the Middle East. The northern kingdom of Israel had fallen to them in 722 B.C., and in 663 B.C. they even occupied the Egyptian capital of Thebes.

Needless to say, Assyria's revival troubled the people of Judah. Some wanted to join Assyria in some kind of alliance. Others looked for help to a confederacy of local nations. Still others hoped that Egypt might come to Judah's aid.

What Judah needed, in other words, was hope—hope that told them the bad guys *could* be defeated and *would* be defeated.

That's why God sent the prophet Nahum. "Evil may return with a vengeance," God said through him, "but the good guys still win in the end."

What you'll learn in Nahum

One of the most common myths of our day is the idea that evil may be wrong, but it sure is efficient. "Look at Mussolini," some people will say. "He may have been a dictator, but at least he made the trains run on time."

Some people even use this as an excuse for their own lack of decency. How often have you heard people justify something horrible, after all, with the phrase that "you can't make an omelet without breaking eggs"?

But Nahum reminds us that evil always comes to a bad end. "Sure," he says, "right now the Assyrians may be riding high, but their days are numbered."

And Nahum was right. In 609 B.C., the Assyrian Empire was completely destroyed.

Likewise, Mussolini may have *said* he made the trains run on time—actually, he never did; that saying was just propaganda—but he came to a bad end, all the same.

And those nasty little people who go around treating others as though they were eggs to be broken? Rest assured, their day is coming too.

The bad guys lose; the good guys win. It may be difficult for us to believe this at times, but God will see to it that justice is done.

GoodWords

- **Assyria:** A wealthy, cultured, and refined people of the Middle East whose "traditional values" included torture, murder, and ethnic cleansing. Their empire lasted from 933 to 612 B.C.

- **Bashan, Carmel, Lebanon:** Agricultural areas known for their productivity.

- **Belial:** Literally, "uselessness" or "wickedness"—a name given people who possess these qualities.

- **Egypt:** "The Empire of the Nile" had been on the skids since 1100 B.C. In 670 B.C., Assyria captured its capital of Thebes. The Assyrians weren't able to rule it for more than a few years, however, and Egypt enjoyed relative prosperity for the next hundred years or so.

- **Elkosh:** No one knows where Nahum's hometown might have been. Assyria? Galilee? Judah?

- **Ethiopia:** Black Africans who ruled Egypt from around 750 to 670 B.C., when the Assyrians took over. Experts often refer to this period as Egypt's twenty-fifth dynasty.

- **Libyans:** Rulers of Egypt from around 950 B.C. until its conquest by the Ethiopians in 750 B.C. or so.

  Nahum: Outside of the fact that he wrote flawless Hebrew poetry, we know almost nothing about this prophet. Yes, his name means "consolation." And yes, he must have written sometime between 670 B.C. (when the Assyrians captured Thebes) and 612 B.C. (when the Babylonians destroyed Nineveh). Beyond that, we can only speculate.

- **Nineveh:** Capital of Assyria from 750 to 612 B.C.

- **Put:** Probably another name for Libya.

- **Thebes:** Known to the Israelites as "No," it served as capital of Egypt through most of the second and first millennia B.C.

- **Wrath:** What we call it when God sees to it that people get exactly what they deserve. (When this doesn't happen, we call it "grace.")

 ## Were the Assyrians really that nasty?

The wall carvings show Assyrian officials in a garden. The officials themselves are elaborately dressed, their hair carefully cut and curled. The garden is alive with flowers and trees. But dangling from the trees—almost like Christmas tree ornaments—are the severed heads of their enemies.

That's the kind of empire it was.

The Assyrians were among the first to use organized terror as a weapon of war. If they didn't accept an offer of peace, for instance, they would skin the person who had brought it to them and send back his hide as their answer. Prisoners (male and female) were routinely raped—and if no other use could be found for a prisoner, he would be impaled on a long pole where the people who were still fighting could see him.

When Assyria finally fell to Babylon, it fell hard. Outside of the Bible, as a matter of fact, its memory vanished until some English diplomats began digging up its remains in the nineteenth century—almost 2,500 years after Assyria came to an end.

Habakkuk
Waiting for Answers

3 CHAPTERS — READING TIME: 15 MINUTES

" 'The earth will be filled with the knowledge of the glory of the LORD, as the waters cover the sea' " (Habakkuk 2:14).

HighLight

- Habakkuk's Song of Faith (Habakkuk 3).

Why was it written?

"If you don't like the answers," say the people of Cameroon, "then don't ask the questions."

Wise words—and if you want proof of that, then take a look at Habakkuk.

Habakkuk was a prophet with a beef. "Why don't You do something about all the crime and corruption we have here in Judah?" he complained to God. "Why don't You see to it that the bad guys are punished?"

"No sooner said than done," God replied. "Even as we speak, I'm sending in the Babylonians. They'll see to it Judah gets what it deserves."

"Whoa! Wait a minute! Time out!" said Habakkuk. "I've heard about these Babylonians; they're even worse than we are! So how can a God as good as You are use bad guys to punish people who are better than they are?"

"And while I'm at it," Habakkuk continued, "what's a nice God like You doing with scum like them? You're holy and righteous; the Babylonians are not. So how can You use people like them?"

187

Good questions! And Habakkuk isn't the only to ask them. Most of us have wondered why God doesn't do more to bring about justice in this world of ours. Most of us have wondered how we're supposed to hang on while we wait for God to act.

And most of us have wondered if the end can justify the means. What if someone does something bad for bad reasons . . . but it all ends well? Does that mean God *wanted* that person to do something bad *so that* it would end well? Does the fact that things ended well mean that God won't punish that person for all the terrible things they did?

These are questions we've all asked. And if the answers we get aren't always satisfactory . . . well, welcome to the world of Habakkuk.

What you'll learn in Habakkuk

One of the most important lessons of Habakkuk is also one of the easiest to overlook: it's the simple fact that we can ask God questions. And if we don't like the way He seems to be running the universe, we can tell Him so.

God listens to our complaints—that's a pretty radical idea. And if you've grown up on the idea that God prizes unquestioning obedience (or if you work around people who continually tell you to "sit down and shut up"), then Habakkuk can be a little scary. Once you get used to asking questions, however, you'll be amazed at the things God is willing to discuss.

But if we're going to question God, then we need to stick around for the answers—and that's another lesson we can learn from Habakkuk. We live in a fast-food world, after all, and it's easy to approach God with the attitude of "hurry up and give me what I want." But Habakkuk had to wait for God's answers. And sometimes, so do we.

Finally, Habakkuk teaches us the importance of memory. The book ends with a poem—a hymn—that lists the dramatic ways in which God has shown His care for His people in the past. God's people have been through tough times, it says, but

God has never failed them yet. In remembering this, Habakkuk found the courage he needed to wait for God's answers. As one author put it, "We have nothing to fear for the future, except as we forget how God has led us in the past."

GoodWords

- **Chaldeans:** Another name for the Babylonians. Babylon was part of the Assyrian Empire before its revolt in 626 B.C. The Babylonians quickly grew to rival Egypt as the dominant power of the Middle East. Lying between these two empires as it did, Judah was in an extremely precarious position during the time of Habakkuk.

- **Cushan:** This usually refers to Ethiopia, but in Habakkuk, it seems to refer to the nomadic people who once inhabited Canaan.

- **Habakkuk:** Nothing is known of this prophet, though the contents of his book suggest he wrote shortly before 605 B.C., when the Babylonians defeated the Egyptians at the battle of Carchemish.

- **Midian:** The northern part of the Arabian desert, inhabited by a nomadic people whom the Bible (not surprisingly) refers to as "Midianites." Moses' father-in-law was a Midianite, but once the Israelites settled in Canaan, the Midianites came to be viewed as a threat. Gideon's famous battle was fought against the Midianites.

- **Mount Paran:** Probably a reference to Mt. Sinai—the mountain on which God gave His law to the people of Israel after their escape from Egypt.

- **Selah:** Even though it occurs seventy-four times in the Bible, nobody knows what this word means. Suggestions range from "Hallelujah!" to "turn up the volume!"

- **Sheol:** Sometimes translated as "hell," this word actually means "the grave."

- **Shigionoth:** The plural of "shiggaion." (Aren't you glad you asked?) Seriously, this word probably means "dirge" and indicates either the name of the tune or the manner in which Habakkuk 3 was to be sung.

- **Tablets:** This can mean simply "writing material," though some believe it refers to the clay tablets used by the Babylonians for permanent records. Habakkuk 2:2 says that Habakkuk should make a permanent record of God's answer.

- **Teman:** Probably refers to the land of Edom, southeast of the Dead Sea. The Israelites skirmished with the Edomites on their way to Canaan, and relations between the two nations never improved after that.

Aftermath

Habakkuk's prophecy came true. The Babylonians invaded Judah in 605 and 597 B.C.; they did so again and destroyed Jerusalem in 586 B.C. The Babylonians, in their turn, lost to the Persians in 539 B.C. God's people were finally able to return home in 538 or 537 B.C.

Other prophets

If you would like another prophet's perspective on the times in which Habakkuk lived, try the books of Isaiah and Jeremiah.

Clothing

Countless children have appeared in Christmas programs, clad in their father's bathrobe. And yes, that's pretty much the way that people dressed in biblical times.

The basic garment was a loose shift or shirt that went down to your ankles. (No buttons—they hadn't been invented yet.) Over that, you wore a cloak or mantle that could double as a head covering. Add a belt and shoes or sandals, and you were ready to go.

The fabric would be pure linen, pure cotton, or pure wool—mixed fabrics were forbidden by Jewish law as "unclean." Both solids and stripes were popular, in shades of blue, black, tan, white, yellow, or red. (Purple and green dyes were both rare and expensive.) And many Jews—both men and women—also carried baskets for those bulky items they couldn't tuck into their belts.

The cost of such an outfit? Probably as much as a new car today—remember, all of this clothing was hand-made, and the cloth as well. That's why you probably owned no more than one set of clothing.

Zephaniah
The Awesome God of Wrath

" 'I will leave within you the meek and humble,
who trust in the name of the LORD' " (Zephaniah 3:12).

HighLight

• The Day of Wrath (Zephaniah 1).

Why was it written?

With hand grenades, maybe. In a game of horseshoes, certainly. But when it comes to life, "close" just doesn't count.

And that was a shame, because Josiah had done so much for God's people. King of Judah between 640 and 609 B.C., Josiah had repaired the temple in Jerusalem. He had destroyed the places where God's people had worshiped false gods. And he had seen to it that Passover was celebrated—"the best Passover since the days of Samuel," says the Bible . . . and Samuel had been dead for more than 400 years!

Then too, the Assyrian Empire was crumbling; God's people now had little to fear from their old enemy to the north. And with Babylon on the rise, it looked as though Judah might have a new ally—one that could protect it from Egypt, its old enemy to the south.

Josiah had done a lot for God's people . . . but it wasn't enough.

Josiah's father had been Amon, you see, and his grandfather had been Manasseh—two of the most wicked kings ever to rule Judah. Both had led out in the worship of foreign gods; Manasseh had even killed one of his own sons and offered him as a sacrifice to a foreign god.

To be sure, Manasseh did turn back to God at the end of his life. And Josiah had repaired much of the damage done by his father and grandfather.

But God's people had not changed their ways—not all the way. They still blended the worship of God with that of foreign gods. They still put their trust in politics rather than in God's protection. And they still made military alliances with their neighbors.

As a result, Judah was still on the road to disaster. And as much as Josiah had done, it still wasn't enough . . . not unless God could turn things around through Zephaniah.

What you'll learn in Zephaniah

Strange as it may seem, God's people had been looking forward to Judgment Day! They actually longed for the day when God would in wrath destroy all His enemies.

That's because they had a long list of enemies whom they wanted God to destroy!

"You just wait," they said to the people around them. "The day is coming when God is going to fix you, and fix you good!"

"Now wait a minute," Zephaniah said in effect. "It's true that the day will come when God destroys all of His enemies, but if you don't shape up, that means that God will go after you too!"

In short, Zephaniah warns us not to use a double standard when we compare ourselves with others. God doesn't play favorites, after all, and the same behavior that will get our enemies in trouble with God will get us in trouble as well.

What's more, the same love that can save us can also save our enemies. "I won't just judge My enemies," God says through Zephaniah. "I will save and purify My people as well. And that means *all* of My people, no matter where they come from."

GoodWords

- **Ammonites:** Judah's enemies to the northeast.

- **Assyria:** On the surface, the empire has never been stronger. It stretches from the Persian Gulf to the Nile and north into Turkey. But rival factions within the government are fighting for power, and the eastern provinces—Babylon and the Medes—are in revolt.

- **Baal:** The Canaanite god of thunder, rain, and growing plants.

- **The Day of the Lord:** Judgment Day. The Latin hymn *Dies Irae* is based on Zephaniah 1:14.

- **Foreign attire:** Some say Zephaniah was condemning those who showed their political allegiance to foreign powers by dressing in the national costumes of those countries. Others say he was condemning those who dressed in the garb of foreign priests.

- **Ethiopians (or Cushites):** This may be another name for the Egyptians. Ethiopia invaded Egypt sometime around 750 B.C. and ruled it for ninety years. The Assyrians had pushed out the Ethiopians by Zepaniah's day, but old names have a way of sticking.

- **Leaping over the threshhold:** A common superstitious practice, based on the belief that the door of a house was guarded by a god. You "leaped over the threshhold" so that you wouldn't make this god angry by stepping on him.

- **Milcom:** Although it sounds like it should be the name of the telephone company in Milwaukee, Milcom was an Ammonite god—his name means "lord," the same as does Baal. (It doesn't pay to be original when you're naming a god.) Little else is known about him.

- **Moab:** Judah's enemy to the east.

- **Philistines and Cherethites:** Judah's enemies to the west. These were the "sea people" who swarmed out of the Aegean in the second millennium B.C. and caused trouble for everyone from the Egyptians to the Hittites. In Palestine (which means "the land of the Philistines"), they settled in a small group of coastal cities, and proceeded to make life miserable for the Israelites.

Aftermath

Zephaniah was right. A few years after his book was written, Pharaoh Necho of Egypt tried to help the dying Assyrian Empire by attacking its greatest foe: the army of Nabopolassar, king of Babylon.

Josiah could have stayed out of the fight; instead, his army attacked the Egyptians near the town of Megiddo. Josiah may have hoped that his attack would give him some "bargaining chips" in his dealings with the Babylonians; instead, Josiah was killed. His reform of Judah's religion came to an end. And in less than a generation, the Babylonian army would destroy the temple in Jerusalem.

Hedgehogs and other *hapax legomenon*

My eldest daughter has a pet hedgehog named "Fast Eddy," and she has asked me to find some way of including him in this book.

I thought I could do it—after all, in speaking of Assyria's destruction, Zephaniah 2:14 says that "herds shall lie down in the midst of her . . . and the hedgehog shall lodge in her capitals."

Unfortunately, the Revised Standard Version is the only translation I could find that mentions hedgehogs in this verse. Other versions speak of "screech owls" (New International Version), "crows" (Today's English Version), "noisy ravens" (Contemporary English Version), and "the bittern" (King James Version).

So what's going on here? What kind of people can't tell the difference between a hedgehog and a screech owl?

The problem is that the Hebrew word *kippode* appears only three times in the Bible— once in Zechariah, and twice in Isaiah. The context of each quotation indicates that a *kippode* is a small creature that lives in desolate places, but that's all we know about it. So if you're translating the Bible, you have a choice. You can plug in the original Hebrew word (and leave your readers scratching their heads and wondering what a *kippode* might be) or you can cross your fingers and make your best guess.

Zephaniah 2:14 is not the only text with this kind of problem. Many of the animals, plants, and jewels that appear in the Bible, for instance, do so only once. That's why you'll often see different names in different translations for the jewels in the high priest's breastplate or the perfumes in the Song of Solomon or the foundation stones of the New Jerusalem. Words such as these that appear only once are known as *hapax legomenon*, and they are the bane of every translator's existence.

Myself, I don't worry about them. I don't know of *any* important text whose meaning is affected by a *hapax legomenon*. And as for Assyria, I like to think that the hedgehogs might have had the last laugh, after all.

Haggai
God Rebuilds a Dream

" ' "Be strong, all you people of the land," declares the Lord, " and work.
For I am with you," declares the LORD Almighty' " (Haggai 2:4).

Highlight

*   If You Keep Doing What You're Doing, You'll Keep Getting What You're Getting (Haggai 1).

Why was it written?

Sometimes, it's the important things that get overlooked.

When the Babylonians destroyed the temple in Jerusalem, for instance, all Judah mourned. The temple had been the place where God met with people to make things right between them and Him. So when it was destroyed in 586 B.C., salvation itself seemed threatened.

You can imagine, then, the excitement when Cyrus, emperor of Persia, announced in 539 B.C. that the Jews could rebuild Jerusalem. Led by Zerubbabel, 50,000 of them had returned to Jerusalem. And they had done their best to restore everything that had been lost. By 536 B.C., as a matter of fact, they were laying the foundation for a new temple.

But while the Jews were in exile, a new people had settled the land. These people saw the renaissance of Jerusalem as a threat. They tried to co-opt the reconstruction of the temple, and when that failed, they persuaded the Persians to ban it.

For seventeen years, the work languished. True, the emperor Darius reauthorized the temple's restoration in 521 B.C. But even then, nothing much happened.

That's not to say the Jews were idle during this time. In fact, they seem to have been quite busy—rebuilding houses, replanting vineyards, and restoring their own fortunes. That the temple remained a ruin, in other words, was not the result of laziness. Just misplaced priorities.

That's why Haggai spoke up. Beginning late in the summer of 520 B.C., he encouraged the people to start working on the temple again. And Haggai wasn't alone. The prophhet Zechariah was active at the very same time, with the very same message (see Ezra 5:1; 6:14).

All of which suggests that rebuilding the temple was important to God. Haggai's task was to make it important to God's people as well.

What you'll learn in Haggai

Haggai is often overlooked, even by Bible scholars. Its prose is flat and businesslike; its message so rooted in a particular time and place that most people despair of finding any wider significance in it.

Still, Haggai is a useful reminder of the need to keep our priorities straight. Like the Jews of Haggai's day, we can become so absorbed in "minding our own business" that the community as a whole suffers. And like the people of Jerusalem, we will find that everything else falls into place when we put God first.

"Put God first," Jesus said in words drawn from Haggai, "and everything else will fall into place" (see Matthew 6:33).

True, this may sound hopelessly idealistic. We live in a cynical age, after all—one in which it's easy to assume that the bad guys always win and God's voice is always ignored.

That's why it's important to remember that Haggai has a happy ending. The people of God did listen! They did rebuild the temple! And God even went so far as to promise that the new temple would be better than the old. " ' "The glory of this present house will be greater than glory of the former house," says the LORD Almighty. And in this place I will grant peace" ' " (Haggai 2:9).

Don't be dismayed by the past, in other words. Don't be discouraged by memories of what you've lost or of what you've endured. Follow God's leading and trust in His future. That's the message of Haggai.

GoodWords

- **Chariots:** The fighter aircraft of their day. A chariot weighed approximately seventy-five pounds. Pulled by a team of horses in good condition and on favorable terrain, it could reach speeds of twenty miles per hour. The Persian reliance upon chariots would prove their undoing, however. Even in Haggai's day, chariots were giving way to war horses and the infantry phalanx.

- **Darius:** Known both for his generosity and his extreme cruelty, he was emperor of Persia from 522 to 486 B.C. Haggai's Darius was the man whose army was defeated by the Greeks at Marathon in 490 B.C.

- **Haggai:** Pronounced *HAG-guy,* not *HAH-gee-yi.* Haggai 2:3 suggests he had seen Solomon's temple with his own eyes. If that's true, he would have been at least eighty years old when he wrote this book. Nothing else is known about him.

- **Holy:** Not a moral quality so much as a statement of ownership. To be holy means to be given over completely to God for His use alone.

- **Hosts:** Armies. Calling God "the Lord of hosts" is Haggai's way of emphasizing God's authority and power to a people who sorely needed reminding of these things.

- **Joshua:** Also known as Jeshua; both names mean "Yahweh is salvation." As high priest, Joshua worked with Zerubbabel to restore the worship of God in Jerusalem. He figures prominently in a vision of Zechariah (see chapter 3 of that book). His son Joiakim is mentioned in Nehemiah 12:10-12.

- **The Lord's house:** The temple in Jerusalem. Destroyed by the Babylonians in 586 B.C., its restoration was complete by 515 B.C. or so.

- **The Persian Empire:** Stretching from Greece to India, it was founded by Cyrus the Great sometime around 550 B.C. and was destroyed by Alexander the Great in 330 B.C. The official religion of the empire was Zoroastrianism—the belief that the forces of light (led by the god Ahura Mazda) were in perpetual battle with the kingdom of darkness (led by the god Ahriman).

- **Remnant:** If a catastrophe sweeps away most of a community, the part that remains is what the Bible calls a "remnant." God has promised that no matter how great the danger, there will always remain a remnant—a community of people who are faithful to Him.

- **Signet ring:** A sign of authority. A signet ring was carved with the seal of the person who wore it. That person could leave his or her mark on a document by pressing the signet ring onto a blob of wax. In saying that Zerubbabel would be like God's signet ring, Haggai was saying that Zerubbabel would speak and act with all the authority of God.

- **Zerubbabel:** Though his name means "shoot of Babylon," he was Jewish and a descendant of King David. Grandson of Judah's king Jehoiachin, he was appointed governor of Judah by the Persian emperor Cyrus around 537 B.C. and served as such for at least twenty years. He supervised the return of more than 50,000 exiles to Judah and saw to the rebuilding of the temple.

Clean and unclean

Like most societies, the Jews had rules about diet, clothing, and bodily functions—what to eat, what to wear, what to do if you start going bald, and that sort of thing. And like most societies, anyone who failed to abide by these rules was cut off from society, either temporarily or permanently.

A person who touched a dead body, for instance, was "unclean," and was cut off from human contact until he or she had gone through the proper rituals. Only then could that person rejoin society.

In short, the point of Haggai 2:10-19, is that it's a lot easier to ruin something than it is to make it special.

Other voices

Chapters 1 through 8 of Zechariah deal with the same problem and were written at the same time as Haggai; you may find their perspective helpful. The books of Ezra, Nehemiah, and Malachi will also shed light on life in Palestine during Persian rule.

The temple

The temple was a place where God's people could worship Him through prayer and sacrifice. The temple built during Haggai's day was actually the third such place:

- *The sanctuary* was a movable tent built at God's command during the Exodus. It had an outer court that any Israelite could enter, an inner tent (or "Holy Place") that could be entered only by the priests, and an inner-inner tent (or "Most Holy Place") that could be entered only by the high priest once a year, on the Day of Atonement. The ark of the covenant was kept inside the Most Holy Place.

- ***The temple of Solomon*** was planned by King David, but built by his son Solomon c. 960 B.C. in Jerusalem. It followed the same general plan as the sanctuary—an outer court, a Holy Place, and a Most Holy Place—but was obviously a lot bigger and more permanent. The building containing the two holy places measured roughly thirty-five feet by 110 feet; it was destroyed by the Babylonians in 586 B.C.

- ***The temple of Zerubbabel*** was begun in 536 B.C. and completed around 515 B.C. It seems to have followed the same plan as Solomon's temple, though the people who saw it thought otherwise. King Herod the Great began the enormous project of enlarging and rebuilding this temple in 20 B.C.; the work continued until A.D. 62 or so. Herod's temple was then destroyed during the Great Jewish War in A.D. 70; a fourth temple was planned during the reign of the Emperor Julian (A.D. 361-363), but was never built.

Zechariah

God Restores His Kingdom

" *'As you have been an object of cursing among the nations, O Judah and Israel, so will I save you, and you will be a blessing. Do not be afraid, but let your hands be strong' " (Zechariah 8:13).*

HighLight

- Zechariah's Vision of Joshua the High Priest (Zechariah 3).

Why was it written?

The nightmare was over. God's people had survived the destruction of Jerusalem. They had endured captivity in Babylon. And now they were back in their native land of Judah, enjoying the tolerant rule of the Persians. Had this been a fairy tale, in other words, you would have expected them to live "happily ever after."

But fairy tale endings are rare, and freedom had brought with it new problems for God's people. Relations between those who had returned and those who had never left were strained. The Persian Empire was going through a crisis in leadership—one that was being exploited by the enemies of the Jews. And all efforts to rebuild the temple had come to nothing.

It's no wonder, then, that God had to send not one, but *two* prophets to deal with this situation—both the straightforward Haggai and the imaginative Zechariah. Together, they worked to get God's people back on track and the temple rebuilt.

What you'll learn in Zechariah

If nothing else, Zechariah will give you a new respect for the power of the human imagination. It's the kind of book that Salvador Dali or Pablo Picasso might have written—a book full of riderless horses, flying scrolls, a lead-covered basket with a woman inside, and other strange pictures as well.

Odd as its imagery might be, however, Zechariah's theme is a simple one: restoration. The first eight chapters contain eight visions about the restoration of Israel; the last six contain two oracles about the Messiah who will come and rule over God's people. Together, these chapters tell us that God will restore *everything*—the temple, the priesthood, the land, and the people themselves.

God's people may have suffered much in the past, in other words, but God will see to it that they have a glorious future.

GoodWords

- **Adament:** Something extremely hard—possibly corundum.

- **Ashkelon, Aram, Ashdod, Ekron, Gaza, Hadrach, Hamath, Sidon, Tyre:** Cities associated with the enemies of God's people.

- **The branch:** Literally, "a shoot," "sprout," or "sucker." A common title for the Messiah, since His ancestry was "rooted" in David.

- **Darius:** Darius the Great was king of Persia from 522 to 486 B.C. Though he had to fight his way to the throne—he was only a distant cousin of his predecessor, Cambyses—he proved to be a wise, strong, and tolerant ruler. His decision to invade Greece in 490 B.C., however, was a big mistake; he was defeated at the Battle of Marathon.

- **Ephraim:** Another name for the ten tribes that formed the northern kingdom of Israel prior to its destruction in 722 B.C.

- **Hadadrimmon:** Some think Zechariah may be referring to the place near Megiddo where King Josiah died. Others say he was talking about the Syrian god of thunder and rain.

- **Joshua:** The high priest. His stay in Babylon may have caused some to question his ritual purity.

- **The Messiah:** Literally, "the one anointed" or "the one God has chosen and blessed." Prophecy predicted that a future king would restore David's kingdom and rule as he had ruled; this king was given the title of "messiah." (The Greek word for "messiah" is "christ.")

- **Persia:** The number one power in the Middle East from 539 to 331 B.C. Many Persians followed the teachings of Zoroaster; they sought to help the "wise lord" Ahura Mazda in his fight against the wicked Angra Mainyu by living a life free of dishonesty, laziness, or ritual impurity.

- **The River:** The Euphrates River.

- **Shinar:** Another name for Babylon.

- **Teraphim:** Images of minor "household gods" that were thought to promote fertility.

- **Zechariah:** Prophet, priest, and author of the biblical book that bears his name. Born in Babylon, he moved to Judah at the same time as Joshua the high priest and Zerubbabel. His first recorded message was given in 520 B.C.

- **Zerubbabel:** Grandson of Judah's king Jehoiachin, he was appointed governor of Judah by the Persian emperor Cyrus around 537 B.C. and served as such for at least twenty years. He supervised the return of over 50,000 exiles to Judah and saw to the rebuilding of the temple.

The wisdom of Zerubbabel

An apocryphal story has it that Zerubbabel once entered a contest in which he was asked to name the strongest thing of all. He won by answering, "Women are the strongest, but truth always wins." Go figure.

Contemporaries

Zechariah and Haggai both served as prophets at the exact same time in Judah's history—but they weren't the only religious leaders of their day.

- In China, Kung Fu-tse (or "Confucius") was developing the teachings that would later be compiled in his *Analects,* and Lao-Tse (if he actually existed) was responding with Daoism.

- In India, Siddhartha Gautama was perfecting Buddhism, and Mahavira Jina was developing the religion that would be known as Jainism.

- And in Greece, the philosopher Pythagoras was teaching his own blend of mathematics and mysticism.

Malachi

God Challenges His People to Greatness

" 'But for you who revere my name, the sun of righteousness will rise with healing in its wings. And you will go out and leap like calves released from the stall' " (Malachi 4:2).

Highlights

- God Offers a Money-Back Guarantee (Malachi 3).

- The Promise of Elijah to Come (Malachi 4).

Why was it written?

"Any idiot can face a crisis," wrote columnist Molly Ivins. "It's the day-to-day living that wears you out."

True words—and if you need proof, take a look at Malachi. It was written sometime around 420 B.C.—roughly a hundred years after God's people had returned from their exile in Babylon. When they had first arrived, they had been greeted by total devastation. Jerusalem had been in ruins, its temple destroyed, its prospects for the future almost nonexistent.

But rallied by the prophets and the governor Nehemiah, the people pulled off a miracle. They restored the city walls, rebuilt the temple, reestablished religious services, and recommitted themselves to the God of Israel. By Malachi's day, it would seem they had resurrected a way of life that had been all but dead.

But what kind of life? Did this success encourage them to move on to even greater things?

No. Instead, they had . . . well, there's no other word for it but to say they had drifted. Things had gotten slack. People were "forgetting" the offerings they should have been bringing to the temple. Their marriages were going to pot. Their businessmen were cutting corners.

Worst of all, a pervasive cynicism was taking over. " 'All who do evil are good in the eyes of the Lord, and he is pleased with them,' " they were saying. " 'Where is the God of justice?' " (Malachi 2:17).

In other words, what was killing God's people was not a sudden attack, but a slow rot. That's why God sent Malachi—He wanted to turn things around before they reached a crisis.

What you'll learn in Malachi

Jesus once said, "Whoever is faithful in little things will also be faithful with much, but whoever is dishonest in little things will also be dishonest in much" (see Luke 16:10). He may have had Malachi in mind.

Why is that? Because Malachi is a book about little things—the little attitudes and tasks that define our everyday lives. Written in the form of eight questions and eight answers, it's a book about the "little" sins we commit every day—sins such as snickering at those who are less fortunate. Fudging the truth. Betraying our friends in our efforts to get ahead.

"These things add up," says Malachi. "And dishonesty in these 'little' things is going to cost God's people more than they could possibly imagine."

Malachi is not all gloom and doom, however. If little sins add up, so do little acts of faithfulness, kindness, and mercy. In fact, Malachi ends with the promise that the greatest of all God's prophets—the prophet Elijah—will again step in to help God's people. For " 'he will turn the hearts of the fathers to their children, and the hearts of children to their fathers' " (Malachi 4:6).

GoodWords _____

- **Covenant:** An agreement or contract. In Malachi, this refers to the agreement that God made with the people of Israel in the time of Moses that "He would be their God, and they would be His people."

- **Divorce:** It's worth remembering that divorce was permitted by God's law at this time. Judah's sin was not so much that it was breaking the law, but that it was using the law to its own selfish advantage.

- **Elijah:** The greatest of all God's prophets. He was caught up to heaven in a "fiery chariot." Orthodox Jews still look for him to come and prepare the earth for the Messiah's arrival. Jesus said the work of John the Baptist was a fulfillment of the promise of Malachi 4:5.

- **Esau:** The brother of Jacob and traditionally thought to be the father of the Edomites. Edom was a kingdom to the southeast of Judah.

- **Jacob:** Also known as Israel. Jacob was the father of the Jewish people; both of his names were used of their kingdom.

- **Judah:** The tribe of David. It was associated with political leadership. As a geographical term, Judah refers to the area around Jerusalem.

- **Levi:** The tribe of Moses and Aaron. It was associated with religious leadership.

- **The Lord of hosts:** A name for God that emphasizes His power and authority as Commander of the armies of heaven.

- **The Lord's table:** The altar on which sacrificial animals were burned as an offering to God.

- **Malachi:** His name literally means "messenger," but little else is known about him. The book's context strongly suggests it was written after the Babylonian captivity—a time when Judah was a province of the Persian Empire. But it's impossible to know precisely when it was written.

- **Messenger:** A term that may refer to either earthly messengers (prophets) or heavenly messengers (angels). It may also be used as a personal name, for example, "Malachi."

- **Tithe:** One-tenth of a person's net income. The tithes given by God's people supported both religious workers and the poor.

Weights and measures in the Old Testament

There was no Bureau of Standards in ancient Israel; weights and measures varied from place to place and from task to task. If you're willing to settle for "good enough," however, here's a list of some of the common units of measurement:

Weight: The basic unit was the *shekel*—about half an ounce.

- Sixty *shekels* made a *mina* (a little over two pounds).

- Sixty *minas* made a *talent* (about sixty-seven pounds, although the "heavy talent" weighed roughly 134 pounds).

Length: Arms and hands provided the basic yardstick for measuring length—and since arms and hands come in different sizes, this made for some confusion.

- A *finger* is the width of your thumb: figure a smidgeon under an inch.

- A *handbreadth* is the width of your palm: roughly three inches.

- A *span* runs from the tip of your outstretched thumb to the tip of your outstretched pinkie: a smidgeon under nine inches.

- A *cubit* goes from the tip of your middle finger to your elbow: roughly eighteen inches.

Wet measure: start with a *log*—about one-third of a quart.

- Twelve *logs* make a *hin* (not quite a gallon).

- Six *hins* make a *bath* (about five and a half gallons).

- Ten *baths* make a *cor,* which is also known as a *homer* (roughly fifty-five gallons).

Dry measure: start with a *kab*—a little over a quart.

- Two *kabs* make a little more than an *omer* (roughly a half gallon).

- Ten *omers* make an *ephah* (about five and a half gallons or two and a half pecks).

- Ten *ephahs* make a *homer* (about fifty-five gallons—the largest amount of grain that a donkey could carry).

QUICKSTART

New Testament:
The Gospels

Matthew
Jesus as King

28 CHAPTERS — READING TIME: 3 HOURS

" 'Come to me, all you who are weary and burdened, and I will give you rest. Take my yoke upon you, and learn from me, for I am gentle and humble in heart, and you will find rest for your souls. For my yoke is easy and my burden is light' " (Matthew 11:28-30).

Highlights

- The Birth of Jesus (Matthew 1; 2).

- The Sermon on the Mount (Matthew 5–7).

- Seven Stories About God's Kingdom (Matthew 13).

- The Transfiguration (Matthew 17).

- The Rich Young Ruler (Matthew 19; 20).

- The Triumphal Entry (Matthew 21).

- Jesus Talks About the End of Time (Matthew 23–25).

- The Death of Jesus (Matthew 26; 27).

- Jesus Comes Back to Life (Matthew 28).

Why was it written?

If you're feeling overwhelmed by change, you'll appreciate the Gospel of Matthew. More than just a biography of Jesus, it's a survival manual—a guidebook that was originally meant to help believers survive one of the most wrenching changes ever to take place in Christianity.

Matthew wrote for Jewish Christians—believers who had accepted Jesus as Messiah without giving up the rituals, customs, and laws of their parent religion. But being a Jewish Christian was growing more difficult all the time. Nationalism was growing as a force within Judaism; the idea that a suffering king would rule over a heavenly kingdom was rapidly losing its appeal. And a flood of Gentile converts was threatening to dilute the Jewish identity of the church. Even the law of Moses was losing ground, its role threatened by those who claimed that Jesus had done away with the law.

Members of Jesus' original band of followers had already written down their memories of Jesus. Peter had contributed to the *Gospel of Mark,* and someone else had compiled a list of Christ's sayings that experts now call *Q* (from the German word *quelle,* or "source").

But Matthew felt that another Gospel was needed. Under the inspiration of the Holy Spirit, and drawing upon his own memories, as well as *Mark* and possibly *Q,* Matthew wrote an account of Christ's life with Jewish Christians in mind— Jewish Christians who needed help if they were to survive in a rapidly changing church.

What you'll learn in Matthew

The key to Matthew's Gospel is the idea of the "kingdom of heaven." Jesus is Lord, and we are His subjects. We give Him our loyalty; He gives us the security that comes from belonging to something that will last forever.

Continuity is an important part of this kingdom—Matthew makes it clear that Christ's reign is the natural outgrowth of God's historic agreements with Israel. As such, the Old Testament is still a reliable guide to knowing God's will. Its laws are still important. And the Jews still have an important role to play in history.

Yet Matthew makes it clear that this kingdom brings change with it as well. The Sermon on the Mount (Matthew 5–7), for instance, outlines just how a citizen of this kingdom should behave. Its demands are radical. So is the authority of Jesus. Anything that might have been important before joining God's kingdom— wealth, prestige, tradition, or even the simple desire to protect one's own skin— *any* or *all* of these things must come second to God's kingdom.

Continuity and change; a love for the past and the ruthless sacrifice of anything that interferes with God's will—God's kingdom brings both stability and chaos. Frightening? Yes. And perhaps that's why Matthew's Gospel ends as it does, with a command that should daunt the fearless and a promise that should give heart to the timid:

> "Go and make disciples of all nations, baptizing them in the name of the Father and of the Son and of the Holy Spirit, and teaching them to obey everything I have commanded you. And surely I am with you always, to the very end of the age" (Matthew 28:19, 20).

GoodWords

- **Baptize:** Literally, "to immerse," presumably in water. Baptism is the public announcement that you have decided to follow God; Jesus was baptized because all of God's people should be baptized.

- **Galilee:** The early part of Jesus' ministry took place in this hilly, well-populated region of northern Palestine. Roughly half the people there at the time would have been Jewish, the other half Gentile.

- **Gentile:** Anyone who isn't Jewish.

- **Herod:** The Herod of Matthew 2 is Herod the Great, ruler of all the Jews in Palestine from 37 to 4 B.C. His son Herod Antipas is the Herod of Matthew 14; he ruled Galilee from 4 B.C. to A.D. 39.

- **John the Baptist:** The wandering holy man whose imprisonment and death foreshadowed the fate of Jesus. Even in Matthew's day, some thought he might have been the Messiah. Matthew is careful to nip this idea in the bud without denigrating John's ministry.

- **Jerusalem:** The spiritual center and political capital of Judaism. Some experts believe that in Matthew's day, it may have had a permanent population of 50,000 and that during Passover as many as 125,000 additional pilgrims may have crowded its streets.

- **Jews:** The Gospels don't have much good to say about the Jews, and Matthew's Gospel is rougher on them than most. No one will ever know how many people have been killed because of Matthew 27:25. Even though it helps to remember that Christianity was fighting for its very existence at the time when Matthew wrote these words, too many Christians have used this verse in such a way as to make one wish that it had not been written.

- **Judea:** The region surrounding Jerusalem. Herod the Great had willed it to his son Archelaus, but the kid had made such a mess of things that the Romans assumed direct control.

- **Matthew:** A tax collector who quit his job to become a follower of Jesus. Tradition says that he wrote the Gospel that bears his name in Hebrew originally, but the version we have shows no sign of ever having been written in anything other than Greek. Most experts date its composition to A.D. 70 or so.

- **Messiah:** Literally, "the anointed one." Priests and kings were both "anointed" for their office; oil was poured over their heads as a sign of God's blessing.

- **Perfect:** If Matthew 5:48 drives you to despair, try to remember that the Greek word *telos,* tranlsated "perfect," can also mean "mature" or "complete." And if that doesn't help, read Matthew 11:28-30.

- **Pharisees:** Jews whose desire to follow God's law led to elaborate regulations about behavior. Pharisees were generally members of the lower-middle-class; they believed in angels, life after death, and the binding authority of prophets such as Isaiah, Jeremiah, and Hosea.

- **Pontius Pilate:** Probably in his thirties at the time he appears in Matthew's Gospel, he came from a good (but not *too* good) Roman family and had been appointed *procurator* ("governor") by the emperor himself. Pilate would later resign in disgrace; tradition has it that he committed suicide.

- **Romans:** The Jews had invited the Romans into Palestine during the seventh decade B.C.; once they were there, the Romans decided to stay. By and large, Roman rule wasn't all that taxing (ha!)—as long as you paid your dues and kept the peace, the Romans pretty much left you alone.

- **Sadducees:** Jews whose conservatism led them to reject any elaboration on the first five books of the Bible—the ones we know as "the Law of Moses" and that they called the "Torah." Sadducees were generally rich. They did not believe in angels or life after death.

- **Sanhedrin:** The Jewish council of elders.

- **Satan:** Literally, "the adversary." Believers have traditionally considered him to be a nonhuman, created being who led a rebellion against God and was expelled from heaven for his crimes.

- **Talent:** One talent amounted roughly to what a common laborer would earn in twenty years. Christ's parable of Matthew 18:23-35 has a little more bite when you remember that the tax revenue for Herod's kingdom was only 900 talents per year.

- **Wise men:** Also known as "Magi." The magi were Zoroastrian astrologers from what is now Iraq. Matthew includes them to show that Christ's royalty is (and will be) acknowledged by the leaders of other nations.

When did Jesus live?

No, He wasn't born in the year zero—there is no "year zero" in our calendar. And He wasn't born in the "year one." The New Testament says He was born during the reign of Herod the Great, and Herod the Great died most likely in 4 B.C. In other words, when Dionysius Exiguus developed our calendar sometime around A.D. 550, it's obvious he made some mistakes.

It gets worse. Jesus probably lived in Egypt until shortly after A.D. 6—that's when Archelaus was removed as the ruler of Judea. His family then moved to Nazareth, where they lived until Jesus began His public ministry, sometime between A.D. 27 and 30. What

Jesus did in Nazareth is unknown—aside from describing a visit to the temple when He was twelve years old, the Bible says nothing about this time of His life. After three years or so in the public eye, Jesus was executed sometime between A.D. 30 and A.D. 33.

So there you have it. We're not sure when Jesus was born, and we don't know for certain when He died. What's more, 90 percent of His life on this earth is a complete blank to us.

Yet we do know that He lived—and we know that His life was of cosmic, eternal importance. What else really matters?

The Sermon on the Mount

Few chapters in the Bible have stirred more discussion than Matthew 5–7. If you'd like to join the discussion, take a look at Dietrich Bonhoeffer's *The Cost of Discipleship*, John Stott's *Christian Counterculture*, or Ellen White's *Thoughts From the Mount of Blessing*.

The Herods

The Bible speaks of seven people who are all named *Herod*—and if you have trouble keeping them straight, so do I. Here's a list of who's who in the Herod family:

- **Herod the Great (73 to 4 B.C.):** King of all Palestine when Jesus was born, he was hated both for his friendship with the Romans and for his cruelty. (He killed three of his own sons, as well as one of his ten wives).

- **Herod Archelaus:** Son of Herod the Great. When his father died, Archelaus was made king of Judah; he did such a terrible job, however, that the Romans kicked him out and replaced him with an appointed official in A.D. 6.

- **Herod Antipas (also known as "Herod the Tetrarch"):** Son of Herod the Great. He ruled Galilee and Perea during the ministry of Jesus. Married to a Nabatean princess, he fell in love with his sister-in-law Herodias; his subsequent divorce and remarriage angered both the Nabateans and John the Baptist! When he got too "uppity," the Romans kicked him out in A.D. 39.

- **Herod Philip:** Son of Herod the Great. He ruled northeastern Palestine both wisely and well until his death in A.D. 39. He's the one who built Caesarea Philippi; he also married Herodias's daughter Salome.

- **Herod Philip:** Yes, another Philip—this one was the son of Herod the Great and the first husband of Herodias.

- **Herod Agrippa I (10 B.C. to A.D. 44):** This is the Herod mentioned in the first part of the book of Acts—the one who persecuted Christians. His friendship with the Roman emperors Caligula and Claudius eventually made him king over all of Palestine.

- **Herod Agrippa II (A.D. 27 to *c.* A.D. 93 or 100):** This is the Herod who listens to Paul toward the end of the book of Acts. He ruled most of Palestine, but lost it all in the Great Jewish War (A.D. 66-73).

The Immaculate Conception

No, this is *not* the same thing as "the Virgin Birth." The Immaculate Conception is the belief (held by Roman Catholics) that Mary was conceived without any taint of original sin; the Virgin Birth is the belief that Jesus was conceived and born of a virgin.

How many Magi were there?

Actually, the Bible doesn't say. The number three is a tradition, nothing more.

Likewise, the Bible doesn't say that the Magi visited Jesus while He was in the manger; it was the shepherds who did that. In fact, Matthew suggests that some time passed before the Magi saw Jesus—first they had to visit Herod and find out where the King had been born, and *then* they went to Bethlehem.

FlashPoint: What was the Christmas star?

The Magi seem to have been the only ones who saw "the star in the east." When they went to Herod, after all, they had to explain what they were looking for—and Herod's advisers relied on Scripture, not the star, to tell him where the Baby was born.

So what was this star? A comet? A supernova? The planet Jupiter moving through the different constellations? Despite what you'll hear at various planetariums, none of these theories really fit the facts. That's one reason I keep coming back to the oldest theory of all: a band of angels who were singing the praises of God.

Mark
The Power of the Cross

" 'Surely this man was the Son of God!' " (Mark 15:39).

HighLights

- Four Stories About God's Kingdom (Mark 4).

- The Feeding of the Five Thousand and the Death of John the Baptist (Mark 6).

- The Triumphal Entry (Mark 11).

- The Last Supper (Mark 14).

- The Death of Jesus (Mark 14; 15).

- The Resurrection (Mark 16).

Why was it written?

Thirty years can make a lot of difference. In that time, Christianity had spread from Palestine to nearly every major city of the Roman Empire. There was even a group of Jewish Christians meeting in the capital city itself.

But they were meeting under increasingly difficult conditions. Once the Romans had thought Christianity was just a branch of Judaism. More and more, however, Judaism and Christianity were being seen as two separate religions—both competing for Gentile converts; each offering its own views on diet, prayer, Sabbath keeping, and salvation.

And that was dangerous. Judaism was a "licit" religion, after all; its existence was protected by Roman law. But as members of a "new" religion, Christians were on their own. No longer protected as Jews, they were, quite literally, "outlaws" as far as the Roman authorities were concerned.

Troubled times put a premium on good leadership, of course. Unfortunately, the years had done to Christ's disciples what the years do. There had been a time when, if you had a question about the sayings of Jesus on a given subject, you could simply ask somebody who had been there when He had said it. Now those "witnesses" were dead or going fast.

If Christianity was to survive, in other words, it needed an accurate way to pass on the teachings of Jesus. It needed to assure the loyalty of its followers—even in the face of persecution. And it needed effective answers for the questions raised by its opponents.

Mark's Gospel met those needs. It was meant to be a permanent record of Christ's unchanging message for a rapidly changing church.

What you'll learn in Mark

While Mark is often read as history, a quick comparison with the other Gospels shows that Mark arranged his material in the way that would best meet the needs of his audience. In other words, he is not telling a story so much as he is doing theology—a theology of the Cross.

True, the Christ of Mark's Gospel is a man of power. Mark's emphasis is not on teaching, but on action—not on knowledge, but on authority. With a word, Jesus calls disciples, casts out demons, stills a raging sea, and raises the dead to life. Yet Jesus' mighty acts do not lead to faith—not the kind of faith He wants. In fact, Jesus' miracles often inspire opposition and misunderstanding.

That's because Mark wants to make the point that God's power is shown most clearly in service—not miracles. So Jesus fully demonstrates who He is, not when He casts out demons, but when He submits to a humiliating death. Only as an accused criminal will Jesus publicly admit that He is the Messiah; only the centurion who watches Him die can call Jesus the "Son of God" without rebuke.

Mark's Gospel, in other words, is not a "course in miracles," but a call to follow Christ no matter the cost. And, yes, the price may be high: persecution, pain, or even death. But Jesus has promised to be with the believer in all these things, just as He was with the disciples on the road that led to His own death.

GoodWords

- **Christ:** The Greek word for "messiah"—a title that refers to "the one anointed" or blessed by God to rule as king.

- **Gospel:** Literally "the good news." Originally, it referred to an important, official announcement, such as was proclaimed at the birth of an emperor.

- **Jerusalem:** The ancient capital of Judah. During festivals such as Passover, it would swell to three times its normal population of 50,000. That's why the authorities feared the outbreak of a riot during the trial of Christ.

- **Mark:** Legend has it the apostle Peter dictated this Gospel in Rome to his translator, John Mark. Mark was the cousin of Barnabas and the sometime traveling companion of Paul. His mother was a leader in the early Christian church; believers met at her home when Peter was in prison (see Acts 12:12) and may have met there for the Last Supper. Some experts feel the young man mentioned in Mark 14:51 may have been John Mark himself.

- **Son of God:** A Messianic title that stresses the divinity of Jesus.

- **Son of man:** A Hebrew phrase that means simply "man" or "human being." But Daniel 7 refers to a "Son of man" who will judge the earth; this gives the phrase a Messianic meaning.

Fourteen Greek words you should know

- **Agape** *(uh-GAH-pay)*: A love that does the right thing for someone else, regardless of your feelings about that person.

- **Apostolos** *(ah-POSS-to-loss)*: Apostle—literally, "the one sent." Originally it was a title used for ambassadors and business agents, but Jesus used it to describe those who would carry His message to others.

- **Christos** *(CHRIS-toss, with the "ch" pronounced as it would be in the Scottish word "loch")*: The Christ or Messiah—literally, "the one anointed." Priests and kings had oil poured over them at their inauguration; this "anointing" symbolized God's blessing. When God's people fell on hard times, they began to look for a king who would rule as David had ruled—victoriously and with justice. Their name for this future king was the "messiah"; the Greek word for *messiah* is *christ*.

- **Doulos** *(DOO-loss)*: Often translated as "servant," this word actually means "slave."

- **Ekklesia** *(ek-KLAY-see-uh)*: Church—literally "the ones called out." This word was originally used for any caucus or assembly of people.

- **Epistolae** *(eh-PIH-stoh-lay)*: Epistle or letter.

- **Euaggelion** *(Oi-ahn-GEH-lee-on)*: Gospel—literally, "the good news." Originally used for official announcements that concerned the emperor, this word was applied to the life story and teachings of Jesus.

- **Hagioi** *(HAHG-ee-oi)*: Saints—literally "holy ones." A term used for all of God's people, not just super-achievers.

- **Hamartia** *(HAH-mahr-TEE-uh)*: Sin—literally "to miss the mark." Just as an archer might miss the target, so we often "miss the mark" when it comes to doing what God wants.

- **Mathaetaes** *(MAH-thay-TAYS)*: Disciple, student, or follower.

- **Martus** *(MAHR-toos)*: Someone who testifies that Jesus is Lord—literally, "a witness." The fate of most early witnesses is indicated by the fact that we get "martyr" from this word.

- **Metanoia** *(meh-TUH-NOI-yuh)*: Repentance—literally "to turn around."

- **Mustaerion** *(moo-STAY-ree-on)*: Often translated as "mystery," this word actually refers to something that used to be a secret, but now has been revealed to God's people.

- **Pistis** *(PIHS-tiss)*: Faith or trust.

What did Jesus look like?

Nobody knows what Jesus looked like. None of the Gospels say anything about His appearance, and the earliest portraits were done hundreds of years after the fact. In fact, it's difficult to know what *any* Jew might have looked like at this time—by and large, they didn't go in much for statues or paintings.

Still, we can guess. Since Jesus was Jewish, He probably had dark hair, dark eyes, and an olive complexion. Since He was a working man (the Greek word *tektonos* can refer to anyone who works with his hands, not just a carpenter), He was probably muscular—even burly. He had a voice that would carry over the noise of a crowd . . .

And that's it. That's all that we really know about the appearance of Jesus.

The twelve disciples

- **Andrew, son of John:** A fisherman and the brother of Simon Peter.

- **Simon Peter, son of John:** Peter is the nickname given him by Jesus; it means "rock."

- **James, son of Zebedee:** A fisherman and the brother of John; he was the first disciple to be martyred.

- **John, son of Zebedee:** "The beloved disciple" and author of five books in the New Testament. Together with his brother James, he was known as "Boanerges" (a "son of thunder").

- **Philip:** His name means "fond of horses."

- **Nathanael:** Also known as "Bartholomew."

- **Matthew:** A tax collector, also named "Levi."

- **Thomas:** Known as "doubting Thomas." Tradition says he carried the gospel to India.

- **James, the son of Alphaeus:** He may have been the brother of Matthew Levi.

- **Simon the Zealot:** A member of a violently nationalist, anti-Roman group.

- **Judas, brother of James:** Also known as Thaddaeus.

- **Judas Iscariot:** The disciple who betrayed Jesus. The name "Iscariot" is thought to mean "man of Kerioth"—a town in southern Judah.

Why were the Romans in Palestine?

The Persians ruled Palestine until their empire was taken over by Alexander the Great. When he died, his generals split up his empire. The general Seleucus got Syria. Ptolemy got Egypt. And the two agreed to argue over Palestine.

Stay with me—it gets better. Antiochus IV, a descendant of Seleucus, tried to turn all the Jews into Greeks. Instead, they kicked him out in 165 B.C. and set up their own kingdom.

Now Judah was ruled by the Hasmoneans—priestly descendants of the Maccabee family that had led the revolt against Antiochus IV. But when one of the Hasmonean kings died, his two heirs—Hyrcanus II and Aristobulus II—fought over who should rule. Both asked the Romans for help. Both got more than they had bargained for.

The Roman general Pompey invaded Jerusalem in 63 B.C. and tried to sort out things, but continuing quarrels among the Hasmoneans led the Romans to install one of their good buddies Antipater II as king. After the death of Antipater II's son—Herod the Great—the Romans divided Judah into three sections, with the area around Jerusalem under the direct control of a Roman procurator.

The Jews managed to kick out the Romans in A.D. 66 . . . and when the Romans came back in A.D. 70, they were not happy. When the Romans weren't happy, they made sure a lot of other people weren't happy either. Millions of people died as a result, and the Jews lost control of their homeland.

FlashPoint: The ending of Mark

All of the earliest and best manuscripts of Mark that we have end with Mark 16:8. Having seen the empty tomb of Jesus, "trembling and bewildered, the women went out and fled from the tomb. They said nothing to anyone, because they were afraid."

Now what kind of an ending is *that?!?*

"A brilliant ending," some scholars say. "Once again, it demonstrates the failure of Jesus' followers to realize who He is, and what He has done."

Others disagree—in fact, some very early Christians *must* have disagreed, because they came up with two additional endings for Mark! One is quite brief. In it, the women report the empty tomb to Peter, and Jesus tells them to spread the good news everywhere. Another is quite long—eleven verses that record Jesus meeting with Mary, His meeting with His twelve followers, and His ascension into heaven.

Now there's nothing wrong with either ending—in fact, most experts agree that they draw upon authentic stories about Jesus. But the experts *also* agree that these were not the original endings to Mark's Gospel!

So what happened? Did Mark *really* want to end his Gospel at verse 8? Is there another ending—the *original* ending—still floating around out there somewhere? Or what?

Luke
A Jesus for Strangers

24 CHAPTERS — READING TIME: 3 HOURS

" 'There will be more joy in heaven over one sinner who repents
than over ninety-nine righteous persons who do not need to repent' " (Luke 15:7).

Highlights

- The Birth of Jesus (Luke 2).

- The Temptation of Jesus (Luke 4).

- The Faith of a Roman Soldier (Luke 7).

- The Story of the Good Samaritan (Luke 10).

- The Story of the Prodigal Son (Luke 15).

- The Story of Zacchaeus the Tax Collector (Luke 19).

- The Death of Jesus (Luke 22; 23).

- Jesus Appears on the Road to Emmaus (Luke 24).

Why was it written?

Success can bring problems of its own.

Take the early Christian church, for example. In just a few decades, it had gone from the villages of Palestine to the great cities of Athens, Alexandria, and Rome.

And the people listening were no longer just Palestinian Jews. No, they came from every nation and religion. Persians and Libyans, Romans and Greeks, rational Stoics and ecstatic followers of fertility cults—all of these people wanted to hear about Jesus.

That was the problem. Jesus, after all, was a Jew. His first followers were all Jews. The first few accounts of His life and teachings were all written *by* Jews and *for* Jews. Telling Jews about Jesus, in other words, was something that early Christians knew how to do.

But how could you explain Jesus in a way that made sense to people who weren't Jewish? After all, you couldn't talk about the way He fulfilled Bible prophecy; your audience didn't know Scripture. You couldn't appeal to their patriotism—why should they care that Jesus was the royal son of David?

And you couldn't assume that your audience would understand *why* Jesus said and did some of the things He did. They didn't have the background needed to "read between the lines" of Christ's words. They didn't know enough about Palestinian Jewish laws and customs in order to do so.

In other words, Christianity needed a translator. It needed someone who could take the good news about Jesus and put it into words that non-Jewish (or Gentile) readers could understand.

That's what Luke did in his Gospel. A Gentile himself, Luke was a Greek-speaking physician that the apostle Paul had met during his travels. Though Luke had never met Jesus himself, he had carefully interviewed those who had, and he had read everything he could find about Jesus.

Based on this research, Luke drew up an account of Jesus' life for Gentile readers. In it, he highlighted Jesus' dealings with Gentiles. He explained Jewish laws and customs. And he traced Jesus' ancestry, not just to Abraham, the ancestor of all Jews, but all the way back to Adam, the ancestor of all peoples.

In short, Luke wanted his Gospel to be something that *anyone* could read and understand. That's why it is the Gospel that many modern readers find to be the easiest of all to read.

What you'll learn in Luke

When Mary learned she was pregnant with Jesus, she sang that God " 'has brought down rulers from their thrones but has lifted up the humble. He has filled the hungry with good things, but has sent the rich away empty' " (Luke 1:52, 53).

That's an important theme in Luke—the theme of a God who turns the world upside down. In this book, Jesus favors the outcast. He blesses the poor (and not just the "poor in spirit"). He befriends those who have no other friend— foreigners, children, even sinners. In short, Luke shows us that Jesus rooted for the underdogs and the losers of this world.

What's more, Jesus wants us to do the same. " 'Be merciful,' " He said, " 'just as your Father is merciful' " (Luke 6:36). Like Jesus, our job is to " 'preach good news to the poor, . . . proclaim freedom for the prisoners and recovery of sight for the blind, to release the oppressed, to proclaim the year of the Lord's favor' " (Luke 4:18). When we do this, we are the "sons and daughters of God."

GoodWords

- **Centurion:** A noncommissioned officer in the Roman army. A centurion began his career as a common soldier, but worked his way up to the command of a hundred men.

- **Herod:** In the first chapter of Luke, this is Herod the Great (73 to 4 B.C.), the unscrupulous king of all Palestine. In the rest of Luke, it's his son Herod Antipas, who ruled northern Palestine (or Galilee) from 4 B.C. to A.D. 39. Both Herods were great friends of the Romans.

- **Luke:** The "beloved physician" and companion of Paul. Little is known about him, but experts speculate that he was a Greek-speaking Gentile with medical training. Luke also wrote the book of Acts. Archaeologists report they *may* have discovered the body of Luke; it will be interesting to see what comes of this.

- **Pharisees:** Jews whose desire to follow God's law led to elaborate regulations about behavior. Pharisees were generally members of the lower-middle-class; they believed in angels, life after death, and the binding authority of prophets such as Isaiah, Jeremiah, and Hosea.

- **Pontius Pilate:** The Roman governor (or procurator) of southern Palestine (or Judah from A.D. 26-36. Palestine had been a client-state of the Romans since 63 B.C., but they had assumed direct control of Judah soon after the death of Herod the Great. Pilate treated the Jews with such cruelty and contempt, however, that he was dismissed from his post. Legend has it that he was banished to France, where he committed suicide.

- **Sadducees:** Jews whose conservatism led them to reject any elaboration on the first five books of the

Bible—the ones we know as "the Law of Moses" and that they called the "Torah." Sadducees were generally rich. They did not believe in angels or life after death.

- **Theophilus:** The name means "friend of God." Whether this was the real name of a real person, or a literary device used by Luke is something that the experts love to argue about. But if he really did exist, Theophilus was probably a member of the upper-class in Rome.

Crucifixion

Crucifixion was the kind of death that made you glad to be a Roman citizen. Because as such, you couldn't be crucified—only beheaded.

Crucifixion was definitely not a good way to die. It wasn't even a respectable way to die. The victim was flogged with a cat-o-nine-tails, then made to carry a huge, heavy crossbeam to the place of his execution. There he was stripped naked, his hands or wrists nailed to the crosspiece, the crosspiece nailed to the upright, and his ankles nailed to the upright post. A sign over his head proclaimed his crime, with its underlying message to the reader—"Let this be a lesson to you!"

It was a painful, agonizing death, but it wasn't a quick one. Victims of crucifixion were known as "food for the crows," because these birds would go for their eyes. Dying on a cross could take days unless the legs of the victims were broken; suspended by his arms alone, he would quickly suffocate. Once dead, the victim would usually be left on the cross until his body rotted.

Roman Caesars

While the Roman Empire was officially a republic that was ruled by the senate, in practice it was a military dictatorship ruled by the emperor. Here are some of the emperors who ruled during the New Testament era:

- **Octavian, or "Caesar Augustus" (31 B.C.-A.D. 14):** Balding, short, and utterly unscrupulous, he left the symbols of the Roman republic in place while he consolidated all the real power in himself. By and large, his reign was marked by peace and prosperity.

- **Tiberius (A.D. 14-37):** Gloomy, paranoid, and prone to fits of rage, he was not someone you wanted to offend. So it's no wonder that Pontius Pilate feared the crowd's shout that if he let Jesus go, he was "no friend of Caesar."

- **Gaius, or "Caligula" (A.D. 37-41):** Vicious, vain, and quite possibly insane, he threatened to install a statue of himself in the Jerusalem temple—something the Jews would have considered a scandalous sacrilege. Fortunately, local authorities stalled the project until Caligula's death brought the idea to an end.

- **Claudius (A.D. 41-54):** His limp and stutter ensured that no one took him seriously—and that enabled him to survive long enough to become emperor. Claudius expelled all the Jews from Rome in A.D. 49 because of the disturbance they created over someone named "Chrestus" (Christ?). He was probably poisoned by his fourth wife, Agrippina.

- **Nero (A.D. 54-68):** He began his reign as a tolerant and capable ruler; he ended it as a murderous tyrant. Looking for a scapegoat, he blamed the great Roman fire of A.D. 64 on Christians and killed many of them . . . including Peter and Paul.

- **Vespasian (A.D. 69-79):** Capable and wise, he was an old-fashioned Roman who had won fame by his war against the Jews.

- **Titus (A.D. 79-81):** The eldest son of Vespasian, he successfully concluded his father's campaign against the Jews with the capture of Jerusalem in A.D. 70.

- **Domitian (A.D. 81-96):** The youngest son of Vespasian, he was vain, suspicious, and very, very touchy about his dignity. When he was finally assassinated, few mourned.

The birth of Jesus

Only two Gospels—Matthew and Luke—tell us anything about the birth of Jesus. Matthew tells us that Jesus was visited by royal "Magi"—wise men from the east. Luke tells us about the humble shepherds who came to see Jesus. Both have selected the details that help them make their main points: Matthew wants us to know that Jesus was a King, and Luke wants to emphasize that Jesus was a Friend of common people.

FlashPoint: The synoptic problem

Read the Gospels of Matthew, Mark, and Luke, and you'll notice that they have a lot in common. They all use roughly the same chronology, and they tell many of the same miracles and sayings of Jesus—often in almost exactly the same words. That's why experts call these three Gospels "the synoptics" (from the Greek words *syn optik,* or "same view").

Keep reading these three Gospels more closely, however, and things start to get more complicated. Almost everything you find in Mark, for instance, is also in Matthew and Luke. But Matthew and Luke contain a lot of stuff that you won't find in Mark. Some of this extra stuff is common to both Matthew and Luke, but some of it is unique to one or the other.

So what's going on? Most experts believe that Mark's Gospel came first and that both Matthew and Luke used it in preparing their own gospels. They believe that Matthew and Luke *also* used a collection of Jesus' sayings (called *Q,* from the German word *quelle,* remember?), and that each had an additional source of materials that the other did not.

Everything clear?

Then I should also tell you that some experts *don't* believe all this. Instead, they insist that Matthew came first. They think that Mark and Luke relied on Matthew in order to prepare their Gospels—with Mark *cutting* material from Matthew, while Luke *added* material.

Confused? So are the experts—in fact, one of them once told me that "eternity will consist of biblical scholars, all trying to solve the synoptic problem"!

Village houses

Start with one room—the walls made of stone or adobe brick, the flat roof made of mud slathered over brush that has been laid over the roof beams. Inside is everything you own—a mortar and pestle to grind grain, a few dishes, some tools, and perhaps a chest to hold all these things. Food is stored in jars, sacks, and pits; any money you've saved has been safely buried. The bed is a raised platform at one end of the room; at night, everyone sleeps there—mom, dad, the kids, and grandma too.

As you have money and time, you'll add to your house, room by room. Your major constraint is probably the wood needed for the roof beams; wood is scarce and expensive. Water will still come from the community well; baking will still be done at the community oven. But in time, you might have a rambling structure of a half dozen rooms or more—enough to make you one of the wealthier citizens in your village.

Medicine in the New Testament

In ancient times, most medical treatment was little more than magic—a case of "Wear this charm around your neck, and call me in the morning." Germs were unknown. Sanitation was nonexistent. Drugs were harmless at best and poisons at worst. Then too, there were no screens on the windows to protect against flies or mosquitoes!

Still, life went on. Midwives handled childbirth; "bone-setters" handled broken bones and dislocations. And by New Testament times, a number of medical schools had been set up—schools that educated the slaves who served as most of the physicians in the Roman Empire. There the student would learn how to lance boils, amputate limbs, ease pain with opium, and write effective magic charms.

John

Jesus as the Teacher of Wisdom

21 CHAPTERS — READING TIME: 3 HOURS

*" 'For God so loved the world that he gave his one and only Son,
that whoever believes in him shall not perish but have eternal life' " (John 3:16).*

Highlights

- The Wedding at Cana (John 2).

- Jesus Meets With Nicodemus (John 3).

- Jesus and the Woman at the Well (John 4).

- Jesus Forgives the Woman Caught in Adultery (John 8).

- Jesus Raises Lazarus From the Dead (John 11).

- The Last Words of Jesus to His Followers (John 13–17).

- The Death of Jesus (John 19).

- Jesus Is Raised From the Dead and Appears to "Doubting Thomas" (John 20).

- The Risen Jesus Has One Last Meal With His Followers (John 21).

Why was it written?

Few books state their purpose as clearly as does the Gospel of John:

Jesus did many other miraculous signs in the presence of his disciples, which are not recorded in this book. *But these are written that you may believe that Jesus is the Christ*, the Son of God, and that by believing you may have life in his name (John 20:30, emphasis supplied).

John's Gospel, in other words, is not a history book but an advertisement. It is meant to convince you that Jesus is God's Son so that you can have "life."

What's more, John wrote his Gospel with a particular audience in mind. Most experts believe it was written to educated, philosophically trained Jewish Christians sometime between A.D. 90 and A.D. 100. This was an exciting time for Palestinian Judaism. The temple had been destroyed, and many Jews weren't sure how to cope with the loss. Many were offering solutions: extreme nationalism, wild-eyed mysticism, and even the belief that John the Baptist was the promised Messiah!

But gradually the Pharisees gained control of Judaism. They defined orthodoxy in terms that pleased them . . . and excluded Christians. Jewish Christianity had lost its place in the synagogue, in other words, and many believers weren't sure how to cope.

That's why John wrote his Gospel. It's meant to comfort believers with the knowledge that they are the true people of God. As such, it can be quite harsh in its views of other Jewish groups—an attitude that it shares with the Dead Sea Scrolls. Keep in mind, however, that this was a *family* argument. John wrote his Gospel as a Jew to other Jews, and not as an attack on all Jews everywhere.

Like the Gospels of Matthew and Mark, in other words, John's Gospel was written with a Jewish audience in mind. But if Matthew wrote for the *traditional* Jews, and Mark for *foreign* Jews, John wrote for *educated* Jews—Jews who weren't sure where they fit into contemporary Judaism.

What you'll learn in John

Matthew, Mark, and Luke all present very similar views of Jesus in their Gospels—so similar that they are called the synoptic (or "same view") Gospels.

But the Jesus of John's Gospel is different. He rarely speaks in parables. He doesn't preach about "the time of the end." And even the story of His "last supper" is missing!

Instead, Jesus comes across in John's Gospel as a rabbi—a great teacher who is interested in discussing the deep questions of philosophy. Some experts believe this is because John gives us Jesus' *private* conversations with His followers, while the synoptic Gospels focus on His public sermons to the crowds. And certainly John does give us the words of Christ's most intimate conversations with His closest friends.

But John also makes it clear that Jesus is greater than any rabbi—greater even than Moses or Abraham. He is greater because He doesn't just teach with wisdom; He *is* wisdom. He is the "light of the world," the "water of life," and the "true vine" that gives life to everyone.

In short, the Jesus of this Gospel is both more personal and more philosophical than those of the synoptic Gospels. Its speeches are longer; its teachings are more abstract. But its purpose, once again, is to introduce us to Jesus—the divine "Word"—who can be both our greatest Friend and our greatest Teacher.

GoodWords

- **Annas:** The Romans made him high priest in A.D. 6 and threw him out in A.D. 15—but still his connections allowed him to retain his title and influence. Five of his sons (as well as his son-in-law Caiphas) also served as high priests.

- **The beloved disciple:** Tradition has it that this was John's way of referring to himself.

- **Bethzaith (also spelled Bethzatha, Bethesda, or Bethsaida):** The site of a pool-side miracle recorded in John's Gospel. Archaeologists discovered its location in 1888. It's a large pool that has been divided into two and surrounded on all sides by a covered porch.

- **Denarius:** A silver coin the size of a dime. It was a day's wages for a common laborer.

- **Disciple:** Literally, "a student."

- **Feast of Dedication:** Also known as the Feast of Lights or Hanukkah. Celebrated in December or early January, it commemorated the rededication of the temple by Judas Maccabees in 164 B.C.

- **Feast of Tabernacles:** A fall festival that celebrated both the harvest and God's care during the Exodus from Egypt. The promise of Ezekiel 47 was an important part of this festival—that's why the words of Jesus are so important in John 7:37.

- **Gospel:** Literally, "the good news."

- **Greeks:** It's not clear whether this term refers to ethnic Greeks or Greek-speaking Jews.

- **Jews:** John's Gospel uses this term more than any other Gospel—a total of sixty-eight times in all. But it doesn't refer to the Jewish *people* so much as it does to the political and religious *leaders* of Judea.

- **John (the apostle):** Son of Zebedee the fisherman, brother of James, bishop of Ephesus, and perhaps a disciple of John the Baptist at one time. A reliable tradition has it that he also wrote the book of Revelation and the three little New Testament letters that bear his name.

- **John (the Baptist):** Born to a priestly family, he preached a message of reform and repentance; the political implications of his message resulted in his execution by Herod Antipas. Some of John's followers continued to think that he might be the Messiah, right up to the fourth century. Curiously, he is the only John mentioned by name in this Gospel.

- **Judea:** The name for southern Palestine. It was ruled directly by Rome from A.D. 6 to A.D. 41, and from A.D. 44 to A.D. 66.

- **Living water:** A phrase that means "flowing water."

- **Nard (or spikenard):** An extremely expensive perfume derived from the roots and stems of *Nardostachys jaramansi*—a plant found in the Himalayas. (And yes, Roman traders routinely traveled as far as India—a fact that someone could use as the basis for a wonderful book!).

- **Passover:** The spring festival that celebrated God's deliverance of the Israelites from slavery in Egypt.

- **Pharisees:** There were only 6,000 or so of these "separated ones" in Palestine during the time of Jesus; they were famous for their attempts to apply God's law to everyday life. Unlike the Sadducees, they believed in angels as well as life after death.

- **Pontius Pilate:** Roman procurator (or governor) of Judea from A.D. 26 to A.D. 36, he was a protégé of the consul Sejanus. The execution of his mentor for treason in A.D. 31 may have made Pilate all the more afraid of being known as "no friend of Caesar."

- **The Prophet:** The references in John 1:21; 6:14; 7:40 are to Deuteronomy 18:15-22—God's promise that He would send a successor to Moses.

- **Samaritans:** They said they were descendants of the ten "lost tribes"; the Jews said they were foreign interlopers who had adopted a degraded form of their religion. As similar as their religions might have been, the Jews and the Samaritans didn't get along together very well.

The Word

"In the beginning," says John, "was the *logos*"—a word that can be translated as "word," "intellect," or "understanding." Stoics taught that "the Word" animated the universe (much as did "the Force" in *Star Wars*). But some experts think that John's use of *logos* owes more to the Hebrew concept of "wisdom" (such as you'll find in the book of Proverbs) than it does to the Greek philosophy of Stoicism.

John the Baptist

Often viewed as little more than the forerunner of Jesus, John the Baptist was an important figure in his own right. The son of a priest, John adopted the lifestyle of Elijah—Israel's most famous prophet. John attracted followers from as far away as Asia Minor (present-day Turkey) and stirred speculation that he might be the Messiah.

But John was imprisoned and then killed by Herod Antipas—an insecure ruler who couldn't abide John's criticism of his marriage to his niece (and ex-sister-in-law) Herodias. Many of John's followers became Christians . . . though not all. Well into the third century A.D., there were "Baptists" who continued to insist that John was the promised Messiah.

When did Jesus die?

Read Matthew, Mark, and Luke, and it's clear that Jesus died on a Friday, the day *after* Passover. Read John, on the other hand, and it's clear that Jesus died on a Friday, the day *before* Passover. So what gives?

The experts aren't sure. It *may* be that there was some disagreement that year about the correct day to celebrate the Passover—with some Jews celebrating it on Thursday and others waiting until Sabbath—but this seems doubtful. If anyone has a better suggestion, please let me know!

FlashPoint: Why is John's Gospel so different?

Experts tell me that the Greek of John's Gospel is beautifully written, while that found in the book of Revelation is . . . well, let's just say that no one is going to mistake the author of Revelation with the person who wrote John's Gospel; it's like comparing *Mother Goose* with *Romeo and Juliet!*

Yet there's a very old and reliable tradition that says *both* books were written by someone named John—presumably John, the son of Zebedee and disciple of Jesus. So why the difference in language between the two?

Some liberals say the Gospel of John and the book of Revelation were written by two men with the same name: the Gospel by John the apostle (or his followers), and Revelation by an "elder" (or bishop) John who lived in Ephesus.

Conservatives tend to argue that both books were written by the apostle John. When he wrote his Gospel, he had friends and followers who could help him polish his Greek; when he wrote Revelation, he had to do so alone and under primitive conditions.

Myself, the whole argument reminds me of Mark Twain's joke about the scholar who spent years proving that *The Illiad* was not written by Homer, but by another man with the same name.

The Dead Sea Scrolls

Discovered in caves between 1947 and 1960, these are the remains of 520 texts, all written on leather by Jewish scribes between the third century B.C. and A.D. 70.

For years, people have speculated about the contents of these scrolls—speculations fueled by the fact that scholars were abominably slow in getting out the results of their discoveries. To be sure, their job wasn't an easy one—the scrolls themselves had to be pieced together from somewhere between 15,000 and 40,000 fragments—but the delay made people suspicious. Were these scholars hiding something? Did the Dead Sea Scrolls tell us something they didn't want us to know—something new and shocking, perhaps, about the birth of Christianity?

Well, as it turns out, they don't. Now that we know what the scrolls actually say, it turns out that all the speculation was for nothing. To be sure, the scrolls themselves are exciting—for instance, we learn from them that Judaism was a pretty lively affair, with a lot of different groups competing for attention. We've also learned that the Hebrew manuscripts we have today are remarkably similar to those of Jesus' time; there has been very little change over the centuries.

Now this is important information—in fact, the Dead Sea Scrolls have been called "the greatest manuscript discovery in modern times." But if you're looking for shocking discoveries that will rattle your faith, then stick to the *National Enquirer*. You won't find such things in the Dead Sea Scrolls.

FlashPoint: The quest for the historical Jesus

All four Gospels were written by believers—a fact that makes some people nervous.

"How do we know that we're getting the straight story?" they ask. "How do we know that those sneaky Christian believers aren't just feeding us propaganda?"

As a result, a number of people have tried to write the biography of Jesus—a biography that would owe nothing to faith, but that would "just give the facts as they happened."

It sounds great, but in his famous book, *The Quest for the Historical Jesus,* Albert Schweitzer noted that every "objective" biography of Jesus always ends up looking like the person who wrote it. The socialist writer ends up with a socialist Jesus. The conservative writer ends up with a conservative Jesus. The revolutionary writer ends up with a revolutionary Jesus. And the "New Age" seeker ends up with a Jesus who wore crystals and sipped herb tea.

"We can't get 'behind' the Gospels," Schweitzer said in effect. "It's a case of 'what we see is all we've got.' " And with that, Schweitzer moved to Africa, founded a hospital, and spent the rest of his life working with lepers.

The life of Jesus

As you've learned by now, no single Gospel tells the whole story of Jesus—but if you would like read some of the more famous stories about Him, try the texts in this list:

• The Birth of Jesus (Luke 2:1-20).

• Jesus As a Boy in the Temple (Luke 2:41-52).

• Jesus Is Tempted by Satan (Matthew 4:1-11).

• Jesus Turns Water Into Wine (John 2:1-11).

• Jesus Heals a Little Girl (Matthew 9:18-26).

• Jesus Calls Twelve Disciples (Matthew10:1-42).

• Jesus Forgives a Guilty Woman (John 8:1-11).

• The Sermon on the Mount (Matthew 5–7).

• Jesus Feeds the Five Thousand (Matthew 14:13-21).

• Seven Stories About God's Kingdom (Matthew 3:1-52).

• The Death of John the Baptist (Mark 6:14-29).

• Peter's Confession (Mark 8:27-30).

• The Mount of Transfiguration (Matthew 17:1-13).

• The Rich Young Ruler (Matthew 19:16-30).

• The Triumphal Entry (Matthew 21:1-11).

• Jesus Cleans the Temple (Matthew 21:12-17).

• Jesus Speaks of the Future (Matthew 24; 25).

• The Last Supper (Luke 22:7-38).

• Jesus' Last Words to His Followers (John 14–17).

• The Garden of Gethsemane (Mark 14:32-42).

• The Death of Jesus (Luke 22:47-23:49).

• Jesus Comes Back to Life (John 20:1-31).

• Jesus on the Road to Emmaus (Luke 24).

• Jesus Goes Back to Heaven (Acts 1).

QUICKSTART

New Testament:

The Book of Acts

Acts
God's People Move Out Into the World

28 CHAPTERS — READING TIME: 3 HOURS

" 'You will be my witnesses in Jerusalem, and in all Judea and Samaria, and to the ends of the earth' " (Acts 1:8).

Highlights

- Jesus Returns to Heaven (Acts 1).

- The Holy Spirit Descends During Pentecost (Acts 2).

- The Conversion of Saul (Acts 9).

- Peter's Vision of Clean and Unclean (Acts 10).

- The Council in Jerusalem (Acts 15).

- The Riot in Ephesus (Acts 19).

- Paul's Arrest and Trial (Acts 21–26).

- Shipwreck! (Acts 27).

Why was it written?

Like the book of Luke, the book of Acts is a "Gentile's Guide to Christianity." It explains the beliefs and practices of the early church in a way that its non-Jewish readers could understand.

And, like the book of Luke, Acts makes it clear that reaching out to the Gentiles was not wrong. It's not something that the apostle Paul brought in as his own personal heresy. No, it has always been God's plan to include both Gentiles and Jews in His church—something that the early church recognized even before Paul came along.

These similarities between the books of Luke and Acts shouldn't surprise us. Tradition has it that both books were written by Luke—a Gentile physician, who accompanied Paul on several of his missionary journeys. Most experts agree, as a matter of fact, that Luke and Acts were originally one book, not two! They were split from each other only because the original book was too long to fit on a single scroll.

But Acts has a different setting than Luke's Gospel. Luke's Gospel takes place entirely in Palestine. In the book of Acts, the scene moves from Palestine to the Gentile lands of Asia Minor (now Turkey), Greece, and Rome. In his Gospel, Luke tells us how Christianity began, but now he wants to tell us how it spread. Luke's Gospel begins in the Most Holy Place of the temple in Jerusalem. Acts ends with Paul awaiting trial before the emperor in Rome.

It's Paul's trial that provides the reason for the book of Acts. Christianity was getting big enough to attract attention—and not all of it was good. The Romans were beginning to wonder if Christianity was a "good" religion like Judaism . . . or if it encouraged lawlessness and revolt.

Luke's answer was that you could be a good Roman *and* a good Christian. Christianity was not an enemy to good government. It did not stir up trouble. And, contrary to rumor, it did not cause riots. As a matter of fact, in every place where Christianity was given a fair hearing, Roman officials declared it to be . . . well, harmless at the very least.

"Don't be swayed by gossip," Luke is telling his readers in Acts. "Learn the facts for yourselves. You may find that Christianity isn't what you thought it was. And you may find that Christianity is exactly what you need in your life today."

What you'll learn in Acts

As J. B. Phillips once pointed out, a good name for this book would be *Some Acts of Some Apostles.* That's because Acts doesn't give us a complete picture of the spread of Christianity. It just shows us how Paul (and to a lesser extent, Peter) contributed to that spread.

If nothing else, Acts would be a wonderful biography of one of Scripture's most fascinating characters. It tells us how Paul, who first opposed Christianity, became one of its most active (and controversial) champions. And in doing so, it provides the background needed to understand many of Paul's letters to the churches.

But the real star of Acts is not Paul, but the Holy Spirit. "Jesus did not leave us when He returned to heaven," Luke is saying in the book of Acts. "The age of miracles is not over. No, Jesus is still leading His people—still calling disciples, still teaching them, still guiding them—through His Spirit."

GoodWords

Luke is very careful to give the exact title and rank of the Gentile officials and governmental bodies that appear in Acts. A few examples:

- **Areopagus:** Named for the limestone ridge that rises above Athens, this council licensed teachers and judged religious crimes.
- **Asiarch:** A fairly common title for high officials in the Roman province of Asia (today's Turkey). Some say an *asiarch* was a priest; others say he was a delegate to the provincial assembly.
- **First man:** Chief official on the island of Malta.
- **Lictor:** Assistant to the Roman *praetor* (or "judge"). A rough equivalent to today's chief of police.
- **Politarch:** A member of the city council in some Macedonian cities. Thessalonica, for instance, was ruled by five or six *politarchs*.
- **Praetor:** A Roman judge who saw to it that the law was enforced in colonies that had not been granted self-rule.
- **Proconsul:** A governor over provinces that were ruled directly by the Roman senate. Unlike a *praetor*, a *proconsul* held both military and civilian authority.
- **Sanhedrin:** The council of Jewish elders.
- **Town clerk:** An important job in Ephesus. He supervised the city's records, drew up new laws, and saw to it that they were publicized.

Other "GoodWords" you'll find in the book of Acts:

- **Circumcision:** Removing the foreskin of the penis. God had told Abraham that this was to be the sign of an "everlasting covenant" (Genesis 17). Paul was so annoyed by those who applied this text to Gentile converts to Christianity—insisting that they should be circumcised—that he said they should go all the way and castrate themselves (see Galatians 5:12).

- **Diana of Ephesus:** Also known as Artemis, Cybele, Atargatis, and Ashteroth, Diana was a fertility goddess whose statues portray her with a chest that is covered by at least twenty-four . . . well, we don't really know what they are. Breasts? Eggs? The skulls of her enemies? Her temple—an enormous building with sixty-foot columns—was almost 300 years old at the time Luke writes about it and was one of the Seven Wonders of the Ancient World. The locals continued to worship Diana until her temple was destroyed by the Goths in A.D. 263.

- **God-fearers:** Some Gentiles attended synagogue services and lived by Jewish laws as best they could . . . but they weren't willing to be circumcised. Known to the Jews as "God-fearers," they provided many of the early converts to Christianity.

- **Paul:** Paul is known by two names: Saul and Paul—one Jewish, the other Roman. This is appropriate, because Paul lived in two worlds. He was a Jew trained in the law by some of the finest teachers in Jerusalem. He was also a Roman citizen who could speak Greek. The combination made him an ideal bridge between Jewish Christianity and the Gentile world of the Roman Empire. Not much is known about Paul himself. He was a leatherworker (which is what a "tentmaker" really means) who was born in Antioch and schooled in Jerusalem. Tradition has it that he was short, bald, and bow-legged . . . but we don't know that for a fact. Neither do we know if he was ever married. Jewish men usually were, but Paul certainly doesn't seem to act like a married man. Finally, we're not sure how he died. Tradition has it that he was beheaded in Rome sometime in A.D. 67 or 68, but who can say?

- **Sanhedrin:** The Jewish council of elders.

Roman ships

Rome was fed by foreign grain, almost all of which came from North Africa and Egypt. The ships that carried grain could weigh as much as 800 tons and measured up to 180 feet in length and forty-five feet in width. Grain carriers could make the trip from Egypt to Rome in fifty days; the return trip might take as little as nine days. No ships moved between November and March, however; winter storms made ocean travel too dangerous.

Roman law

The primary concern of Roman law was order. Governors, towns, private citizens—all were expected to keep the peace. Anyone who did not was punished severely.

Most laws were enforced by private citizens who brought complaints to the ruling council or governor. Acting as judge and jury all in one, the council or governor examined the defendant—an examination that might include torture, since all defendants were considered guilty until proven innocent. Once guilt had been determined, the sentence was passed: a fine, flogging, or death. Death might be commuted to exile or slavery, but criminals were rarely imprisoned after their trial.

A city's laws applied only to its own citizens; in theory, at least, a Roman citizen could ignore the rulings of local courts. (In practice, this wasn't a good idea!) What's more, someone who had been found guilty in one city could flee to the safety of the next. And Roman citizens always had the right to appeal their sentence to the emperor.

Paul's journeys

Paul makes four trips in the book of Acts—three voluntarily, and one as a prisoner:

- **The first missionary voyage (A.D. 45-47):** Paul travels from Antioch to Cyprus with Barnabas and John Mark. John Mark returns home; Paul and Barnabas continue on to the southern coast of present-day Turkey. They move inland, establish several churches, then return to Antioch.

- **The second missionary voyage (A.D. 49-52):** Paul and Silas move overland from Antioch to central Turkey. There they pick up Timothy (and eventually Luke) and move east into Greece. Moving south through Athens and Corinth, Paul founds several churches, then sails back to Turkey and lands in Ephesus. A riot follows. Paul sails for Palestine, visits the church in Jerusalem, and then returns to Antioch.

- **Third missionary voyage (A.D. 53-58):** Paul sails from Antioch for southern Turkey, then makes a circuit of ports in the Aegean Sea and stops at Corinth. He then reverses course, makes another circuit of the Aegean, then sails for Palestine and Jerusalem.

- **Paul as a prisoner (A.D. 58-63):** Paul is arrested in Jerusalem and transported to Caesarea, where he waits two years for his trial. He appeals to the emperor and is removed by ship . . . only to be shipwrecked on Malta. Paul survives and continues on to Rome, where he waits two years for his trial.

FlashPoint: The ending of Acts

The ending of Acts seems abrupt to some. Paul travels to Rome, where he is placed under house arrest. And the last we see of him in the book of Acts, he is patiently awaiting trial.

That's it? Luke isn't going to tell us what happened next? What kind of an ending is that?

Some experts believe that Luke did *not* plan to end Paul's story there; they speculate that Acts was only the second volume in a trilogy that Luke had planned to write on the early Christian church. The abrupt ending of Acts, in other words, was a cliff-hanger—"Stay tuned for part three!" But the third book was lost or (more likely) never written, and that's that.

Others believe that Luke ended Acts right where he wanted to end it. The gospel has been taken to "the ends of the earth" (i.e. Rome), and the outcome of Paul's trial has already been foreshadowed by the fact that Paul has been declared innocent (or close enough) in every other trial he's been through.

"Luke has done all that he needed to do," is what these experts say. "And if he leaves you wanting more at the end of the story . . . why, that's the mark of a good storyteller!"

QUICKSTART

New Testament:
Pauline Epistles

Romans
The Gospel According to Paul

16 CHAPTERS — READING TIME: 1 HOUR

"For the wages of sin is death, but the gift of God is eternal life in Christ Jesus our Lord"
(Romans 6:23).

Highlights

- We All Need God's Forgiveness (Romans 2).

- Nothing Can Separate Us From God's Love (Romans 8).

- How Should God's People Live? (Romans 12; 13).

Why was it written?

Paul wrote the book of Romans for much the same reason that you might put together a résumé or portfolio. He did so to introduce himself.

In the past, Paul had tried to preach only where the Christian message had not yet been heard. In three epic journeys, he had visited most of the cities that lined the Mediterranean's northeast coast.

And now, after a three-year stay in Ephesus, it was time to move on. He would make a short stop in Corinth, deliver an offering for the poor to Jerusalem, then travel to his ultimate destination: Spain.

But to preach in Spain, Paul needed the help of the church in Rome. Just why this was so is not clear—perhaps Paul hoped to use Rome as a home base; perhaps he just wanted to avoid stepping on toes. Whatever the reason, he needed the cooperation of Christians in Rome.

Unfortunately, Paul had not started the church in Rome, so he couldn't count on the gratitude of Christians there. What's more, there's evidence that Roman Christians had already heard of Paul . . . and didn't care for him. Some Jewish Christians saw Paul's work among the Gentiles as a snub; others feared his emphasis on grace was little more than a license to sin.

That's why Paul wrote to the Roman church from Corinth, sometime between A.D. 55 and 58. Hoping to gain their support, he explained his views on righteousness, salvation, and God's covenant with Israel.

Whether Paul's letter would have done the trick, we'll never know. While in Jerusalem, Paul was arrested. When he finally saw Rome, he was in chains—a prisoner charged with the capital crimes of subversion and sacrilege.

What you'll learn in Romans

Most of us consider ourselves to be pretty good people. After all, we know people who are a lot worse than we are. Besides, we love our children, pay our taxes, and brush our teeth. (Most of the time, anyway.) What more could anybody want?

Lots more—because we all know what it's like to *wish* that we could do something without having the ability to follow through. (Think of the last time you went on a diet, for instance!) And even when we do something good, it's rarely for motives that are absolutely pure. "A conscience," as H. L. Mencken once remarked, "is that still, small voice that tells you someone might be watching."

That's why we need help—the kind of help only God can give. We need help in dealing with our past mistakes and help in avoiding future ones. What's more, we need the kind of help that comes to us, not because we've earned it, but only because God loves us. That's the kind of help that Paul talks about when he talks about "grace."

And "grace" is what the book of Romans is all about. It's a "gospel of grace"; it's the good news that we can be right with God because God wants us to be right with Him.

GoodWords

- **Apostle:** Literally, "the one sent out"—a title given ambassadors and other authorized representatives.

- **Elect:** Those whom God has chosen. The word often carries with it the idea of a "remnant" or "those who have survived a great disaster."

- **Epistle:** A fancy word for a "letter."

- **Flesh:** Literally, "the body," but used by Paul as a symbol of everything that keeps us from being what God wants us to be. Heredity, environment, weird allergies, whatever—if it fouls up your life, it's "flesh."

- **Faith:** Trust or confidence.

- **Grace:** God's saving love for us. Protestants generally define this as an attitude, Catholics as the power of God.

- **Justify:** A legal term that means "to declare someone not guilty."

- **Law:** Not just the Ten Commandments. Not just the body of ritual, moral, and legal requirements that made up the Judaism of Paul's time. No, to grasp the full impact of Paul's message, you need to think of *any* blueprint for behavior—even if it's *The One-Minute Manager* or *Thin Thighs in Thirty Days*—and realize that Paul's statement about "the law" applies to it as well. It's one thing to know what you should do. It's quite another to do it.

- **Paul:** The Roman name of Saul—a Jew from the city of Tarsus who opposed Christianity as a perversion of Judaism, then turned around and began to spread the message of Christ among the Gentiles! He made three voyages as a missionary to the northeastern part of the Roman Empire, and a fourth to Rome as a prisoner. Following his imprisonment, he may have traveled to Spain. If so, he was re-arrested and returned to the capital; legend has it that he was martyred in Rome.

- **Redeem, redemption:** To pay the price needed to free a slave or to ransom the victim of a kidnapping.

- **Sin:** Not just wrong deeds, but the selfishness that motivates even our finest acts. Literally, "to miss the mark."

- **Wrath:** God "breaking in" where His power has not yet been acknowledged.

Paul's list of sins in Romans 1

Both Greek philosophers and Jewish rabbis loved to make long lists of the sins that were common in their day. Paul's list in Romans 1 is fairly typical of the lot; what makes it different is the way Paul turns on his audience in Romans 2—after describing those who commit all these sins—and says, "But you're no better than they are!"

FlashPoint: The importance of context

True story—the sea captain finds the first mate drunk on duty, so he writes in the ship's log: "The first mate was drunk today."

This makes the first mate mad. So the next day, he writes in the log: "The captain was sober today."

OK, so maybe it's not a true story—but the point it makes is important: What you leave *out* can be just as important as what you leave *in*. What the first mate wrote about the captain was perfectly true—after all, he *was* sober! What the first mate left out, however—the fact that the captain was sober *every* day—made it look as though the captain was habitually drunk.

Keep this in mind the next time someone "proves" something from the Bible. Ask yourself what that person may be leaving out. Take Romans 9, for instance—a chapter in which Paul states that God chooses who will be saved and lost. Sounds pretty grim, right? Keep reading. Because in Romans 10 and 11, Paul says that *we* can choose to be saved or lost.

Now how you put these chapters together is up to you. Myself, I believe that we should *live* as though it were all up to us, and *pray* as though it were all up to God.

But my point is that you need to read *everything* Paul says on a subject before you draw any conclusions. Context is important, after all; you don't want to leave out *anything* that might affect the truth.

And if you don't believe that, then just ask the captain.

The role of Jews in Roman society

Gentiles in Roman society both admired and hated the Jews. They admired the Jews for their honesty, their love of children, and their belief in one God. They hated the Jews because "they stood apart" from the rest of society—they didn't feast in the temples, take part in the games, or serve in the army. The Romans were also appalled by circumcision. Jews were always in demand as fortunetellers and exorcists . . . but if there was a riot, the Jews were the first to be attacked.

FlashPoint: Expiation or propitiation?

In Romans 3:25, Paul says that God presented Jesus "as an *hilastairion* through faith in his blood." Some versions translate *hilastairion* as "expiation"; others as "propitiation" or "sacrifice of atonement." And yes, there's an important difference between the two.

Expiation carries with it the idea that you've done something wrong and need to make it right; *propitiation* that you've made somebody mad and need to make him happy. If I dent the fender of your car, for instance, I have two choices: I can repair it (expiation), or I can apologize and hope you'll forgive me (propitiation).

Scholars that translate *hilastairion* as "expiation" tend to view the death of Jesus as an example of God's love for us; scholars that translate it as "propitiation" tend to view the death of Jesus as a sacrifice that takes away the penalty of our sin. In the first view, the death of Jesus changes *us;* in the second, His death changes our *relationship* with God.

Again, think of the dent I made in your car. Imagine that Jesus comes along while we're looking at the damage I've done. Do you want Jesus to pound out the dent (expiation), or to make things right between us (propitiation)?

What do you mean, you want Him to do both?!?

OK—then keep in mind that *hilastairion* literally means "the cover for the box that contained the copy of the Ten Commandments that God gave Moses." This box (or "ark"), was kept in the Most Holy Place of the temple, and visited only once a year by the high priest. During this visit, the priest sprinkled lamb's blood on the ark's cover; as a result, anything that separated us from God was now "covered" and taken care of.

In other words, when Paul calls the death of Jesus our *hilastairion,* he means that this death was the place where God and humanity got back together. And whether that means *expiation* or *propitiation* is up to you; I just call it our *initiation* into salvation.

Rome

Rome was the capital of the . . . well, it was the capital of the Roman Empire. (And you thought this was going to be difficult!) In Paul's day, Rome had anywhere between 800,000 and 1,600,000 people.

The emperor Claudius expelled all Jews from Rome in A.D. 49 because of the disturbance they made about someone named *Chrestus;* the similarity of that name to the Greek word for messiah *(Christos)* has tantalized experts ever since.

1 Corinthians

The Wisdom of Love

50 CHAPTERS — READING TIME: 5 HOURS

"And now these three remain: faith, hope and love. But the greatest of these is love"
(1 Corinthians 13:13).

HighLights

- True Wisdom (1 Corinthians 1; 2).

- Christian Marriage (1 Corinthians 7).

- Spiritual Gifts (1 Corinthians 12).

- Paul's Famous Chapter on Love (1 Corinthians 13).

- Life After Death (1 Corinthians 15).

Why was it written?

Sometime around A.D. 49, a wandering tentmaker named Paul set up shop in the Greek city of Corinth. As a Jew, he worshiped in the local synagogue. As a Christian, he preached about Jesus. As a result, two things happened: one was a riot that forced him to leave Corinth for Ephesus. The other was a new Christian church in Corinth.

Soon after he left Corinth, however, Paul heard disturbing news about the church he had founded. The precise cause of these problems is unclear—the Corinthians may have been influenced by Jewish mysticism. They may have fallen victim to the kind of "New Age" thinking that later would develop into gnosticism. Or they may have fallen prey to the temptations that come from living in a town such as Corinth.

What's clear is that the Corinthian church members were behaving badly. Some claimed to have spiritual "gifts" that others lacked. Others denied Paul's teachings about the resurrection of the dead. Still others claimed that Christians were not bound by society's rules about sexual morality. And Paul's earlier attempt to answer their questions by letter had stirred up even more controversy—controversy on issues such as divorce, church discipline, and food offered to idols (see 1 Corinthians 5:9).

So Paul tried again to help. The result is 1 Corinthians—a long-distance attempt to deal with the specific problems of a real church. And in reading it, we need to remember that we're hearing only half the conversation; we can only guess what the Corinthians said or did to make Paul write the things he did in this letter.

What you'll learn in 1 Corinthians

If nothing else, 1 Corinthians should kill any longing you might have had for "the good old days" of Christianity. Far from modeling apostolic purity, the church in Corinth was a mess. It's members fought, got drunk, and even committed incest. What's more, they justified all these things in the name of Jesus!

Jesus had told His followers to "judge not," after all.

And He had promised them the guidance of the Holy Spirit.

Therefore, if a church member in Corinth said that the Spirit had led him or her to do something really awful, who could disagree?

Certainly Paul disagreed . . . but in dealing with these problems, Paul had to carefully define what it means to be a "spiritual" person. He had to make it clear that spirituality is not a substitute for action. It is not a license for bad behavior. And it should not result in arrogance or pride.

No, a spiritual person models his or her life after that of Christ. And, as Paul says in 1 Corinthians 13, a spiritual person "is patient and kind. [He] does not envy, [he] does not boast, [he] is not proud. [He] is not rude, [he] is not self-seeking, [he] is not easily angered, [he] keeps no records of wrong." True spirituality, in other words, is really the same thing as true love.

GoodWords

- **Achaia:** The Roman province that took in southern Greece.

- **Apollos:** A Jew from Alexandria who became a follower, first of John the Baptist, then of Christ. Like Paul, Apollos traveled around the Roman Empire and spread the good news about Jesus. Though Paul was careful to point out that he and Apollos were "one," there appears to have been some rivalry among their disciples.

- **Crispus Gaius:** Superintendent of the Jewish synagogue in Corinth.

- **Grace:** God's saving love for us. Protestants define this as God's willingness to forgive us; Catholics as His power to change us.

- **Paul:** The Roman name of Saul—a Jew from the city of Tarsus who had first opposed Christianity, then turned around and began to spread it among the Gentiles! Most experts believe Paul wrote 1 Corinthians while in Ephesus, probably around A.D. 54 or 55.

- **Sosthenes:** Acts 18 speaks of a Sosthenes who was head of the synagogue at Corinth and led a demonstration against Paul. When the Romans refused to try Paul, the mob attacked Sosthenes. Could this be the man Paul refers to as "brother" in 1 Corinthians 1:1?

- **Timothy:** A native of Lystra in Asia Minor (present-day Turkey). He met Paul and became a Christian in A.D. 49 or so. Apparently, his mission to Corinth did not succeed—and together with the tone of Paul's two letters to him (1 and 2 Timothy), this has given him a reputation for timidity.

- **Wisdom:** Gnostics (the Greek word for "wisdom" is *gnosis*) taught that "wisdom" was a god that had been trapped in our material world; the task of a "spiritual" person was to free it. Jewish mystics, on the other hand, followed Proverbs and proclaimed wisdom to be the means by which God manifested Himself in our world; they used the term much as we would "providence."

 **Paul in Corinth**

Acts 18 offers a brief history of the founding of the Corinthian church.

Love

The Greek language had four words that we translate as "love":

- **Eros:** To love something because it is beautiful or valuable. ("I just *love* your chocolate brownies!")

- **Philos:** To love someone as you would a brother. ("After all we've been through, all of us guys on this team have learned to really *love* each other.")

- **Storgay:** To love someone as you would a member of your own family. ("Well, at least his mother *loves* him!")

- **Agape (pronounced "ah-GAH-pay"):** To love someone deliberately and by choice. ("Your mother and I haven't always gotten along, but we've always *loved* each other.") This is the word Paul uses when he speaks of "love" to the church in Corinth.

Earthly versus spiritual

Then as now, many religions divided people into two groups: "earthly" and "spiritual." "Earthly" people were the caterpillars; "spiritual" people, the butterflies. "Earthly" people were novices; "spiritual" people were the experts. "Earthly" people were literal-minded; "spiritual" people perceived truth mystically. And as befitted their exalted status, "spiritual" people were not bound by the fussy little rules and regulations of religion; these applied only to the clodhoppers of this world.

Obviously, Paul disagreed with this distinction between "earthly" and "spiritual" people in the Christian church . . . but in doing so, he faced a problem: Anything he said against it would only confirm him as "earthly" in the eyes of the "spiritual" people to whom he was writing!

Corinth

A large city in southern Greece, Corinth was the capital of the Roman province of Achaia and an important seaport in its own right. Corinth's reputation is summed up in the fact that the Greeks coined a verb from the name of that city: To *corinthianize* meant to fornicate.

Food offered to idols

Business contracts, social events, volunteer organizations—almost every aspect of public life in a Roman city, as a matter of fact—would have involved a "sacred" meal at one of the many local temples. And even the meat for sale at butcher's shops probably came from an animal that had first been offered to one of the gods and then resold.

This presented a problem for church members. As Christians, they weren't supposed to have anything to do with idolatry. But if you didn't eat food that had been offered to idols, you were cut off from almost every contact with the society around you.

Understandably, some Christians chose not to eat food that had been offered to idols. And equally understandably, others swallowed their objections and swallowed the food; they reasoned that food offered to a god who didn't exist was no different than the food of an ordinary meal. And given these differences, it's understandable that Christians who dealt with this issue in different ways were prone to judge each other unmercifully.

FlashPoint: Speaking in tongues

In Acts, "the gift of tongues" is clearly the supernatural ability to speak a foreign language; in 1 Corinthians, no such clarity is possible. Some say it was an ecstatic babbling; others argue it was a foreign language. Some say it was a legitimate gift of the Holy Spirit that was being wrongfully used. Others lean toward identifying it with possession by an evil spirit or a naturalistic explanation (such as self-hypnosis). Again, it's not clear just what "tongues" might have been; what is clear is that it should be used to build up the church, not tear it down.

2 Corinthians

Leadership That Loves

12 CHAPTERS — READING TIME: 40 MINUTES

"For you know the grace of our Lord Jesus Christ, that though he was rich, yet for your sakes he became poor, so that you through his poverty might become rich" (2 Corinthians 8:9).

Highlights

- Paul's Trials and Tribulations (2 Corinthians 4; 6).

- Paul Forces Himself to Boast (2 Corinthians 11; 12).

Why was it written?

Things were not going well in Corinth; what's more, everything Paul had done to try to make things better had only made things worse. In fact, no sooner did Paul leave Corinth than he began to hear disturbing reports about the church he had founded there. Paul had sent the Corinthian church a letter—now lost—in an attempt to deal with this situation. The church's reply had led him to send yet another letter—the one that we know today as 1 Corinthians. But still, the problems persisted.

So Paul wrote another letter—now lost—and even paid a personal visit to Corinth. But these overtures only stirred up more opposition to him. Following the lead of some people who called themselves "the super-apostles," the Corinthians said Paul didn't have what it took to be a true leader. He was not a polished speaker. He was unspiritual. He vacillated—wavering between timidity and arrogance. And his "offering" for the poor in Jerusalem was just a trick meant to cheat the Corinthians out of their money.

That's why Paul wrote yet *another* letter to the church in Corinth—his fourth letter—the letter we know today as 2 Corinthians. In this letter, he defends his status as an apostle, encourages the Corinthians to donate money to his offering, and warns them to prepare for his upcoming visit.

We don't know if this was the last letter Paul wrote to the Corinthians, but we do know that Paul's third visit was a success. During this visit, as a matter of fact, Paul wrote his famous letter to the church in Rome—and in Romans 15:26ff, Paul says that church members in Achaia (of which Corinth was the capital) were "pleased to make a contribution for the poor among the saints in Jerusalem." Compare that statement with Paul's words in 2 Corinthians chapters 8 and 9, and you'll see the difference a letter can make!

What you'll learn in 2 Corinthians

What does it take to be a leader—especially a spiritual leader? Most would point to training. Some might say that the only requirement is the ability to get results. A few might argue that a leader should be popular—what is a leader, after all, without followers? And humanly speaking, there is nothing wrong with any of these answers.

But as Paul points out in 2 Corinthians 5:16, "We [should] regard no one from a worldly point of view." And this is true even of leaders.

So far as Paul is concerned, a leader's job is to glorify God. A leader doesn't have to be inspiring—in fact, Paul goes out of his way to point out that he was not a very "inspiring" person. A leader doesn't have to be "successful"—Paul's life was a series of disasters. A leader doesn't even have to be popular—Paul has nothing but scorn for the "super-apostles" with their eager little bands of spiritual groupies.

No, the true leader models the life of Jesus. That's why Paul can say that he is a leader . . . and that's the kind of leadership that was needed by the church in Corinth.

GoodWords _____

- **Achaia:** The Roman province encompassing southern Greece.

- **Amen:** A Hebrew word, literally meaning "so be it."

- **Apostle:** Literally, "the one sent." It was a title given ambassadors and business agents. Jesus used it of those who would carry the good news of His life and teachings to other people.

- **The brother:** The man who goes by this title in 2 Corinthians 8 is otherwise unknown. It appears as though the churches had appointed him as an independent auditor—someone who would see to it that the money contributed for the relief of poor church members in Jerusalem actually went to poor church members in Jerusalem.

- **Corinth:** Capital of the Roman province of Achaia and an important seaport in its own right.

- **"Leads us in triumph":** Roman generals celebrated a victory by leading their captives through the streets of the capital; the technical term for this parade was a "triumph." 2 Corinthians 2:14, in other words, points out the humble status of every believer.

- **Paul:** The Roman name of Saul—a Jew from the city of Tarsus who opposed Christianity, then spread it among the Gentiles! Most experts believe Paul wrote 2 Corinthians while in Macedonia, probably around A.D. 56 or so.

- **Macedonia:** The Roman province that took in northern Greece.

- **Third heaven:** The Jews believed heaven had seven levels, with paradise on the third.

- **Thorn in the flesh:** No one knows the nature of Paul's affliction; guesses range from eye trouble to epilepsy.

- **Titus:** A Gentile who had joined the church in Antioch as a result of Paul's preaching.

- **Troas:** A large coastal city located in what is now northwestern Turkey.

Money in the New Testament

It's almost impossible to figure out the exact value of any coin mentioned in the New Testament. Inflation was a problem back then (as well as today), and the standard of living was so different that it's difficult to compare values.

If you're willing to settle for "good enough," however, here's a list of common coins and their values:

- A *lepton* was a bronze coin that was smaller than a dime. (This was the "widow's mite" Jesus spoke about.)

- Two *leptons* made a Jewish *peruta*.

- Two *perutas* (or four *leptons*) made a Roman *quadrans* (also known as a *kodrantais*).

- Two *quadrans* made a Roman *assarion*—a bronze coin the size of a quarter. (Some Bibles translate *assarion* as "farthing," and others as "penny.")

- Roughly twenty *assarions* made one *denarius*—a silver coin about the size of a dime that was worth a day's wages for a working man. (Some Bibles translate *denarius* as "penny.")

- A Roman *denarius* had roughly the same value as the *drachma* of Tyre. (The thirty "pieces of silver" paid to Judas were probably *drachmas*.)

- Four *drachmas* made a *stater* (which was also known as a *tetradrachma*. Some Bibles translate *stater* as "piece of money," others as "shekel.")

- One hundred *drachmas* made a *mina* (which was actually a unit of weight. Some Bibles translate *mina* as "pound.")

- And sixty *minas* (or 6,000 *drachmas*) made a *talent*.

  Again, it's difficult to compare the value of money in New Testament times with that of today, but if you figure that today an unskilled worker makes about fifty dollars a day, that would mean that a *denarius* or a *drachma* was worth fifty dollars, a *lepton* was worth roughly thirty cents, and a *talent* was about $300,000.

Life in a Roman city

If you lived in a Roman city, you probably lived in an *insulae*—an apartment building with a central courtyard and possibly six stories high. The ground floor would be shops and the next floor "luxury apartments" (more or less). After that, the higher up you went, the cheaper the rent.

Most families lived in a single room. The "kitchen" was a charcoal grill; the "bathroom" a pot under the bed. (You were supposed to empty this pot in one of the public latrines that dotted the streets, but it was easier just to pitch the contents from the balcony.) Fires were common, disease even more so, and many buildings were so shoddily built that they simply collapsed.

For all that, life in a big city like Corinth or Rome had its advantages. The government subsidized food; wealthy patrons sponsored free tournaments, games, and theater performances. And then there were the baths—giant "health clubs" that gave people a chance to work out, clean up, and socialize.

Roman cities were crowded, messy, and dangerous; they were also a place where people came to get a new start in life. Not surprisingly, Christianity spread the most quickly in the cities; if you lived in the country, after all, you were almost guaranteed to be someone who liked life the way it was and felt no need for change.

FlashPoint: How many letters did Paul write to Corinth?

We know that Paul wrote at least four letters to the church in Corinth—his first (now lost), 1 Corinthians, a third (now lost), and 2 Corinthians.

But chapters 10–13 of 2 Corinthians are completely different in tone than the rest of the book—so different, as a matter of fact, that some experts think these chapters were a *fifth* letter to the church in Corinth, one that was added on to 2 Corinthians later so that it wouldn't get lost.

Others argue that Paul may have received some good news from Corinth while he was writing this letter; that's why it changes tone. Still others argue that Paul was using the "carrot and stick" approach; 2 Corinthians chapters 1–9 are the "stick," while 2 Corinthians chapters 10–12 are the "carrot."

Galatians
Jesus Brings Freedom!

6 CHAPTERS — READING TIME: 30 MINUTES

*"It is for freedom that Christ has set us free. Stand firm, then,
and do not let yourself be burdened again by a yoke of slavery" (Galatians 5:1).*

HighLights

- Paul's Meeting With Church Leaders (Galatians 1; 2).

- Our Freedom as Believers in Jesus (Galatians 5).

Why was it written?

To us, it's obvious that Judaism and Christianity are different religions. To be sure, the Hebrew Bible is the same as the Christian Old Testament. But Jews interpret the Hebrew Bible by means of the Talmud, and Christians by means of the New Testament. And for close to two thousand years, each religion has viewed the other as something apart.

But in the beginning, it was not so. Jesus was a Jew, after all, and so were His disciples. And the early Christians worshiped in the temple as observant Jews. They kept the Jewish festivals, such as Hanukkah and Tabernacles. And they were circumcised as Jews—at least the men were, anyway!

That's why so many early Christians were shocked by Paul's notion that you could be a Christian and still be a Gentile! The customs, the laws, the God-given commandments that defined what it meant to belong to God's people—how could Paul say that these things were no longer binding?

Obviously he couldn't—not if he were a *real* apostle!

So when Paul began a church among the Gentiles of Galatia, it's only natural that some Jewish Christians were concerned. And when they heard that Paul had moved on to other fields, it was only natural that those Jewish Christians would go to Galatia and try to straighten things out. And when the confused Galatian Christians protested that this was not what they'd been taught by Paul . . . well, it was only natural for those Jewish Christians to point out that Jesus could not have commissioned Paul as an apostle, since Paul hadn't even become a Christian until well after the death of Christ!

When Paul heard about this, of course, he was appalled. Unless he acted fast, he knew that both his message and his authority to preach that message would be undermined. And so he dictated a letter to try and straighten things out—the letter we know as Paul's Epistle to the church in Galatia.

What you'll learn in Galatians

The experts love to argue about Paul's message to the church in Galatia—both what it meant back then and what it means to us today. And to be honest, it's not always easy to understand Paul's argument about the roles played by law and grace in the believer's life.

At the very least, Galatians tells us that action must follow belief, rather than the other way around. No custom, no ritual, and no lifestyle can reconcile us to God— not by itself. No, everything must flow from faith or it is worse than useless.

Galatians also lays down the principle that there is no such thing as a "second-class Christian." Nothing we do can make us more "saved" than anybody else; nothing we do can increase our status with God. Jew or Gentile, male or female, young or old, Harvard alumnus or high-school dropout—we are all saved by grace.

GoodWords _____

- **Apostle:** Literally "one sent forth"—a title given ambassadors and business agents. Twelve of Christ's original followers were commissioned as apostles; Paul, Barnabas, Apollos, Silvanus, and Timothy are also described as such although they came along after Jesus had already returned to heaven.

- **Cephas:** An Aramaic word meaning "rock." The Greek equivalent is "petros," and this is the nickname—"Peter"—that Jesus gave Simon bar Jonah. Today we would call him "Peter Johnson."

- **Circumcision:** Removing the foreskin of the penis. God had told Abraham that this was to be the sign of an "everlasting covenant" (Genesis 17). Paul was so annoyed by the people who applied this text to Gentile converts—insisting that they should be circumcised—that he said they should go all the way and castrate themselves (Galatians 5:12).

- **Epistle:** No, an epistle is not the wife of an apostle, but a synonym for "letter."

- **Faith:** Trust or confidence in God.

- **Flesh:** The word can mean simply "the body," but Paul also uses it for the life lived apart from God or for anything that keeps us from following God.

- **Gentiles:** Non-Jews.

- **Grace:** God's saving love for us. Protestants generally define this as God's willingness to forgive us, Catholics as God's ability to change us.

- **Justification:** Literally, "acquittal." The act by which God declares us righteous.

- **Paul:** The Roman name of Saul—a Jew from the city of Tarsus who violently opposed Christianity, then began to spread it among the Gentiles!

- **Schoolmaster:** Also translated as "custodian" (RSV), "guardian" (JB), and "a strict tutor" (Phillips). The actual word is *paidagogos* or "a leader of children." It referred to a slave whose job it was to supervise (not teach!) young boys. He protected them from harm, disciplined them when they misbehaved, and made sure they got to school on time. Perhaps the best translation of this word is "nanny."

- **The Spirit:** God's presence in the believer's life.

Paul in Jerusalem

In Galatians 2:1-10, Paul describes a meeting with church leaders in Jerusalem. Most experts identify this meeting with the one described in Acts 15; some identify it with the "famine visit" described in Acts 11.

Paul's "illness."

Speculation abounds about the "illness" Paul mentions in Galatians 4:13, 14. Epilepsy? Weak eyes? Dysentery? Nobody knows.

FlashPoint: Galatia

Galatia was the name for two places in what is now Turkey—an ancient kingdom, and the much larger Roman province that followed it. Experts have been arguing for the last 200 years which of these two "Galatias" Paul meant.

If Paul was writing to people in the old *kingdom* of Galatia, then he wrote this letter during his third missionary journey—perhaps during the winter of A.D. 57/58. (This is known as the "North Galatia" or "territorial" hypothesis.)

But if Paul was writing to people in the *Roman province* of Galatia, then he may have written this letter around A.D. 49—or possibly even as early as A.D. 45. (This is known as the "South Galatia" or "provincial" hypothesis.) Good arguments exist for both sides.

FlashPoint: The law in Galatians

Exactly what did Paul mean by "the law"? Did he mean the Ten Commandments? The ritual laws of Judaism that concerned sacrifices and holidays? The first five books of the Bible? Everything contained in the covenant that God had made with His people? All of these were known at one time or another as "the law."

Or did Paul condemn *any* attempt to codify behavior? Was he saying that no believer should *ever* draw up a list of "do's" and "don't's"?

In a sense, every church is an experiment that is trying to discover the answer to that question. Some churches draw up long lists of rules; others leave everything up to the conscience of the believer. Perhaps it is time that we looked at the results of these experiments and decided which approach seems to glorify God the most.

Ephesians
The Church as the Body of Jesus

6 CHAPTERS — READING TIME: 25 MINUTES

"There is one body and one Spirit—just as you were called to one hope when you were called—one Lord, one faith, one baptism; one God and Father of all, who is over all and through all and in all" (Ephesians 4:4-6).

Highlights

- Why Follow Jesus? (Ephesians 1).

- Unity in the Body of Jesus (Ephesians 4).

- Put on the Whole Armor of God (Ephesians 6).

Why was it written?

A comedian once noted there are two kinds of people in this world: those who divide the world into two kinds of people and those who do not.

Be that as it may, it's amazing how often our decisions boil down to two choices: *Pepsi* or *Coca-Cola*. *Windows* or *Macintosh*. *Democrat* or *Republican*. And while other options may exist (such as root beer, *Linux,* and the Libertarian party), the third choice often trails far behind the first two.

That was the problem early Christians faced: They were the third choice. Neither Jew nor Gentile, Greek nor barbarian, they were the "third race" of the Roman Empire—and the empire wasn't happy about that. That's because the Romans divided religions into two groups: those that were legal and those that were not. As long as Christianity had been considered a part of Judaism, it had been "licit." But now it was in danger of becoming an outlaw religion.

What Christians needed to do, in other words, was settle the issue of who they were. They didn't fit into any of the usual categories; old ways of thinking didn't apply to them. But if they didn't forge a clear identity for themselves, then others would do it for them . . . and the results of *that* weren't worth thinking about.

Establish their own identity, or die. There was no third alternative.

What you'll learn in Ephesians

Like the pastoral epistles—1 and 2 Timothy as well as Titus—Ephesians is concerned with the church: what it's like and what it should do.

While the pastoral epistles take a "nuts and bolts" approach, however, Ephesians is more philosophical. Its author doesn't list the qualifications for a bishop; you won't learn from Ephesians how to run a welfare program for widows. In other words, Ephesians is not concerned with the *how* of a church so much as it's concerned with the *why*.

And that's important. For then as now, some saw church as a hindrance—a halfway house for spiritual misfits who didn't have the guts to make it on their own. Others saw the church as an arena—a place where only the gifted could perform. And still others saw it as a hothouse—a sheltered place where one withdrew to cultivate the spirit.

But Ephesians defines the church as the body of Christ. As such, it is important. It is essential. It is not an afterthought. Indeed, even before the world began, God had already made His plans for it. And as a part of this body, every believer has a role to play. God gave His spirit, Ephesians says, not to help us excel as individuals, but "to prepare God's people for works of service so that the body of Christ may be built up" (Ephesians 4:12).

Finally, everything we do as a part of Christ's body affects the rest of the body. That's why our conduct is important—we're a part of something bigger than ourselves. The gospel is not just the good news that God *saves* people; it is the good news that God is *creating* a new people—a people that He calls His church.

GoodWords

- **Apostle:** Literally, "the one sent"—a name given ambassadors and business agents.

- **Church:** Literally, "those called out"—a name given any small group or caucus.

- **The dividing wall of hostility:** Most experts agree this refers to the wall in the Jerusalem temple that divided the court of the Gentiles from that of the Jews. In other words, God has removed everything that used to separate Jews from Gentiles.

- **Ephesus:** Located on the main road from Rome to the eastern part of the empire, Ephesus was an important center for government, banking, and religion. Paul was nearly lynched in Ephesus by silversmiths whose income depended on the temple of Artemis.

- **Epistle:** A letter.

- **Faith:** Trust or confidence in God.

- **Fullness:** You wouldn't think it to look at it, but this is actually a very significant theological word. It means "to fill completely"—just as water fills a bottle or smoke fills a room. Gnostics would later use this word to describe God's glory; Paul uses it to describe the relationship of Jesus to the Father. "Everything that you have in God," Paul says in effect, "you have in Jesus as well."

- **Grace:** God's saving love for us. Protestants generally define this as an attitude of God; Catholics as the power of God.

- **Law:** Probably refers to the Torah—the first five books of the Bible—and by extension, to the whole Hebrew Bible or Old Testament.

- **Mystery:** Something once hidden that has now been revealed to us.

- **Paul:** The Roman name of Saul—a Jew from the city of Tarsus who violently opposed Christianity, then began to spread it among the Gentiles!

- **Prince of the power of the air:** The devil or Satan.

- **Principalities and powers:** While this phrase may refer to human political rulers, it's more likely that it refers to the demonic forces that can make this world such a miserable place to live. Whatever they are, Ephesians says that we are more than a match for them.

- **Tychicus:** A frequent companion of Paul. He also delivered Paul's letter to the church in Colossae.

How did Paul deliver his letters?

The Roman *cursus publicus* worked like the Pony Express, with relay teams that could carry a message as far as 170 miles in a twenty-four-hour period. But it carried only official government documents; private citizens were on their own. Most often, they found a trader or ship's captain who was traveling to the city needed, and paid him to carry the letter.

Jewish leaders in Jerusalem, however, sent out teams of messengers on a regular basis; these made the circuit of Jewish communities abroad—carrying news and new ideas *out* to the people and money *back* to Jerusalem. In time, Christian leaders may have adopted a similar system.

Roman soldiers

The Roman army was an infantry force of 150,000 men, divided into thirty legions. Most legions served on the frontiers; only the emperor's bodyguard (known as "the praetorian guard") was allowed in Rome. Since the empire itself had over 50 million people, that made the army a distant reality for most citizens.

Life in the army was harsh for the common soldier. Marriage was forbidden. Pay was low—300 denarii a year—and didn't include food, clothing, or weapons. Retirement came only after twenty years of service . . . and roughly half of those in the army didn't survive that long.

Those who did survive, however, got a retirement bonus of 4,000 denarii—and often a farm as well. Foreigners who had served as "auxiliaries" (usually cavalry or archers) didn't earn as much, but did become Roman citizens upon their retirement.

FlashPoint: Did Paul write this letter?

The language and theology of Ephesians is so different from the other letters of Paul, that many liberal scholars believe he didn't write it. Instead, they believe it may have been written by one of his disciples late in the first century A.D.

But conservative scholars point out that a difference in circumstances may lead to a difference in styles. *Studies in Medieval and Renaissance Literature,* for instance, is a very different book than *The Chronicles of Narnia,* yet both were written by C. S. Lewis.

FlashPoint: Did Paul write this letter to the Ephesians?

Some early manuscripts lack Paul's greetings "to the saints in Ephesus"—a fact that has stirred speculation about who was supposed to receive this letter. For instance, could it have been a "general epistle" intended for all churches? Or was it intended for another church?

In Colossians 4:16, Paul implies that he wrote a letter to the church in Laodecia—a town that was roughly one hundred miles to the east of Ephesus. And Marcion (who died around A.D. 160) said that the letter we know as Ephesians is really Paul's missing letter to Laodicea!

Marcion's reputation as a heretic, however, didn't do anything to advance his thesis. All we can say for a fact is that nobody really knows what happened to the letter to the Laodiceans—or who was supposed to get the letter we know as Ephesians.

Philippians
Jesus Is Enough

"I can do everything through him who gives me strength" (Philippians 4:13).

Highlight

• An Early Hymn About the Death of Jesus (Philippians 2).

Why was it written?

Both Paul and the believers in Philippi had been through a lot together. The Philippians were the first converts Paul had made in Europe. And as he noted in 2 Corinthians 11:9, they were the ones who had been the most faithful in supporting his ministry and supplying his needs.

But now Paul was in prison—and if this wasn't bad enough, the believers in Philippi had heard that some of Paul's enemies were using this unfortunate fact to discredit him.

"Look at the results of Paul's message," some of his enemies were saying. "Surely God can't be blessing someone who has ended up in prison!"

This kind of talk upset the Philippians, so Paul wrote to them. The result is the warmest and most affectionate letter in all the New Testament—a letter that assured the Philippians that Paul had not lost hope, that God had not abandoned him, and that they should not be discouraged.

What you'll learn in Philippians

Most religions promise that they can help you get what you want. Need a new car? Say a few prayers. Want to lose ten pounds? Read your Bible. Got your heart set on becoming rich, famous, and powerful? Join our church—we'll put you on the fast track to success.

But things didn't work out that way for Paul. Once there had been a time he had had it all—status, security, and the kind of self-esteem that comes from knowing that you belong to an elite group. But then he had become a Christian. And in doing so, he had lost everything—even his personal freedom.

Did this bother Paul? No, for he had discovered that happiness depends on knowing God. If you don't know Him, then it doesn't matter what else you might have. But if you do know Him, then it doesn't matter what else you may lack. In other words, even if the only thing you have is God, that's more than enough to make you happy.

GoodWords _____

- **Circumcision:** Required of all Jewish men and males who converted to Judaism—and nearly required of all male converts to Christianity.

- **Emperor's household:** This phrase probably includes servants, slaves, and officials as well as relatives . . . but there's good evidence that this phrase may actually have included the emperor's relatives as well.

- **Even death on a cross:** Crucifixion was a slow, agonizing death, and those who died this way were scorned even by decent criminals. Whether our culture has anything equivalent to the abject humiliation of Christ's death is an open question. The electric chair? Lethal injection? "Shot while trying to escape"? None of these combine the cruelty of Christ's death with its nature as a public spectacle—not to mention the shame attached to it.

- **Epaphroditus:** A Philippian Christian who served Paul as a messenger. (Don't confuse him with Epaphras, a native of Asia Minor.)

- **Gospel:** Literally, "good news."

- **Imperial guard (also known as "the Praetorian Guard"):** An elite unit of troops used for guarding the emperor.

- **Libation:** The Greeks would not drink from a cup before they had poured a small amount of its contents on the floor as an offering to their gods. This sacrifice was known as a "libation." In speaking of his own life as a libation, Paul was drawing on the cultural heritage of his readers—not that of Judaism.

- **Paul:** Once an opponent of Christianity, he became the chief reason it spread beyond Judaism. Experts agree that Paul wrote Philippians while in prison; most point to his stay in Rome between A.D. 60 and A.D. 62 as the likely place and time. Others suggest it could have been written in A.D. 56 when Paul was imprisoned in Caesarea.

- **Saints:** Literally, "holy ones"—a name given by Paul to all Christians.

- **Slave:** Roman slaves were the property of the people who owned them and subject to their will. Why Paul would say that Christians are "the slaves of Christ" is worth pondering.

- **Timothy:** A young man who had become Paul's disciple in Asia Minor (now Turkey). Paul spoke of him as "my dear son" (2 Timothy 1:2) and "my true son in the faith" (1 Timothy 1:2), but we also get the impression in Paul's letters to him that he wished Timothy would develop a backbone.

 ## Philippi

Though located in northern Greece, Philippi had more of a Roman flavor, thanks to the large number of Roman soldiers who had retired there, as well as to its location on the road that connected Italy with the eastern empire. Paul founded the Philippian church around A.D. 50 or so.

 ## Other sources

If you would like to read about Paul's experience in Philippi, try Acts 16. And if you would like to read some of the other letters Paul wrote in prison, try Colossians, Ephesians, and Philemon.

 ## Hymns

Both Ephesians 5:19 and Colossians 3:16 imply that music was a regular part of Christian worship. We don't know what this music *sounded* like . . . but we have a pretty good idea what it *looked* like. Most experts agree that Philippians 2:5-11 is an early Christian hymn—though the question of whether it was composed by Paul or merely quoted by him is a matter of debate.

Colossians
Trust Jesus Alone

"God was pleased to have all his fullness dwell in [Jesus], and through him to reconcile all things, whether things on earth or in heaven, by making peace through his blood, shed on the cross" (Colossians 1:19, 20).

HighLights

- Jesus Is Supreme (Colossians 1).

- Rules for Living (Colossians 3).

Why was it written?

Some people like buffets. They like going through line, picking and choosing, trying a dab of this and a spoonful of that. Granted, the result may be an unholy mess of mashed potatoes and lime-green Jell-O with a ladle of gravy on top. But they don't mind. They like to try a little bit of everything.

Likewise, some people approach religion as though it were a buffet. The people of Colossae, for instance, used this approach of "pick and choose." They took a dab of Jewish mysticism, added a spoonful of the local fertility cults, and covered it all with a generous serving of Greek philosophy. And when Christianity came along, they just added it to their plates as well. In other words, Jesus became a part of their beliefs, perhaps the most important part, but still only a part.

Drawing from many sources like this to make your own religion is called *syncretism*—and it's no secret that many people do this today. As a result, Jesus becomes nothing more than one of the many spiritual guides that are out there.

But Paul saw Jesus as something special, something unique, something that had never happened before and would never happen again. And to safeguard the extraordinary nature of Jesus, Paul wrote to the church in Colossae.

What you'll learn in Colossians

Jesus was not just another good man. He was not just another Moses or Confucius; He was not just another "great soul" who shared enlightenment with His followers.

No, Colossians insists that Jesus was actually God in the flesh. His was (and is) the ultimate authority: Nothing came before Him. Nothing comes after Him. Nothing else even comes close.

And the fact that Colossians says this proves that Christians have always believed this; it proves that the divinity of Jesus wasn't something the church dreamed up in later years to enhance its own authority. No, as early as A.D. 60 or so, Paul could write that in Jesus "God was pleased to have all his fullness dwell" (Colossians 1:19).

We may accept Jesus. We may reject Him. But we have to take Him seriously.

GoodWords _____

- **Barbarian:** Literally, anyone who didn't speak Greek. Since the Greeks believed anyone who didn't speak their language was a rude, uncultured slob, the word acquired the meaning it has today.

- **Circumcision:** Removal of the foreskin of the penis. Required of all men who joined Judaism, many found it one of the chief barriers to conversion. Paul's point is that Jesus has removed anything and everything that might have separated us from God.

- **Do not handle. Do not taste. Do not touch:** The Colossians seem to have viewed religion in much the same way we might a dress code—you did things, not because they were morally right, but because they were ritually correct. Paul wasn't saying that there are not things people should avoid (such as marijuana or pornography), but simply that moral concern rather than ritual purity should guide our choices.

- **Elemental spirits:** While the exact nature of Colossian beliefs is unclear, most experts suspect the Colossians saw the spiritual journey as climbing a ladder, with angels and "elemental spirits" in charge of each rung. Jesus could start you on this ladder, in other words, but you also needed to make friends with these "principalities and powers," or you wouldn't make it to the top.

- **Epaphras:** Founder of the church in Colossae and a follower of Paul.

- **Firstborn:** The word doesn't mean "first in time" so much as it means "first in glory." When Paul wrote that "Jesus is the firstborn of creation," in other words, he wasn't saying that Jesus was the first being to be created. He was saying that Jesus is more important than anything in creation.

- **Fullness:** A technical word used by Greek philosophers to mean all of God's attributes, manifestations, and characteristics, with nothing in reserve.

- **Image:** An exact likeness. Jesus is truly God, not just a symbol of Him.

- **Laodicea:** A prosperous city near Colossae. The letter to which Paul refers in Colossians 4:16 has never been found . . . not unless it is actually the letter we know as "Ephesians."

- **Mystery:** In the Bible, this word doesn't mean something puzzling or hard to understand; it means something once hidden that has now been revealed.

- **Paul:** A devout Jew who switched from persecuting Christians to proclaiming their message. Christianity began as a small, Jewish sect. And since many early Christians enjoyed belonging to a small, Jewish sect, they didn't like the fact that Paul preached to the Gentiles.

- **Reconcile:** To restore a broken relationship. Jesus did not reconcile God to us; He reconciled us to God.

- **Sabbaths:** Myself, I don't think Colossians 2:16 refers to the *weekly* Sabbath, but to the *annual* sabbaths of Passover, Pentecost, and Tabernacles.

- **Saints:** Literally "holy ones"—a word Paul uses for all Christians, not just a select few.

- **Scythian:** A nomadic people from what is now southern Russia. Since they lived on the fringes of the then-known world, they were regarded as the barbarian's barbarian.

- **Timothy:** Paul's "beloved and faithful" traveling companion. Acts 16 says Timothy was originally from Lystra in what is now Turkey; he had a Jewish mother and Gentile father.

The written code

When the Romans crucified someone, they nailed a sign to the cross—a sign that listed the charges against that person. Colossians 2:14 does not mean that God's law has been revoked, in other words. It means that the record of our sins was nailed to the cross of Jesus; He has paid the penalty for our crimes.

FlashPoint: Wives, be subject

If you've become a Christian, does this mean that you are no longer married?

Some early Christians said yes! In fact, they said that believers were not bound by *any* of the obligations they had made before conversion. Children no longer had to obey their parents, in other words. Slaves no longer had to obey their masters. And debtors no longer had to pay their bills.

Obviously, this kind of attitude didn't do anything for the church's reputation. Given the Roman fear of disorder, as a matter of fact, this attitude could quickly prove fatal!

Paul's concern, in other words, is not the subjugation of women, but that Christians be known as honorable, decent, and orderly people—people who keep the promises they make. (And women, if your husbands ever quote Colossians 3:18 to you, then go ahead and quote Colossians 3:19 right back at them!)

Colossae

Famous for its red cloth, Colossae was a city in Asia Minor (present-day Turkey) about 110 miles to the east of Ephesus and roughly ten miles from Laodecia. Conservatives believe that Paul wrote his letter to Colossae while he was imprisoned in Rome, sometime around A.D. 58 to 60; some experts argue that he might have written it earlier from Caesarea.

1 Thessalonians

Keeping Hope Alive

"For God did not appoint us to suffer wrath, but to receive salvation through our Lord Jesus Christ. He died for us so that, whether we are awake or asleep, we may live together with him" (1 Thessalonians 5:9, 10).

HighLight

- What Will Happen When Jesus Returns? (1 Thessalonians 4; 5).

Why was it written?

Paul was able to spend only three weeks in Thessalonica before a riot drove him away (see Acts 17). In those few weeks, he had established a church.

Safe in Athens, Paul sent Timothy to see how the Thessalonian church was doing in his absence. When Timothy rejoined Paul in Corinth, he brought with him both good news and bad news. The good news was that there were still believers in Thessalonica. The bad news was that they were discouraged. Persecution was an ongoing problem. Then too, some believers had died—and strange as it may sound to us, some thought that those who had died would not be in God's kingdom!

Obviously, the church in Thessalonica needed cheering up. But Paul was busy establishing a church in Corinth, and it wouldn't be fair to the Corinthians if Paul returned to Thessalonica just then.

So sometime around A.D. 50 or 51, Paul wrote the letter we know as
1 Thessalonians. In doing so, he began the New Testament. That's because
1 Thessalonians is not just the first of Paul's letters to be written; it is also the
very first book of the New Testament to have been written.

What you'll learn in 1 Thessalonians

We often forget that the four Gospels were written *after* Paul's letters—some of
them perhaps as much as thirty years later. In other words, if you want to know
what it was like to be a Christian in the first few decades after Christ's life on
earth, your best guide is not the Gospels. It's the letters of Paul.

Right from the beginning, for instance, Christians worried about complex issues
such as the relationship between faith and works—and the operative word here is
"worried." In spite of everything that Jesus had done, after all, everyday life
seemed to go on much as before. Faith was beginning to flicker. Love was
beginning to die.

That's why Paul talks so much in this letter about hope—the hope that we have
in Jesus. As believers, after all, we have the hope of forgiveness. We have the hope
of holiness—the hope of a life that is fully dedicated to God. Best of all, we have
the hope that Christ will come again. That He will re-unite us with our loved
ones. And that He will make it possible for us to live with Him forever.

GoodWords

- **Achaia:** The Roman province that took in all of what is now southern Greece.
- **Archangel:** Literally, "the first [or chief] messenger." The Old Testament refers to "the angel of the Lord" as a being who announces or prepares the way for God's special acts. In some passages, it's difficult to distinguish the angel of the Lord from God Himself! By Christ's time, the archangel had been given the name of Michael (see Jude 9) and was said to be the special defender of God's people (see Revelation 12:7).
- **Athens:** This Greek city was the Harvard or Yale of the Roman Empire, with all the prestige, intellectual clout, and stuffiness that implies.
- **Day of the Lord:** Judgment Day, when God finally sees to it that the bad guys get what they deserve and everyone else gets something better than they deserve.
- **Gentiles:** Anyone who is not Jewish.

- **Gospel:** Literally, "the good news."

- **Macedonia:** The Roman province that took in what is now northern Greece.

- **Paul:** A devout Jew who first persecuted Christians and then preached the message of Christ to the Gentiles.

- **Prophets:** Old Testament prophets rarely died in bed. By Paul's day, the fate of men such as Isaiah and Jeremiah was a common symbol of human stubbornness and perversity.

- **Silvanus:** The Latin form of "Silas" (which is the Greek form of "Saul"). A Roman citizen, prophet, and church leader, he accompanied Paul during Paul's second missionary voyage. Not only is he mentioned in Paul's letters to the church in Thessalonica, but also in Acts, 2 Corinthians, and 1 Peter.

- **Timothy:** Paul's half-Jewish traveling companion. He was a native of Lystra, a town in what is now central Turkey.

- **Wrath:** What the bad guys call it when God gets involved in history. (The people on God's side call it "grace.")

Greet each other with a holy kiss

People in Paul's day were a lot more "touchy-feely" than we are today, and a kiss—even same-sex kissing—played much the same role that a handshake does today. Every now and then, a church tries to revive this custom; the effort inevitably results in lawsuits, broken marriages, and bad feelings all around.

Thessalonica

Known today as Salonika, Thessalonica was the capital of the Roman province of Macedonia and a prosperous seaport in its own right. Paul first visited it on his second missionary voyage and may have done so again on his third missionary voyage—perhaps around A.D. 57. You can read about Paul's visit to Thessalonica in Acts 17.

FlashPoint: With whom does Jesus come?

In 1 Thessalonians 3:13, Paul speaks of the day when "our Lord Jesus comes with his holy ones." Some use this as proof that the righteous dead are now with Christ and will return to us with Him at His second coming. But 1 Thessalonians 4:13-16 speaks of the dead as "asleep" and makes it clear that they will remain "asleep" in the grave until they are raised to life at Christ's return.

The solution to this problem comes when we remember that "holy ones" can refer to God's angels as well as His people. Jesus does not return with the righteous dead, in other words, but in the company of angels.

2 Thessalonians

Clearing Up the Meaning of Christ's Return

3 CHAPTERS — READING TIME: 10 MINUTES

"We ask you, brothers, not to become easily unsettled or alarmed by some prophecy, report or letter supposed to have come from us, saying that the day of the Lord has already come"
(2 Thessalonians 2:1, 2).

HighLight

- The Man of Lawlessness Must Come First (2 Thessalonians 2).

Why was it written?

It's always difficult to explain yourself—you have to tell people what you *didn't* say as well as what you *did*. What's more, you have to do this without sounding defensive, or confusing the issue even more!

That's the problem Paul faced back in A.D. 51 or so. He had tried to cheer up the church in Thessalonica by sending it a letter—the letter we know as 1 Thessalonians. And in this letter, he had told church members not to get discouraged and give up, because Jesus was coming soon.

The Thessalonians believed Paul. After all, he had warned them that things would get tough just before Jesus came—and sure enough, things were getting tough. That's why they had concluded that Paul was right and that Jesus must be coming soon!

283

But the believers in Thessalonica didn't stop there. If Jesus was coming soon, some saw this as reason enough to quit work. Others used the shortness of time as an excuse to avoid family obligations. And some may even have lorded it over their neighbors—telling them how sorry they would be for the way they had acted when Judgment Day finally arrived.

Paul knew this wasn't healthy; he also knew that the people who did these things would claim his words as justification for their actions. So he carefully wrote another letter—a letter meant to correct any misunderstandings that might have been caused by his first letter to them. Written just a few months after the letter we call 1 Thessalonians, this second letter (surprise!) is known as 2 Thessalonians.

What you'll learn in 2 Thessalonians

If nothing else, 2 Thessalonians teaches the importance of reading widely in Scripture. Most of us have one or two favorite texts—John 3:16, perhaps, or Romans 6:23. And while there's nothing wrong with that, we can run into trouble if we act as though these texts are the only ones that matter. But just as 1 Thessalonians needs 2 Thessalonians to explain and apply its message, so any verse or book of the Bible benefits when it's examined in light of the whole.

You can't hope to understand the real meaning of John 3:16, in other words, unless you've also read the books of Genesis and Deuteronomy. You can't make sense of Romans 6:23 without the help of James.

Then too, 2 Thessalonians warns us not to confuse love with sentiment. Sentiment makes you do something for someone so *you* will feel better; love makes you act in the best interests of the other person. Sentiment feeds the hungry without regard for *why* they're hungry; love may mean letting them take responsibility for their own actions. If they won't work, in other words, love may demand that they not eat as well. (That's not the same as saying someone who can't find work shouldn't eat. Or that people whose work doesn't pay enough shouldn't eat. Or that the children of those who won't work should go hungry. We need to base our actions on more than one or two isolated texts, remember?)

Finally, 2 Thessalonians tells us what it takes to be ready for the return of Jesus. It's not enough to *wait* for Jesus or even to *hope* that He might return. No, we need to use the time we have to do the work He has given us to do. When we do that, then we're ready for Jesus to come again.

GoodWords

- **Angel:** Literally, a "messenger"—a term that often refers to an intelligent, nonhuman creature.

- **The coming of our Lord Jesus Christ:** The word for "coming" is *parousia;* it refers to the public arrival of royalty on an important occasion.

- **Day of the Lord:** Judgment Day—the day when God finally sees to it that bad guys get what they deserve and everyone else gets something better than they deserve.

- **Judgment:** Forget Judge Judy. Think Deborah, Gideon, or Samson. When God judges, in other words, He doesn't just pronounce guilt or innocence. He goes to work and sets things right.

- **The lawless one (aka "the man of sin"):** Most experts agree that this refers to the antichrist. And whatever else that "antichrist" might be, Paul says that it is in real trouble when Jesus returns.

- **The one who is now restraining him:** Most likely a reference to the Holy Spirit.

- **Paul:** The devout Jew who took Christianity to the Gentiles.

- **Saints:** Literally, "holy ones."

- **Sanctification:** To make holy—and "holy," remember, means "belonging to God." Sometimes the Bible describes sanctification as a one-time act, sometimes as a lifelong process. The first is for people whose besetting sin is fear; the second is for those whose main problem is laziness.

- **Satan (or "the evil one"):** The chief of those angels (see above) who thought they could run things better than God.

- **Silvanus:** The Latin form of "Silas" (which is the Greek form of "Saul"). A Roman citizen, prophet, and church leader, Silvanus accompanied Paul during his second missionary voyage. He is mentioned in Acts, 2 Corinthians, and 1 Peter as well as in Paul's letters to the church in Thessalonica.

- **Steadfastness:** A word originally used to describe a city defending itself against a siege. It took on the meaning of "striving by any means to retain what is already yours."

- **Thessalonica:** Capital of Roman Macedonia and an important seaport in its own right. Paul visited it during his second missionary voyage and may have done so again in A.D. 57 or so.

- **Timothy:** The half-Jewish traveling companion of Paul. He was originally from Lystra (in what is now central Turkey).

Patronage

Then as now, the rich were always looking for a way to gain status and prestige—and one way they did this in Roman times was to accumulate "clients." The rich provided their clients with the food and money needed to survive; in return, the clients provided the "retinue" that every important person must have when he went out in public.

When rich people became Christians, they often tried to treat the church as they would their own retinue—they would supply the cash, and the church would do what they said. Not surprisingly, some Christians encouraged this attitude; they were happy to be the "clients" of these wealthy members, if that's what it took to be fed.

Paul dealt with this situation in two ways. To the wealthy, he wrote that they should give cheerfully, without expecting anything in return. And to everyone else, he wrote that they should be self-sufficient and not rely upon the generosity of others.

FlashPoint: Tradition

In 2 Thessalonians 2:15, Paul calls on believers to "hold to the teachings we passed on to you, whether by word of mouth or by letter." Some use this verse as proof that the Bible and tradition are both equally important; they argue tradition is nothing more than "teachings" passed on "by word of mouth" in the church. But conservative Protestants believe that such "teachings" should be confirmed by the Bible; any other method is apt to confuse speculation and wishful thinking with the truth.

FlashPoint: Everlasting destruction

2 Thessalonians 1:9 promises "everlasting destruction" to those "who do not know God and do not obey the gospel of our Lord Jesus." Some use this phrase as proof that the wicked will suffer eternal torment. Then again, if I blow a bridge to smithereens, it has suffered "everlasting destruction." It's gone, in other words, and it's not coming back—but that doesn't mean that the explosion lasts forever. In much the same way, this phrase doesn't mean that the wicked writhe forever in the fires of hell. All it says is that when they're gone, they're gone.

1 Timothy

Faith for the Long Haul

"I am writing you these instructions so that, if I am delayed, you will know how people ought to conduct themselves in God's household, which is the church of the living God, the pillar and foundation of the truth" (1 Timothy 3:14, 15).

Highlight

- Qualifications of Church Leaders (1 Timothy 3).

Why was it written?

Christianity had been around for a number of years by the time this book was written. As a result, the church was more structured then it had been in its early days. A new generation of leaders had taken over—leaders who hadn't met Jesus personally, but knew of Him only secondhand. And an organized "protest movement" had started *within* Christianity—a movement with its own agenda for the church.

Nobody today is entirely sure what this "protest movement" was about. It may have been an early form of *gnosticism*—a sort of "New Age" approach to Christianity. It may have been a new kind of "Jewish Christianity" that emphasized both racial and ritual purity. Or it may have been something else entirely—but whatever it was, it was a threat.

Enthusiasm was no longer enough, in other words. Good intentions were no longer enough. Now those early Christians needed help if their faith was going to survive over the long haul.

And that's why 1 Timothy was written.

288

What you'll learn in 1 Timothy

One of the great myths of our day is that religion should be spontaneous—something that "just happens" without any kind of planning or organization. In fact, there are some who say that *any* attempt to come up with an organized system or a long-term strategy will drive away God's Spirit.

But in 1 Timothy, we learn that faith needs structure in order to survive. After all, what seems "spontaneous" and "natural" to one person, may seem "arbitrary" and "capricious" to another. That's why much of this book resembles an employee manual—right down to its descriptions of employee qualifications, benefit packages, and the like. All this is meant to give believers some idea of how to run a church.

To be sure, you can't replace the Holy Spirit with a policy statement. But 1 Timothy reminds us that creativity can be expressed through order, that structure need not be a barrier to faith, and that God is just as able to lead through the long-term strategic planning of a group as He is through the sudden inspiration of an individual.

GoodWords

- **Alexander:** Ironically, his name means "defender of men."
- **Bishop:** Spiritual leaders in the early church could be called "bishops" (from the Greek word *episkopoi,* meaning "overseers") or "elders" *(presbuteroi).* The titles are synonymous—something that is not true of Episcopalians and Presbyterians.
- **Deacon:** Literally, a "servant." Under the direction of a bishop or council of bishops, a deacon cares for the physical needs of church members.
- **Delivered to Satan:** To be put out of the church.
- **Ephesus:** Located on the main road from Rome to Asia Minor, Ephesus was a center for both banking and religion. Paul preached there and was almost lynched by Ephesian silversmiths whose income depended on the temple of Artemis.
- **Genealogies:** Some think this refers to the ancestor lists kept by some Jews to prove racial purity; others say it refers to gnostic speculations about angelic hierarchies or the "essences" that created our world.
- **Hymenaeus:** Put out of the church because he denied a future resurrection. Hymenaeus was still in trouble when 2 Timothy 2:17 was written.

- **Law:** Probably refers to the Torah—the first five books of the Bible—and by extension, to the entire Old Testament.

- **Macedonia:** A region that takes in both northern Greece as well as what used to be southern Yugoslavia. Paul visited it frequently. Macedonian believers financed Paul's ministry and helped support poor Christians in Jerusalem.

- **Myths:** Legends and stories—all meant to teach some spiritual lesson. These were an important part of both Judaism and gnosticism.

- **Ransom:** The price paid to free slaves, prisoners, or the victims of kidnapping.

- **Widows:** Apparently widows who had no families to support them (and no hope of getting married again) were supported by the church.

 ## Timothy

Timothy's father was a Gentile. But even though Timothy had not been circumcised, his mother Eunice and his grandmother Lois had raised him as a Jew. Sometime around A.D. 49, Paul met Timothy in Lystra (a city in what is now Turkey), converted him to Christianity, and had him circumcised. Timothy then accompanied Paul on his second missionary journey through northern Greece (A.D. 49-52). Four or five years later Paul sent Timothy to Corinth from Ephesus; his job was to settle a church fight there. Apparently, Timothy failed to do this—and together with the general tone of 1 and 2 Timothy, this has given him a reputation for being both timid and sickly.

FlashPoint: What does it mean to be "the husband of one wife"?

There's no agreement on the meaning of this phrase. On the face of it, it would seem to be nothing more than a ban on bigamous bishops—but bigamy was extremely rare in the Roman Empire at this time, so it's curious that 1 Timothy should raise it as an issue. Others believe that it prohibits the remarriage of a church leader in the case of his wife's death. Still others say the phrase is a figure of speech that means nothing more than that the bishop should be faithful to his marriage vows.

FlashPoint: Who wrote the pastoral epistles?

Together, 1 Timothy, 2 Timothy, and Titus are known as the *pastoral epistles*—and everyone agrees that they differ greatly in language and subject from books like Galatians or Romans. And while Acts closes with Paul awaiting trial in Rome, the author of 1 Timothy is obviously a free man.

That's why liberals agree that Paul did not write 1 Timothy. Instead, they say that another church leader wrote it in his name, sometime late in the first century A.D. This leader may have been a student of Paul or he may have used fragments of a real letter from Paul, but he definitely was not Paul.

Then again, conservatives believe that Paul may have sketched the broad themes of his letter to a secretary, but left it up to him to come up with the exact words. And the muddle over Paul's imprisonment is solved if we assume he was released from Roman captivity, traveled to Spain, and then returned to Rome . . . only to be re-arrested and executed in A.D. 67 or so. If this is the case, then Paul wrote 1 Timothy sometime between A.D. 63 and A.D. 66.

2 Timothy

Handbook for Survival

"Do your best to present yourself to God as one approved, a workman who does not need to be ashamed and who correctly handles the word of truth" (2 Timothy 2:15).

HighLight

- Paul's Last Words (2 Timothy 4).

Why was it written?

Like 1 Timothy and Titus, 2 Timothy is a handbook for pastors. As such, the three letters all deal with problems that were common to churches toward the end of the first century A.D.

Most of these problems could be summed up as stuff that was coming in the front door, and stuff that was going out the back door. Coming in the front door, for instance, were new church members . . . some of whom had some pretty far-out ideas. They would talk of "secret knowledge" that could be known only by special believers—talk that would later crystallize into gnosticism. Then too, many Jewish Christians retained their interest in racial and ritual purity. Clearly, a new pastor would have his hands full with church members like this!

What made a pastor's job more difficult, however, was the way many long-time church members were disappearing out the back door. Some drifted out, their enthusiasm gone. Others were lured out by nonbelieving friends or business partners. Still others were driven out by persecution. As a result, the church grew more and more unstable.

"Out with the old and in with the new" makes a fine slogan for New Year's Day. But as 2 Timothy proves, it's a terrible strategy for a church.

What you'll learn in 2 Timothy

We value words like "new" and "improved"—a fact that may make it difficult for us to appreciate the message of 2 Timothy. This is not a book that encourages innovation, reform, or even much in the way of curiosity. Rather, the emphasis in this book is on continuity, stability, and persistence. It tells us to "hold fast" to established authorities—the Bible, church leadership, and traditional beliefs.

Some may find this approach to religion stifling—and it's true that 2 Timothy is not a book that every church might need.

But there are times when a church needs to "hunker down" if it's going to survive—just as there are times when we need to be reminded that too much change can be dangerous and that "boundaries" and "landmarks" are important. And it's at times such as these that 2 Timothy is valuable.

GoodWords

- **Alexander the Coppersmith:** This may be the lapsed Christian mentioned in 1 Timothy 1:19.
- **Antioch:** With a population somewhere between 250,000 and 800,000, this city, known as the "Queen of the East," was second only to Rome and Alexandria in the Roman Empire. When believers in Jerusalem heard that Christians were meeting in Antioch, they sent Barnabas. Barnabas then sent for a new convert to assist him . . . a convert whose name was Paul.
- **Asia:** The Roman province of Asia Minor, now known as Turkey.
- **Claudia:** A Roman Christian, possibly the mother of Linus.
- **Crescens:** Tradition has it he was a bishop in Galatia.
- **Dalmatia:** A Roman province northwest of Greece.
- **Demas:** Once an associate of Paul. He is also mentioned in Colossians 4:14 and Philemon 24.
- **Ephesus:** Located on the main road from Rome to Asia Minor, Ephesus was a center for government, banking, and religion. Paul was almost lynched there by silversmiths whose income depended on the temple of Artemis that was located in Ephesus.
- **Erastus:** An associate of Paul. He had gone ahead of Paul to Macedonia and stayed behind when Paul left Corinth. He may be the Corinthian commissioner of streets and public buildings who is mentioned in Romans 16:23.

- **Galatia:** A Roman province in what is now central Turkey. It also included the old kingdom of Galatia. Experts like to argue just exactly which "Galatia" was meant.

- **Jannes and Jambres:** Tradition gives these names to the Egyptian magicians who opposed Moses.

- **Linus:** Possibly one of Rome's first bishops, but no relation to the character in *Peanuts*.

- **Luke:** A Gentile physician who may have been converted by Paul in Antioch. He accompanied Paul on his second and third missionary journeys and wrote both the book of Acts and the Gospel of Luke.

- **Mark:** Also known as "John Mark." He was the cousin of Barnabas and author of the Gospel that bears his name. Mark went with Paul and Barnabas on their first missionary journey, but abandoned them in Asia Minor. Paul broke with Barnabas rather than take Mark on another trip, but Colossians 4:10 and Philemon 24 indicate that Mark and Paul were later reconciled.

- **Paul:** The Jewish Christian who did more than anyone else to make Christianity a Gentile religion. Paul wrote 2 Timothy probably around A.D. 66, while in prison in Rome.

- **Prisca and Aquila:** A married couple who worked with Paul as tentmakers (or leatherworkers) in Corinth. They accompanied Paul to Ephesus and converted Apollos to Christianity there. Though the Romans usually named the husband first, Aquila's name usually follows that of his wife. This suggests that Prisca (or Priscilla) may have been the more gifted of the two.

- **That day:** Judgment Day.

- **Timothy:** A young man, half-Jewish and half-Greek, who was converted and circumcised by Paul sometime around A.D. 49. Timothy then went with Paul on Paul's second missionary journey through Greece. Three or four years later, Paul sent him to settle a church quarrel in Ephesus. His apparent lack of success (along with the general tone of 1 and 2 Timothy) has given him a reputation for timidity.

- **Titus:** A member of the church in Antioch and a Gentile convert of Paul. He delivered Paul's second letter to the church in Corinth.

- **Trophimus:** A Gentile convert and a native of Ephesus. He helped Paul bring an offering to Jerusalem. Paul was accused of bringing him into the "Jew's only" section of the temple—an accusation that started a riot and resulted in Paul's arrest.

- **Tychicus:** A frequent companion of Paul. He delivered Paul's letters to the churches in Ephesus and Colossae.

Scripture

Much of the New Testament did not yet exist when 2 Timothy 3:16 was written. At that time, the word "scripture" referred only to the Hebrew Bible (also known as the "Old Testament").

Names

Most people in Palestine went by only one name. So did slaves. But Roman women went by two names, and Roman men had three.

The *praenomen* was a formal name given Roman men; by Paul's time, there were only twelve possible *praenomina:* Gaius, Gnaeus, Decimus, Flavius, Lucius, Marcus, Numerius, Publius, Quintus, Rufus, Sextus, Titus.

The *nomen* was the clan or family name of a Roman man or woman. A man who belonged to the "Julius" clan, for instance, would have the *nomen* of Julius; a woman would be called Julia.

The *cognomen* was a man's personal name or nickname, though it might be shared with his father. (If that was the case, he probably had a different *praenomen*.) The famous general Gaius Julius, for instance, had the *cognomen* of "Caesar."

A woman might be given the feminine form of her father's or mother's *cognomen;* she might also be named *Prima* or *Secunda* ("first" or "second") to show the order of her birth. Women did not change their name when they got married; legally, they were still part of their parents' family.

"Paul" (or *Paulus*) was the apostle's *cognomen;* unfortunately, we have no idea what his *praenomen* and *nomen* might have been. When double names do appear in the New Testament (such as Claudius Lysias), they are always the *nomen* and *cognomen;* the *praenomen* is never given.

The New Testament church

There were no church buildings as such in New Testament times; believers met in whatever house or rented hall might be available. Of necessity, this meant they met in small groups—perhaps thirty or forty members at most. Leadership was *ad hoc.* Elders (also known as "overseers") were the spiritual leaders, while deacons (or "servants") cared for the physical needs of members.

Jewish Christians probably attended Jewish synagogue services on Sabbath mornings, then a Christian "believers' service" in the afternoon. Gentile Christians probably met just once—in the morning. In either case, the worship service consisted of singing, scripture reading, an "exhortation" or application of the scriptures that had been read, and the Communion service.

Titus

Obedience by Faith

*"For the grace of God that brings salvation has appeared to all men.
It teaches us to say "No" to ungodliness and worldly passions, and to live self-controlled,
upright and godly lives in this present age" (Titus 2:11, 12).*

HighLight

- Teach People to Behave Themselves! (Titus 2).

Why was it written?

Like 1 and 2 Timothy, Titus is a handbook for pastors. And one thing that troubled many pastors when Titus was written was the way that church members took advantage of God's forgiveness.

You *can* force people to be good, after all. All you have to do is play upon their fears, punish their transgression, and subject them to overwhelming peer pressure. Using such tactics, you can produce outward conformity to almost any standard that you might set for them.

The problem with forcing people to be good, however, is that you have to *keep* forcing them. You can't back off the pressure even for a moment. If you do, they'll immediately go back to their bad, old ways—just like recruits who have been allowed off base on a three-day leave.

That's what happens when you tell some people that God will forgive them—they immediately make sure He has something to forgive! Freed from the fear of punishment, they take joy in doing the wrong thing. If you tell them that we "all are one in God's eyes," they will refuse to acknowledge any authority. Assure them that "there is no condemnation in Christ," and they will lie, steal, get drunk . . . and then ask God's forgiveness so that they can lie, steal, and get drunk some more.

Needless to say, this kind of behavior does nothing for a church's reputation. Yet anyone who tried to stop it was going to be called a "legalist." So what could a church leader do? How could he or she convince people to be good, when they know that Jesus came to save people who were *not* good?

That is the dilemma faced in Paul's letter to Titus.

What you'll learn in Titus

Titus makes its purpose clear right from the start: It is meant to strengthen "the knowledge of truth that leads to godliness" (Titus 1:1). In other words, true religion is not just "empty talk" (Titus 1:10). No, those who believe in God should "be careful to devote themselves to doing what is good" (Titus 3:8).

Now for some people, this message would be disastrous. After all, some people already feel guilty that they don't do enough. And they are just the kind of people who would take the message of Titus to heart. As a result, they would feel even more guilty than they did before.

But Titus was written to people who already knew that God loved them—and knew it all too well! What they needed to hear was that creeds must lead to deeds, that faith must show itself in works, that what you do shows who you are. True, Paul makes these points in Titus more forcefully than some of us might like. But this was an extreme situation—and extreme situations call for extreme words.

Titus reminds us that we shouldn't abuse God's love. Yes, God does love us. And we never should doubt God's love. But God does ask us to love Him in return—and He wants that love to show.

GoodWords _____

- **Apollos:** Born a Jew in Alexandria, this follower of John the Baptist became a Christian in Ephesus through the efforts of Priscilla and Aquila. Though some saw him as a rival to Paul, Paul stated he and Apollos were "laborers together" (1 Corinthians 3:6-9).

- **Artemas:** Tradition says he was the bishop of Lystra, but outside of the fact that his name is Greek, we know nothing about him.

- **Bishop:** The word *episkopos* literally means "overseer" or "superintendent."

- **Crete:** The large (thirty-five miles by 160 miles), mountainous island sixty miles southeast of Greece. Paul visited it while on the way to Rome as a prisoner.

- **Doctrine:** Literally, "that which was taught." Some use Titus 2:1, 2 as proof that Christian beliefs were passed on in oral form (tradition) as well as written down (the Bible). Others say that's a pretty big conclusion to hang from such a small text.

- **Elder:** *Presbuteros* is a synonym for bishop.

- **Elect:** Literally, "the chosen." Once used only of the Jews, the term is used in Titus 1:1 to refer to all Christians—both Jewish and Gentile.

- **Factious:** The Greek word *hairetikos* gave us the word *heretic.* It literally means "one who chooses" or "one who divides."

- **Genealogies:** Some think this refers to the ancestor lists kept by some Jews to prove racial purity; others say it refers to gnostic speculations about angelic hierarchies or the "essences" that created our world.

- **The husband of one wife:** Bigamy was so rare at this time that it probably was not an issue. The phrase may simply mean that a bishop should be faithful to his marriage vows.

- **Justified:** Declared righteous by God.

- **Law:** Probably refers to the Torah—the first five books of the Bible—and by extension, to the entire Old Testament.

- **Nicopolis:** A city in western Greece.

- **Paul:** The Jew who made Christianity a Gentile religion. He probably wrote Titus around A.D. 66.

- **Titus:** A member of the church in Antioch and a Gentile convert of Paul's. He delivered Paul's second letter to the church in Corinth.

- **Tychicus:** A frequent companion of Paul. He delivered Paul's letters to the churches in Ephesus and Colossae.

- **Zenas:** An expert in the law—whether Jewish or Roman law, we don't know. A very untrustworthy tradition has it that he was the first bishop of Lydda.

 "Cretans are always liars"

Titus 1:12 quotes the poet Epimenides—a Cretan who lived in sixth or fifth century B.C. The Greek word *kretizo* (literally, "to become like a Cretan") meant "to lie."

Women

Roman women were expected to bear children and raise them—period. They did not run for public office. They did not lead in public worship. They could not even go out in public unless they were veiled; almost by definition, an unveiled woman was a prostitute.

In spite of this, some Roman women did manage to carve out a public role for themselves. Almost all women, for instance, had some kind of job to do. A wealthy woman had plenty to occupy her time in managing her household. A poor woman earned a living any way she could. Then too, widows could manage their own property and run their own businesses. And many wealthy women served as "patrons" to philosophers, poets, and religious groups. (Keep in mind that it was women who bankrolled Jesus' ministry—see Mark 15:41.)

Christianity was popular with women—so popular, as a matter of fact, that it's been called the world's first "feminist" religion. In Christianity, after all, women could take an active role in worship. They also benefited from Christianity's ban on divorce and infanticide—the first, because it stabilized the marriages of many poor people, and the second because infanticide had always killed more girls than boys.

The "don't put beans up your nose" principle

One of the most powerful principles for interpreting the Bible was formulated by Dr. Robert Johnston of Andrews University. He asks you to imagine that you are in a motel—one with thin walls so that you can hear the family next door. It seems that the family on the other side of the wall has a young boy named Johnny, for every few minutes you can hear a woman say, "Johnny, don't put beans up your nose!"

Based on what you've heard, what would you assume that Johnny is doing?

Simple—he is trying to put beans up his nose. Otherwise, his mother would not be telling him to stop!

Likewise, anytime a biblical writer writes, "Don't do *that*," you can assume that his readers were doing just *that*—otherwise, the writer wouldn't have to tell them that they shouldn't do it!

Try this principle when you read a book such as Titus—it just might open your eyes about those early Christian churches and what they were *really* like.

Philemon
Persuaded to Love

"Confident of your obedience, I write to you, knowing that you will do even more than I ask" (Philemon 21).

Highlight

- Welcome This Runaway Slave as You Would Welcome Paul Himself (Philemon 17).

Why was it written?

The apostle Paul had a problem. While in Colossae, he had worked with Philemon—a wealthy man who hosted the local church in his home. But now Paul was a prisoner in Rome. And while in Rome, he had converted Onesimus, a slave who had run away from Philemon!

Legally, Paul should have made sure that Onesimus went back to Philemon. But if he did this, then Onesimus was a dead man. A slave who "stole himself" by running away from his master, could expect torture, mutilation, or even death from his owner.

But if Paul did *not* return Onesimus, he would open Christianity to the charge of subversion. With as much as 10 percent of the people in their empire in chains, the Romans were jittery about anything that might encourage a slave revolt. If word got out that this new Christian religion encouraged slaves to run away from their masters, then many other Christians stood to lose their lives in the persecution that would surely follow.

300

So what was Paul to do? Sacrifice one man for the sake of Christianity? Or sacrifice Christianity for the sake of one man?

What Paul did was to send Onesimus back to his master—but carrying a letter Paul had written to Philemon about the matter!

What you'll learn in Philemon

Paul's letter shows us how to persuade someone to be better than he is. First, Paul compliments Philemon. He points out all the good things Philemon has done for Paul . . . and in the process, he also points out all the good things Paul has done for Philemon!

Having done this, Paul lets Philemon know what he wants, but he is careful to make it clear that he is not *commanding* Philemon to do this. No, he is "merely" *trusting* Philemon to obey.

Finally, Paul closes his letter with the offhand remark that he plans to visit Philemon in the near future . . . and in the process, he drops the hint that Philemon will have to personally answer to Paul for his actions.

In short, Paul maneuvers Philemon into a position where he cannot help but "voluntarily" release Onesimus—and as he does so, Paul shows us how a Christian should exercise authority. Paul is not demanding. He is not harsh or dictatorial. But he does make it clear that he will hold people accountable for the way they act . . . because our relationship with God is tied in to our relationship with other people.

GoodWords

- **Colossae:** A large and wealthy city located in present-day Turkey. A few experts think that Philemon lived, not in Colossae, but in the nearby city of Laodicea.

- **Onesimus:** You won't understand the pun in verse 11 unless you know that this name literally means "useful." A very old legend states that Onesimus was the one who compiled Paul's letters into the form in which we have them today.

Slavery

Slavery in the Roman Empire was not a matter of race, but of circumstances. Slaves might be of any race or nationality, but most were debtors, convicted criminals, abandoned children, or prisoners of war. They worked as cooks and miners, doctors and field hands, bank managers and legal secretaries. Any job requiring physical labor or personal supervision was "slave work."

As a result, roughly 10 percent of all people in the Roman Empire were slaves—and in Italy, the ratio was roughly one out of three.

Slaves could own slaves; what's more, they could use the profits gained to buy their own freedom. Most household slaves could hope to purchase or be given their freedom by age thirty—though even then, they would probably need to visit their "patron" daily, just to see if there was anything he might want them to do.

While a slave, however, no man or woman had any rights at all. Slaves could not legally marry; their children became the property of their owner. Slaves could be tortured or killed with impunity; if a slave-owner was killed by one of his slaves, all the rest of his slaves might be executed in return.

Hebrews

No Turning Back

"How shall we escape if we ignore such a great salvation?" (Hebrews 2:3).

HighLight

- Heroes of Faith (Hebrews 11).

Why was it written?

Few things are worse than making a big decision . . . and then having second thoughts. You've put earnest money on a house or you've accepted a job offer or you've announced your engagement . . . and suddenly, all the things you should have thought about *before* you made that decision now pop into your mind.

"Maybe that wasn't such a smart move," you say to yourself. "Maybe I should cut my losses. Maybe it's not too late to back out."

If you've ever felt like this, then you're in good company—the people for whom Hebrews was written were going through exactly the same thing. But they weren't second-guessing a business decision or even the choice of a spouse. No, they were reconsidering their commitment to Christianity.

Hebrews was written for Jewish Christians—Israelites who saw Christianity as the fulfillment of their faith, not a replacement for it. They had continued to attend Jewish services in the synagogue and temple; they had just added Christian services at church as well. At first, they had no problem doing this . . . but now Jews and Christians were at odds with each other—the Jews because of nationalism, the Christians because fewer and fewer of them had a Jewish background. Then, too, the Romans were cracking down on "illicit" religions, and while Judaism was protected under Roman law, Christianity was not.

As a result, many Jewish Christians were tempted to abandon Christianity and go back to their "old-time religion." After all, as Jews they had been God's chosen people. What could Christianity offer them that was better than that?

In short, Hebrews wasn't meant for people who were trying to decide if they should *become* Christians. It was written for people who were struggling with second thoughts about *staying* Christians—people who were remarkably like you and me.

What you'll learn in Hebrews

Open the book of Hebrews, and you plunge into the world of first-century Judaism—a world that many readers find confusing. Many of the book's main arguments, after all, depend on complicated interpretations of obscure texts. And many of the author's concerns—the purpose of Old Testament ritual, the role of angels, the importance of having the right ancestry—are hopelessly esoteric by today's standards.

Shining through all the confusion, however, is one important theme: Jesus is unique. He is supreme. It doesn't matter in what category you place Him—priest, sacrifice, teacher—Jesus always ranks first.

That point is still worth making, by the way. There are many people today who suggest that Jesus was just another good person—just another prophet, guru, or spiritual leader. Not so, says the book of Hebrews. "God spoke to our forefathers through the prophets at many times and in various ways, but in these last days he has spoken to us by his Son" (Hebrews 1:1, 2).

That's why those Jewish Christians couldn't go back to their old way of life: They had something better now. In a sense, the rituals of their old religion were like the letters that lovers send to each other when they are apart—they were important at the time, but now their beloved has appeared in the flesh. So how could they turn their backs on Him now? What more could they want from God?

GoodWords _____

- **Angels:** God's messengers. Many Jews thought God did not concern Himself with human affairs; instead, angels acted as the "middle managers" that run our planet on a day-to-day basis. Given this idea, Jewish Christians were tempted to believe that Jesus was just another angel—superior to some, perhaps, but still less than the ultimate authority. Hebrews denies this belief . . . and if it had been written today, it would have also pointed out that Jesus is superior to evolution or market forces or whatever else you may be tempted to think is responsible for life being the way it is.

- **Atonement:** Literally, "to make at one." In other words, whatever sets us at odds with God or each other is no match for Jesus.

- **Covenant:** A contract or agreement. In the Bible, this word usually refers to God's agreement with the Jews that He would be their God and they would be His people.

- **Priest:** The person who makes things right between God and humanity.

- **Sacrifice:** The means by which God and humanity are made right with each other. For what it's worth, most of the sacrifices discussed in this book seem to be connected with the inauguration of a new sanctuary.

- **Sanctuary:** The place where God and humanity are made right with each other. Hebrews reflects the common belief that the sanctuary on earth was a copy of a sanctuary in heaven.

Melchizedek

Literally, "the king of peace." Abraham recognized Melchizedek's authority as king of Jerusalem. Aside from that, we know nothing about him—which is exactly the point that Hebrews is making. You see, many Jews believed that only a priest could bring God and people back together, and every Jew knew that priests came only from the tribe of Levi. Since Jesus was from the tribe of Judah, it logically followed that He could not be a priest—which meant that He could not be the one who brought God and humanity back together.

"But what about Melchizedek?" asks Hebrews. "He was a priest—yet he was from the tribe of Levi, not Judah. If he could be a priest, then so could Jesus." Melchizedek is living proof, in other words, that you don't necessarily need the right credentials in order to do God's work. That's a lesson some people have yet to learn.

Background

There's no way you can understand the book of Hebrews without first reading Genesis, Exodus, and Leviticus. Try it, and see if it doesn't help.

Jewish Christianity

Jesus was Jewish; so were His disciples and almost all of His early converts. Yet today, Christianity is almost 100 percent Gentile.

So what happened to Jewish Christianity?

Two events marked the eclipse of the Jewish church. The first was the Jerusalem Council's decision in A.D. 49 that Gentiles did not have to first become Jewish in order to be Christians. This did not mean that Jewish Christians had to stop being Jewish; in fact, they continued to practice circumcision and observe Jewish festivals. But it meant that Jewish Christians would soon be outnumbered by Gentile Christians.

If the Jerusalem Council created an alternative to Jewish Christianity, the Jewish War of A.D. 66-70 struck directly at its roots. The war began with the death of James—the half-brother of Jesus and leader of the church in Jerusalem. It ended with the triumph of the Pharisees—a group with no love for any kind of Judaism other than their own. From now on, Jewish Christians would find themselves strangers in their own land. True, they would survive as a group for another 300 years . . . but only on the fringes of both Judaism and Christianity.

FlashPoint: Who wrote Hebrews?

In a fine display of circular reasoning, early church leaders believed that every book in the New Testament must have been written by an apostle. Hebrews was in the New Testament. Therefore, it must have been written by an apostle—probably Paul.

But Hebrews is unlike any book that Paul ever wrote. Its language is different. Its logic is different. It even quotes a different version of the Bible! That's why liberal scholars all agree that Hebrews must have been written by someone other than Paul.

Then again, the main themes of Hebrews resemble those of Paul. In fact, they're so close that some scholars believe one of Paul's companions wrote Hebrews—someone like Silas, Barnabas, or even Prisca—using notes they'd made of Paul's sermons.

Myself, I don't know who the author was, and I'm not too concerned that I don't know. After all, if we really needed to know who wrote it, then wouldn't Hebrews have told us?

QUICKSTART

New Testament:
General Epistles

James

Faith That Works

"Religion that God our Father accepts as pure and faultless is this: to look after orphans and widows in their distress and to keep oneself from being polluted by the world" (James 1:27).

Highlights

- Rejoice When Bad Times Come Your Way (James 1).

- Taming the Tongue (James 3).

Why was it written?

Truth can't live in an ivory tower. You have to take it out on the street and show people the difference it can make. That's why Greek philosophers didn't spend all of their time talking with other philosophers. They would literally preach on street corners, telling passersby about the meaning of life in short, catchy speeches that came to be known as *diatribes*.

Jewish rabbis did much the same thing. Not content just to read and study the words of God, they sought to make them live. In a process known as *midrash*, they drew lessons from the Bible, explained its difficulties, and applied its principles.

So it's no wonder that early Christians often discussed, not just what Jesus said, but what His words meant. They did this in informal discussions similar to the study groups of today. And they did this formally in sermons that bore a great deal of resemblance to the *diatribes* and *midrashim* of their Greek and Jewish contemporaries.

The epistle of James is just such a sermon. A set piece that could be delivered to any group on any occasion, it explains and applies three of Christ's sayings: "Ask in faith" (James 1:6), "Love your neighbor as yourself" (James 2:8), and "Let your 'Yes' be yes and your 'No' be no" (James 5:12).

James is not an abstract work of "timeless truth," in other words. It's a book about the difference that truth can make in everyday life.

What you'll learn in James

If God loves us no matter what we do, then why bother to be good?

That's a question that has always puzzled believers. And too often, their answers have created even more questions! Emphasize God's love, for instance, and you may end up condoning everything from impertinence to adultery. Emphasize behavior, on the other hand, and you may end up with a God who doesn't love you unless you're good.

Reading between the lines, it appears as though James's audience were sure that God loved them. What they needed to hear was that faith should make a difference in the believer's life—and that if it doesn't, it's probably not real faith.

That's why James spelled out the implications of real faith in three critical areas: the way we speak, the way we relate to suffering, and the way we deal with money. If his words are pointed, it's only because he wants to make them practical. James has no use for an abstract, theoretical faith.

Granted, this emphasis on performance makes some people uneasy. In fact, Luther called James "an epistle of straw." But James is saying nothing more than Paul did in Galatians 5:6 when Paul talked about "faith working through love." These words were not meant to comfort legalists; rather, they challenge us to recognize Jesus as both Savior and Lord.

GoodWords

- **Faith:** In Paul's letters, faith carries the idea of "trust" or "complete confidence" (as in "The rock climber wasn't worried, because she had faith in her equipment and skill."). In James, however, faith might be better understood as meaning "belief" or "opinion."

- **James:** This may be the same man identified in Mark 6:3 as the half-brother of Jesus and in Galatians 2:9 as a leader of the church in Jerusalem. If so, he may also be the brother of the man who wrote the book of Jude.

- **Law:** In James, this word carries much the same meaning as the Jewish *halakha* ("the way to walk"). When he speaks of "law," in other words, James does not mean just the Ten Commandments; he includes all of God's instructions for everyday living (including the Sermon on the Mount).

- **Wisdom:** In Jewish thought, wisdom was not just knowledge or know-how; it carried much the same meaning as "providence"—God's guiding presence in this world.

- **Works:** Those acts that grow from faith. If Paul had written this book, he might have said "fruits of the Spirit" instead of "works."

James's nickname

Tradition has it that James prayed so much he developed thick calluses on his knees—hence his nickname, "the man with the camel's knees."

Midrash

Jewish scholars often wrote "running commentaries" on the Bible that explained and applied its meaning; these commentaries were known as *midrashim*. It's been suggested that James is a *midrash* on Jesus' Sermon on the Mount (Matthew 5–7).

The first book of the New Testament?

Some experts think James may have been written as early as A.D. 44. If that's the case, it is the oldest book of the New Testament.

FlashPoint: Jesus' family

In Mark 6:3, the crowd wonders where Jesus got His knowledge of Scripture and His ability to do miracles.

"Isn't this the carpenter?" they ask. "Isn't this Mary's son and the brother of James, Joseph, Judas and Simon? Aren't his sisters here with us?"

Naturally enough, this list has stirred considerable speculation about Jesus' immediate family. Believing in the perpetual virginity of Mary, Catholics argue that this list refers to *cousins*. Protestants insist that the people named are half-brothers, but can't agree if they are older or younger than Jesus.

"Jesus didn't get the kind of respect the eldest son should get," some argue. "That means Joseph must have been married and had children *before* he married Mary. Then too, Jesus asked His disciple John to care for Mary after His death; He wouldn't have done this if Mary had other children."

"Even if Mary did have other children," others say, "they still might have rejected her because of Jesus. And as for the way they treated Jesus . . . well, even the eldest son would have problems if he made the kind of claims that Jesus did."

In short, both sides make good arguments, but both sides are largely arguing from silence. Fascinating as it may be, in other words, the question of Jesus' family is one that we can't answer just now.

1 Peter

Grace Under Pressure

"Be self-controlled and alert. Your enemy the devil prowls around like a roaring lion looking for someone to devour" (1 Peter 5:8).

HighLight

- How to Endure Suffering When You're a Believer (1 Peter 4).

Why was it written?

Most experts agree that 1 Peter was written somewhere around A.D. 60—a time when religion was not the private, personal affair that it is for many people today.

Instead, religion touched every part of a person's life. If you lived in a particular city, for instance, you worshiped that city's gods. You sealed your business contracts (and did much of your entertaining) in that city's temples. And just as a modern corporation will support a symphony or endow a college in order to improve its image, so too an important citizen of that time would show his "public spirit" by rebuilding a temple or financing a religious festival.

To the ancients, in other words, religion wasn't just a matter of your personal relationship with God. It also took in the things that we mean today when we talk about "patriotism," "public service," and even "the old boys' network." A pagan temple was more than just a church; it was a country club, the Chamber of Commerce, and an Elk's Lodge, all rolled into one.

No wonder the Christians of that day had problems! They were "out of the loop"—cut off by their religion from the local power structures. What's more, they didn't do the things that a "good citizen" should do. And so the rumors began: Christians were said to be clannish. Stuck up. Unpatriotic. Rumors began to circulate that they were enemies of humanity—guilty of atheism, cannibalism, and incest. Others said they weren't evil—just stubborn and stupid. But all agreed that a Christian was not "one of us."

Faced with this, some Christians must have been tempted to despair—to give up and return to their old beliefs. Others must have been tempted to anger—to strike back at the people who were slandering them.

The task of 1 Peter, then, was a difficult one—to encourage relatively new Christians to remain faithful, even when it wasn't easy to do so.

What you'll learn in 1 Peter

The bad news is that suffering is not an exception to the rule, not a fluke, not a temporary "glitch" in a believer's life. First Peter tells us that a Christian can expect to suffer, just as Christ suffered.

What's more, 1 Peter tells us that a Christian should suffer in the same way that Jesus suffered: Patiently. Faithfully. Without striking back at the people who have attacked you or sulking about the unfairness of life. Instead, a believer should try to be a good citizen, a good employee, and a good spouse.

"Do not repay evil with evil or insult with insult," says 1 Peter, "but with blessing, because to this you were called so that you may inherit a blessing" (1 Peter 3:9).

And suffering can be a blessing, says 1 Peter, if you respond to it with the same patience, gentleness, and love that Jesus did.

GoodWords _____

- **Babylon:** Most experts agree that this is a code word for Rome.

- **The dead:** When 1 Peter 4:6 says that "the gospel was preached even to those who are now dead," it means nothing more than that everyone—even the people who are now dead—had a chance to accept or reject God. This does not mean that the dead get a second chance at salvation; 1 Peter 4:5 makes it clear that a person is judged for what he or she did while still alive.

- **The devil:** Literally, "the one who throws against," or "the slanderer"—traditionally thought to be an angel that rebelled against God.

- **The dispersion:** Normally this refers to the Jews who live outside of Palestine. Most experts agree, however, that 1 Peter was written to Gentile Christians. The point? To remind those Gentile believers that they have been adopted into God's family.

- **Pontus, Galatia, Cappaddocia, Asia, and Bithynia:** Roman provinces in what is now Turkey. Apparently this is the order in which 1 Peter was to be circulated among the churches. Why this order (and not another) is unknown.

- **Silas:** A companion of Paul and co-author of this letter.

Peter

Born a poor fisherman, Simon son of John was introduced to Jesus by his brother Andrew. Jesus nicknamed him "Peter" (or "the rock"). He must have been teasing Simon when he did so, for Peter was not a very stable character. For instance, although he was one of the first to say that Jesus was "the Christ," he also denied at the trial of Jesus that he even knew Him. Peter was one of the first apostles to preach the gospel to Gentiles, but fear of criticism made him "draw back" from eating with them in Antioch. Even though he made many mistakes, however, Peter always came back to Jesus. Tradition has it that he was crucified in Rome c. A.D. 66.

Persecution

While persecution did take place during New Testament times, it was usually not wide spread or well organized. A householder might discipline a Christian slave for being "superstitious." A lynch mob might burn down the house of an "atheist" (or Christian). A husband might denounce his wife to the magistrates for "taking up a new religion." But the Roman Empire wasn't organized enough to launch a systematic campaign of oppression . . .

Not usually. While Christians could be arrested and killed at *any* time, five periods in the history of the early church were especially bad:

- **Persecution under Nero (A.D. 64-68):** When fire destroyed much of Rome, the emperor Nero looked for a scapegoat; he found it in the Christian church. As a result, large numbers of Christian believers were crucified, thrown to wild animals, or burned alive. Tradition has it that Peter and Paul both died in Rome at this time.

- **Persecution under Marcus Aurelius (A.D. 161-180):** This period was marked by lynch mobs in the western empire and official executions in the east.

- **Persecution under Septimus Severus (A.D. 193-211):** During this persecution, the authorities targeted adults who had converted to Christianity.

- **Persecution under Decius and Valerian (A.D. 249-260):** This was the first systematic attempt to wipe out Christianity throughout the empire; everyone was required to have a certificate stating that he or she had sacrificed to the emperor as a god. Church leaders were singled out for special treatment; the hope was to make them renounce Christianity and thus, to demoralize the church as a whole.

- **The Great Persecution (A.D. 303-313):** Begun by the emperor Diocletian in a last-ditch effort to restore the "traditional family values" of Rome, it ended with Constantine's legalization of Christianity.

FlashPoint: The spirits in prison

Experts agree that 1 Peter 3:18-20 is one of the most difficult passages in the New Testament to understand. Many interpretations have been suggested, however, most fall into one of the following three categories:

- **The harrowing of hell:** The ancient church fathers (and contemporary Catholics) say, that this passage refers to the descent of Jesus into hell *after* His death, but *before* His resurrection. There Jesus preached to the spirits of the dead, rescued some, and brought them back with Him to heaven.

- **The witness of Noah:** The traditional Protestant view is that Jesus spoke through Noah to warn his contemporaries of the flood that was to come.

- **The proclamation to angels:** Many modern scholars (both liberal and conservative) believe this passage refers to an announcement made by Jesus *after* His resurrection—an announcement made to evil angels that Jesus had triumphed over them.

2 Peter

Dealing With Delay

"The Lord is not slow in keeping his promise, as some understand slowness. He is patient with you, not wanting anyone to perish, but everyone to come to repentance" (2 Peter 3:9).

HighLight

• The Day of the Lord (2 Peter 3).

Why was it written?

Years earlier—just before His death and resurrection—Jesus had promised His followers that He would return and take them to live with Him forever. But the years had passed with no sign of Judgment Day. Many of Jesus' followers had died. And faith in the promise of His return was beginning to flicker and die.

Chief among the doubters were those church members who had tried to combine Christianity with the current philosophies of the day. These *gnostics* (literally, "the ones in the know") prided themselves on their intelligence and courage. They weren't afraid of sin; they "knew" God would forgive them no matter what they did. Neither were they afraid of angels; they "knew" God had made them master of all things.

Most of all, they weren't afraid of Judgment Day. That was because they were too "intelligent" to believe in something as crude as the literal end of this world. In fact, they "knew" that spiritual things were far more important than physical. And so they had spiritualized Christ's promised return into a pleasant tale of personal enlightenment.

As a result, more and more Christians saw their faith as little more than an excuse to do whatever they wanted to do. Their beliefs owed more to philosophy than to the Bible. And their Jesus was neither Creator nor Judge, but just another guru promising wisdom.

In short, 2 Peter was written to Christians who were fast losing sight of heaven—Christians who were just like many people in the world today.

What you'll learn in 2 Peter

The Bible is full of famous last words. You'll find the last words of Jacob, for instance, in Genesis 49, those of Moses in Deuteronomy 31–33, and Paul's final words in 2 Timothy 4.

Like these other "last wills and testaments," 2 Peter follows a pattern. First, the author announces his impending death. Then he reflects upon the past. Next comes a revelation of what was to come and advice about how his readers should respond to it. And last, comes a promise—a promise that even though times will be tough, God's people will be victorious.

Using this framework, 2 Peter makes three important points. The first is that we need to remember the past; we need to "refresh [our] memory" (2 Peter 1:13). Otherwise, we will lose sight of what's important.

Second, we need to make use of the present. After all, it's easy for believers to get lazy—to say that "Jesus did it all, so why should I do anything?" But in 2 Peter, we're reminded of our need to be effective Christians.

Last, we need to remember God's plans for our future. We can't live as though there will be no tomorrow; Judgment Day is sure to come. Granted, it may seem as though this day has been delayed, but that only means we have "extra" time in which to prepare.

> But the day of the Lord will come like a thief. The heavens will disappear with a roar; the elements will be destroyed by fire, and the earth and everything in it will be laid bare. Since everything

will be destroyed in this way, what kind of people ought you to be? You ought to live holy and godly lives as you look forward to the day of God and speed its coming (2 Peter 3:10-12).

GoodWords

- **The fathers:** Whether this phrase refers to the twelve disciples (such as John and Thomas) or to Old Testament patriarchs (such as Abraham and Israel) is a matter of much discussion—and little importance.

- **The glorious ones:** Angels. Gnostics had an extraordinary fascination with angels and loved to speculate about their foibles, follies, and dealings with human beings. This could get pretty rank. Many thought Genesis 6:2, for instance, meant fallen angels had engaged in sexual intercourse with human beings. No wonder 2 Peter comes down pretty hard on this kind of discussion!

- **Goodness:** 2 Peter 1:5 lists *araytain* as the second thing we should add after faith. This word has also been translated as "virtue," "courage," "excellence," or even "expertise." Greek philosophers considered *araytain* to be the chief of all virtues. You might want to think of it as "whatever it takes to make something happen."

- **Hell (or hades):** Often this word simply means "the grave," but in 2 Peter it refers to *Tartarus*—the place in Greek legend where the Titans were confined by the gods of Olympus. The Jews adapted this story and made Tartarus the prison of evil angels after their fall.

- **Knowledge:** 2 Peter uses an unusual word—one that is better translated as "increasing knowledge" or "full and complete knowledge."

- **Lot:** Genesis chapters 18 and 19 tell his story. The fact that this "righteous man" got drunk and committed incest should remind us just how willing God is to save people who don't deserve it.

- **Paul:** Yes, the same man who wrote all those books in the New Testament. Even way back then, Paul's letters were already regarded as Scripture—and even way back then, people had trouble understanding what he meant.

- **Peter:** The best known of Christ's twelve disciples. He is widely believed to have been the author of 1 Peter and the source for the Gospel of Mark.

 **Balaam**

One of the oddest stories in the Old Testament is found in Numbers 22–24. It tells how the prophet Balaam was offered money to curse the Israelites. He ended up blessing them instead . . . but you get the impression that he would rather have put a hex on them, collected his money, and gone home.

Second Peter refers to the belief, common among the Jews of that time, that the sexual goings on recorded in Numbers 25 were the result of Balaam's scheme to lure the Israelites away from God. "Balaam must have done something really dreadful," they thought, "since Numbers 31:8 goes out of its way to tell us that the Israelites killed him."

FlashPoint: Who wrote 2 Peter?

At first glance, the question of who wrote 2 Peter seems ridiculous. After all, the letter begins with the statement that it was written by Simon Peter! What could be clearer or more obvious than that?

Unfortunately, the vocabulary of 2 Peter is *very* different than that of 1 Peter or Mark. First Peter uses 369 words that do not appear in 2 Peter, for instance, while 2 Peter uses 230 words that do not appear in 1 Peter! What's more, the *style* of 2 Peter is what you would expect from someone who had learned Greek in Asia Minor—not Palestine.

That is why liberals believe that, sometime around A.D. 120, someone else used Peter's name to write a letter—a letter that said what that person *thought* Peter would have said about the problems of the day. This kind of practice was common, after all. Writers often "borrowed" a famous pen name in order to give their work authority.

Conservatives don't agree; they believe Peter wrote this book (possibly with the help of a scribe) shortly before his death in A.D. 60 or so.

Out of this debate, a third option has emerged: the idea that someone could have drawn upon the collected sayings of Peter to compose this letter sometime toward the end of the first century A.D.

FlashPoint: Should 2 Peter be in the Bible?

Second Peter has never been a popular book. In fact, no one even mentioned it until A.D. 200 or so. The fourth-century historian Eusebius included it on his list of "disputed books." Even today, 2 Peter is probably the least known (and least quoted) of all New Testament books.

The Letters of John
Lessons in Love

7 CHAPTERS — READING TIME: 20 MINUTES

"Everyone who loves has been born of God and knows God.
Whoever does not love does not know God, because God is love" (1 John 4:7, 8).

Highlight

- Love Tells Us What Is True (1 John 3; 4).

Why were they written?

No one knows exactly what caused the split in the Ephesian church. The likeliest candidate seems to have been a form of *gnosticism,* but whatever it was seems to have caused problems both with doctrine and behavior. And even after they had been forced out of the church, the dissenters were still causing problems. Some members were still fascinated by their teachings; others wondered if the church had done the right thing in expelling them.

What the church needed, in other words, was a reason to move on. They needed help in understanding what they had been through and where they should go from here.

That's why 1 John was written. It's a letter—probably meant to be read as a sermon—that tells a church how to cope with the aftermath of a church fight. More than that, it's good advice for anyone who's wondering why he needs to keep taking the risk of loving other church members.

The second and third letters of John also deal with the aftermath of a church fight. In 2 John, the problem was dissenters who continued to take advantage of church hospitality; in 3 John, the problem was a church leader who continued to make trouble. In short, these letters dealt with the question of how you can show love to people who are determined to do you wrong.

What you'll learn in the letters of John

Like a cross, love must reach out in two directions—it must stretch out to other people, and it must stretch up to God. As 1 John 4:19, 21 says: "We love because he first loved us. . . . And he has given us this command: Whoever loves God must also love his brother."

But if 1 John is a sermon about the *importance* of love, then 2 and 3 John are letters about the *limits* of love. Second John, for instance, urges "the chosen lady and her children" not to extend hospitality to dissenters. In other words, just because you're a Christian doesn't mean you have to be a patsy for the bad guys. And 3 John says that the person who is causing trouble will be held accountable for the damage he has done.

In short, John's letters show us that love is important—but knowing *how* to love is more important still.

GoodWords _____

- **Abide:** Not the passive verb you might think. It carries with it the idea of "standing fast against pressure" or "enduring despite the odds."

- **Antichrist:** The word literally means "in place of Christ." Notice that John saw the condition of the church in his day as a fulfillment of prophecies about "the last days."

- **Command:** If you don't like this word, substitute "commission"—the Greek word *entolay* can be translated either way.

- **Elder:** A synonym for bishop—and the common title given church pastors.

- **Ephesus:** An important port city and government center on the Mediterranean coast of Asia Minor (or Turkey).

- **Sin:** Literally, "to miss the mark." Despite what you saw in *Time Bandits,* evil is not a "thing"; it is our failure to be all that God intended us to be.

- **World:** The word *kosmos* literally means "that which is well-ordered or arranged." While it usually carries the sense of "creation" or "universe," in 1 John it specifically refers to that part of creation which is in rebellion against God.

Single-page letters

The length of both 2 and 3 John indicate that each of them was written on a single sheet of papyrus.

Was Jesus human?

Strange as it may seem, early Christians had little problem believing that Jesus was divine. What troubled them was that He might be human. That's because most philosophers in their day split reality between spirit and matter. The world of the spirit was thought to be heavenly, perfect, and changeless; the world of matter was thought to be earthly, corrupt, and in a continual state of flux.

Given this view, it seemed obvious that perfect, changeless divinity could have nothing to do with corrupt human flesh—especially when that flesh was said to have died! As a result, the idea grew that Jesus only *appeared* to be human (a belief known as *Docetism*). Another idea was that He adopted a human body at its baptism and left it just before its death. (This belief was known as *adoptionism;* it is also known as *Cerinthianism,* after one of the people who taught it.)

In the face of these beliefs, John insists that he had seen Jesus with his own eyes and knew for a fact that Jesus was human.

FlashPoint: Which John?

Experts believe that the three letters of John were all written during the last part of the first century A.D. by a church leader in Ephesus named John.

The problem is that there were two men named John both of whom served as church leaders in Ephesus during the latter part of the first century. So which one of the two wrote these letters? Was it the "beloved disciple" who followed Christ as one of His twelve closest followers? Or was it "the elder" spoken of by the early church leader Papias? Did the same person write the Gospel of John? And what about the book of Revelation?

It is questions such as these that keep experts awake at night. Myself, I'm not worried. Whoever wrote these letters was obviously respected by church members as a man of God. If that was good enough for them, then it ought to be good enough for us.

Jude
Strong Words for a Weak Church

1 CHAPTER — READING TIME: 5 MINUTES

*"Keep yourself in God's love as you wait for the mercy
of our Lord Jesus Christ to bring you to eternal life" (Jude 21).*

HighLight

- Jude's Blessing on God's People (Jude 24, 25).

Why was it written?

One of the sad facts of life is the ease with which some people can be misled.
Honest people. Sincere people. People who want to follow God—but who end
up following any charlatan who comes along with fancy words and a loud voice.

Take the church to which Jude was written, for instance. Obviously it was made
up of devout people—after all, Jude writes to them of "our common faith." Then
too, Jude assumes they are familiar with the stories of Moses, Cain, Michael,
Balaam, and Enoch—something he could not have done unless they knew the
Bible well.

Yet this group of godly, Bible-reading believers had been misled by outsiders who
claimed to have special knowledge of spiritual things. These "false teachers" were
arrogant. They stirred up trouble. And they used religion as a tool to achieve their
own selfish purposes.

So why did these church members believe them? Why did they follow them?
Why had they allowed these "wild waves," "fruitless trees," and "wandering stars"
to take over their church?

324

Most experts agree that these church members had fallen victim to an early form of gnosticism—a "New Age" blend of Christianity, Greek philosophy, and anything else that came along. Gnosticism was endlessly flexible; it could be adapted to almost any circumstance or system of belief. By and large, however, gnostics taught that the world was divided into two realms: the spiritual (which was good) and the physical (which was bad). Christ had come to give His followers the secret knowledge *(gnosis)* they needed to liberate their (good) spirits from their (evil) bodies.

"Now since religion is entirely a matter of the spirit," some gnostics said, "you can do whatever you like with your body."

And they did. Some gnostics even went so far as to say that Christians were free from any law, any rule, and any standard of behavior. Drunkenness, murder, even incest—none of these things, they said, could harm the "spirit" of a true Christian.

Gnosticism attracted church members for many reasons. Some were attracted because it allowed them to do anything they wanted. Others were attracted by the way gnosticism "made sense" of so many different religions. But most of all, the gnostics gained a following because they claimed to know the meaning of life, and they taught it with authority. And when they taught, church members listened—or at least some of them did.

That's why Jude had to change his plans. He had wanted to write about truth. But now he had to warn against error. He had wanted to write about the gift of salvation. But now he had to warn against the misuse of that gift.

What you'll learn in Jude

Jude's main point is that we shouldn't take God's grace for granted. And to make this point, he gives example after example of God's wrath against sin—as well as example after example of people who followed God, only to fall away from Him.

In other words, rather than directly attack the *beliefs* of gnosticism, Jude attacks the *attitude* of the people who believe it. "Don't be too smug," Jude warns them. "Don't be so sure of yourselves. God has condemned cities, believers, and even angels for the same type of behavior in which you take such pride."

In short, Jude's letter is for Christians who've grown smug and comfortable with their own goodness. It's not for unbelievers—or even for timid Christians. It's not a letter that tells us how to be right with God; it doesn't go out of its way to assure us of God's love. Instead, it warns against arrogance. It warns against complacency. And it tells us to beware of people—even "spiritual" people—who tell us only what we want to hear.

GoodWords

- **Balaam:** A prophet of God who was bribed to curse Israel. Though that didn't work, he *was* able to lure the Israelites into idolatry and immorality (see Numbers 22–25).

- **Cain:** The first murderer (see Genesis 4).

- **Enoch:** Genesis 5:24 simply says that "Enoch walked with God; then he was no more, because God took him away." Jude is apparently quoting from 1 Enoch—an apocryphal book that resembles Revelation.

- **Jude:** Traditionally, this "brother of James" was thought to be the half-brother of Jesus. Some experts disagree, since they think Jude was written much too late for a half-brother of Jesus to still be alive. Others say it may have been one of the earliest books in the New Testament to have been written.

- **Korah:** He led a revolt against Moses during the Exodus (see Numbers 16).

- **Love feasts:** The Communion service.

- **Michael:** The name of the archangel in Jewish belief. This story is apparently drawn from an apocryphal work known as *The Assumption of Moses.*

Pseudipigrapha

During the Greek and Roman eras, Jewish authors combined folk tales, speculation, and wishful thinking into a number of books—and to give these books added authority, they used the names of ancient prophets and kings as "pen names."

Known as *pseudepigrapha* (or "false writings"), these books include *The Ascension of Isaiah, The Testament of Job,* and *The Life of Adam and Eve.* Jude apparently quotes from at least two of these books: *1 Enoch* and *The Assumption of Moses.* However, this proves only that Jude was familiar with these books and knew that his readers would be too. It doesn't mean the books he quoted were inspired of God.

FlashPoint: Jude and 2 Peter

Jude and 2 Peter are so similar that some experts feel that one writer may have borrowed from the other. Unfortunately, no one can agree which book came first and which author borrowed from the other!

FlashPoint: Should Jude be in the Bible?

Jude's use of nonbiblical sources troubled some eastern Christians; his letter drifted in and out of favor before it was finally accepted as a part of the New Testament during the fourth century.

QUICKSTART

New Testament:
The Book of Revelation

Revelation
Revealing Jesus

22 CHAPTERS — READING TIME: 90 MINUTES

" 'Now the dwelling of God is with men, and he will live with them. They will be his people, and God himself will be their God. He will wipe every tear from their eyes. There will be no more death or mourning or crying or pain, for the old order of things has passed away' " (Revelation 21:3, 4).

HighLights

- The Seven Churches (Revelation 2; 3).

- God's People Survive the Great Time of Trouble (Revelation 12–14).

- The New Jerusalem (Revelation 21).

Why was it written?

It's hard to wait. It's harder still to wait for someone you love. And it's hardest of all to wait for someone you love when you're beginning to fear that you might not see that person again.

That's the position in which John found himself. As a young man, he had been a close companion of Jesus. He had watched Jesus die. He had been there when Jesus rose into the heavens and heard His promise that He would return to set up His eternal kingdom.

So John had waited.

And waited.

331

And waited.

Now he was an old man. It had been fifty years—maybe even sixty—since Jesus had promised to return . . . and in that time, John had seen many of his fellow-believers die. He himself had been sentenced to exile on Patmos—a small, rocky island in the eastern Mediterranean. And still, Jesus had not come.

Is it safe to guess that John found this waiting hard?

Certainly other Christians did. By the end of the first century A.D., we know that many Christians were beginning to grow discouraged. They were beginning to doubt Jesus' promise. And they were beginning to drift off into other religions that promised more in the way of results.

That's why Jesus appeared to John. He did so to assure John that He *would* keep His promises. That He was in control. That no matter how long they waited, He would be with them until the end (and even longer).

In other words, the book of Revelation is more than just a book about the future. It's a book that tells us how to live until that future comes to pass.

What you'll learn in Revelation

Start with the title. It's not "Revelation*s*." It's "Revelation"—singular, not plural.

That may seem like a small difference, but it's an important one. You see, too many people try to make this a book of "revelations"—a book full of mystic dreams and visions about life, the future, and everything. But it's not. It's a book of *revelation*—to be specific, it's "the revelation of Jesus Christ" (Revelation 1:1).

In short, you can use this book to learn about Jesus—and you won't go wrong. But use it to learn anything else while you ignore what it says about Jesus? Do that, and you'll miss what it's really saying.

So what does Revelation reveal about Jesus? Lots of things. In fact, one of the reasons the book is so difficult to understand is the very richness of its message. Almost every major theme of Scripture is taken up, reworked, and applied in new and different ways.

Take the theme of Creation, for instance. In Genesis we read that God gave structure to this world in seven days. Revelation repeatedly portrays events in terms of this same "sevenfold" structure—there are seven churches, seven trumpets, seven thunders, seven bowls, and seven blessings. The point of all these "sevens" is that life is not just one crazy, random thing after another. No, Jesus is in charge of history just as He was of Creation—and when He does things, it all comes out "sevens."

Other themes abound in Revelation: the Exodus, the temple, the psalms, the captivity in Babylon, and others. Each brings with it new insights; each is used to show us something about Jesus that we could not have learned in any other way. He is both the Lion of Judah and the Lamb that was slain, both conquering King and suffering Servant. Priest and sacrifice, Judge and Advocate, forgiving Savior and avenging Warrior—in Revelation, Jesus is all of these things, and more.

GoodWords

- **Armageddon:** Literally, "the mountain of Megiddo." While Megiddo was the site of many famous battles, it's not a mountain, but a plain. It may be that John wants us to think about the *kind* of battles that have taken place at Megiddo, but doesn't want us to take the location seriously.

- **Babylon:** This city was the ancient enemy of Israel. In Revelation, it's used as a symbol of every earthly power that opposes God. Compare Revelation's description of Babylon with that of its heavenly counterpart, the New Jerusalem.

- **John:** Close friend and disciple of Jesus. He served for many years as the bishop of Ephesus—a city on what is now the Turkish coast. Most experts agree that John wrote Revelation while in exile somewhere around A.D. 95, though some push for a date as early as A.D. 68.

- **The Lord's Day:** While many translate this as "Sunday," this term was not generally used for the first day of the week until much later. A better translation might be "the day of the Lord" or Judgment Day.

- **Michael:** The Jews thought him to be the greatest of all angels, as well as the one assigned to guard God's people from harm. Some think this term refers to Jesus as He was before the Incarnation, and as long as you don't suggest this proves Jesus was a created being, that seems a harmless-enough speculation.

- **Patient endurance:** A phrase originally used to describe people in a city under siege who are actively resisting the enemy. "Don't just fold your hands and wait," John tells his readers. "Fight to keep what is already yours!"

- **Revelation:** Literally, "the unveiling of something that used to be hidden."

- **Seal of God:** A symbol of God's protection and ownership, one that goes right back to the mark God placed on Cain to guard him from his enemies. Its demonic equivalent, of course, is the "mark of the beast." Anyone who thinks these are literal marks that could be read by a supermarket checkout scanner should memorize 2 Corinthians 1:21, 22.

- **The seven churches that are in Asia:** Real churches in real cities, listed in the order that a letter would have followed if it were handed on from one church to another on the usual postal route of the day.

- **666:** Whenever God does something, it's a seven; He always finishes the job, just as He did at Creation. Whenever God's enemies try to do something, however, it always comes up "six"—the day on which humanity was created. And no matter how often they try, it just keeps coming up "six."

- **Stadium (plural, "stadia"):** One Roman mile (or eight furlongs)—about 4,855 feet.

Background

Revelation combines elements of every book in the Bible, but if you want to gain special insight into its meaning, try reading the books of Daniel, Ezekiel, and Zechariah as well.

Reading prophecy

Prophecy is like dynamite—it's powerful, but it needs careful handling. That's why, anytime that you read a prophetic book such as Daniel or Revelation, you need to ask yourself three questions:

- **What else does the Bible say about this?** The themes of prophecy are the same as those of the whole Bible: God's love, His care, His justice and mercy. So if your understanding of prophecy contradicts the rest of the Bible and what it says on these subjects, take another look!

- **What was going on when these prophecies were written?** Most prophecies were meant to be understood by the people of their day. And if you know the questions *they* were asking, you're more likely to understand the answers that God gave in this prophecy.

- **So what?** Prophecy should make a difference in the way you live your life *today*—not just in the plans that you make for tomorrow. So as you read, ask yourself such questions as, "What sin does this text warn me about?" or "What task does it urge me to do?" When you apply prophecy, after all, it's always a good idea to apply it to your own life first.

The 144,000

Far from symbolizing a spiritual elite, this number is used to symbolize the fact that an enormous number of people will be saved, with not one missing.

The number twelve, after all, signified that all of God's people were present and accounted for—think twelve tribes, for instance. Likewise, a "thousand" was one of the biggest numbers you could say in Greek.

In other words, ask John how many people will be saved, and he'll tell you "all of them, times all of them, times the biggest number you can imagine."

FlashPoint: Reading Revelation

There is no general agreement as to how Revelation should be interpreted. Most commentaries, however, fall into one of these four categories:

- **Preterist:** This is the belief that Revelation refers to events that took place in the first century of the Christian era. Those holding this view see Revelation's seven churches, for instance, as literal churches with no symbolic significance. For an example of this approach, see the *Anchor Bible Commentary*.

- **Historicist:** This is the belief that Revelation describes events taking place between Christ's first advent and the end of time. In addition to being literal churches, for instance, Revelation's seven churches also symbolize seven periods of church history. A good example of this approach is C. Mervyn Maxwell's *God Cares*.

- **Futurist:** This is the belief that most of Revelation refers to events that will take place just before the end of time. In this view, Revelation's seven churches are literal churches, for instance, but everything after Revelation 3:22 will take place in the future. Hal Lindsay's books provide the best-known examples of this approach.

- **Symbolic:** This is the belief that Revelation sketches out the broad themes of history, but doesn't tie them too closely to specific events. This view would say that while Revelation's seven churches are literal churches, their significance is primarily spiritual. A good example of this approach is Eugene Peterson's *Reversed Thunder*.